KU-623-696

Women and Japanese management

Women and Japanese management

Discrimination and reform

Alice C.L. Lam

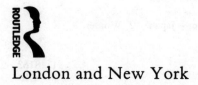

London and New York

First published 1992
by Routledge
11 New Fetter Lane, London EC4P 4EE

Simultaneously published in the USA and Canada
by Routledge
a division of Routledge, Chapman and Hall, Inc.
29 West 35th Street, New York, NY 10001

©1992 Alice C.L. Lam

Typeset in 10 on 12pt Bembo by LaserScript Ltd, Mitcham, Surrey
Printed and bound in Great Britain by
Mackays of Chatham PLC, Chatham, Kent

All rights reserved. No part of this book may be reprinted or
reproduced or utilized in any form or by any electronic, mechanical or
other means, now known or hereafter invented, including photocopying
and recording, or in any information storage or retrieval system, without
permission in writing from the publishers.

British Library Cataloguing-in-Publication Data

A catalogue reference for this title is available from the British Library

ISBN 0–415–06335–3

Library of Congress Cataloging in Publication Data

Lam, Alice C.L. (Alice Cheung-Ling), 1955–
  Women and Japanese management: discrimination and reform/Alice
C.L. Lam.
  Includes bibliographical references and index.
  ISBN 0–415–06335–3
  1. Sex discrimination in employment – Japan.   2. Women –
Employment – Japan.   I. Title.
  HD6060.5.J3L36   1992
  331.4′133′0952–dc20   91-48163
                                                              CIP

To my parents and David

Contents

List of figures   ix
List of tables   xi
Acknowledgements   xv

Introduction

1 Introduction and background   3

**Part I Discrimination against women in employment:
theory and practice**

2 Internal labour markets and discrimination   27

3 Sexual inequality in the Japanese employment system:
     discriminatory company practices   45

4 The emerging situation: changing company practice in
     response to market pressures   68

Part II Legislation and reform

5 Legislating for change? The Equal Employment
     Opportunity Law   89

6 The management response   117

Part III A case study

7 The Seibu case: an introduction   143

8 The Seibu case: changing company practice   155

9 Changing roles and attitudes of Seibu women: towards
     equal opportunity?   185

Part IV Conclusions

10 Equal employment for women in the Japanese
      employment system: limitations and obstacles   221

     Appendix A   241

     Appendix B   249

     Notes   252
     Bibliography   261
     Index   273

Figures

1.1 Women's labour force participation by age, 1975 and 1990 15

3.1 Women's average earnings as a percentage of those of
men, by age group, in selected countries, various years 49

4.1 Changes in the occupational distribution of female
university graduates, 1965–89 76

4.2 A model of the female group leader system 80

4.3 The career conversion system 82

4.4 Career conversion in company A 83

4.5 Grading system in company B 84

5.1 Outline of the EEO Law 102

5.2 Model of change underlying the Japanese EEO Law 111

6.1 Extent of coverage of career tracking system by firm size,
1989 129

8.1 Seibu's specialist career system (*Senmonshoku-seido*) 159

8.2 Seibu's job rotation chart 170

9.1 Number of men and women recruited annually, 1978–87 189

9.2 Number of women recruited annually, by educational
levels, 1978–87 190

Tables

1.1 Number and proportion of women workers by work status, 1955–90   10

1.2 Distribution of the labour force by industrial sector, 1950–90   11

1.3 Distribution of female employees by occupation, 1960–90   12

1.4 Female earnings as a percentage of male earnings, selected countries and years   16

1.5 A ten country comparison of women workers' responses to the statement 'I can use my abilities at work'   17

3.1 Monthly earnings of male and female full-time regular employees, 1960–89   46

3.2 Wage differentials between male and female standard employees, with senior high school education, by age and length of service, 1989   47

3.3 Occupational distribution of male and female employees, 1990   51

3.4 Distribution of male and female employees by firm size, 1990   53

3.5 Distribution of male and female employees by firm size and age groups, 1990 in percentages   54

3.6 Number and proportion of part-time employees, 1960–90   55

4.1 Male and female employees in clerical, professional and managerial occupations as a percentage of all employees in the sector, 1955–80   71

4.2 Educational composition of women entering employment, 1960–89   74

4.3   Number of male and female university graduates
      entering employment, 1960–89   75
4.4   Percentage of companies with the female group leader
      system, 1968 and 1982   79
6.1   Policy orientations on women employees, before and
      after 1985   121
6.2   Extent of response to the EEO Law   122
6.3   Proportion of companies admitting direct discrimination
      against women (1977, 1981 and 1987)   124
6.4   Changes in starting wages for new recruits, 1975–87   126
6.5   Examples of companies which recruited female graduates
      for managerial career track (sogoshoku) in the spring of
      1987   132
6.6   Distribution of male and female employees by career
      tracks, 1987   132
6.7   Type of policy changes in job assignment, job rotation
      and promotion   134
8.1   Changes in the proportional distribution of women
      recruited annually, by educational levels, 1976–85   157
8.2   'Which career route do you intend to pursue at this
      company?' (1984 survey)   165
8.3   'How satisfied are you with your present position?'
      (1984 survey)   166
8.4   Distribution of male and female employees by job
      position (1983)   166
8.5   Distribution of male and female specialists by job
      functions (1983)   167
8.6   Characteristics of the 'global women'   178
9.1   Composition of male and female employees by
      employment status (1983 and 1988)   187
9.2   Composition of contract employees (1987)   191
9.3   Job position of male and female regular employees (1983
      and 1988)   194
9.4   Number and share of women in specialist and
      managerial jobs (1983 and 1988)   195
9.5   Distribution of male and female regular employees by
      grade (1984 and 1988)   197
9.6   Analysis of variance (1984 and 1988 data)   198
9.7   The 'pure sex effect' on job status (1984 and 1988 data) 199
9.8   Women's perception of equality (by age cohorts): 1984
      and 1988 compared   200

9.9   Job preferences of men and women (1988); young
      women only, 1984 and 1988 compared   203
9.10 Women's promotion aspirations: 1984 and 1988
      compared   205
9.11 Promotion expectations of men and women: 1984 and
      1988 compared   207
9.12 Women's promotion expectations: 1984 and 1988
      compared   208
9.13 Women's attitudes to career continuity: 1984 and 1988
      compared   211
A.1   The interview sample   243
A.2   Sample population, sample size and response rates   246
A.3   Characteristics of the samples   247
B.1   Multiple classification analysis (1984 data)   250
B.2   Multiple classification analysis (1988 data)   251

Acknowledgements

I am grateful to Keith Thurley for his advice and intellectual stimulation throughout the various stages of the research. I should like to thank Hiroshi Hazama who helped to design the initial study while I was a *Monbusho* research scholar at Waseda University. I have also benefited a great deal from his advice on the many occasions I have visited Japan since then. I should also like to thank David Guest for his many constructive comments.

The research for this book would not have been possible without the generous help and co-operation of many of the staff in the personnel department of Seibu Department Stores Ltd and the employees who took part in the interviews and surveys. I owe a great debt to many Seibu women whom I met through the interviews and during the month when I worked as a shop assistant.

This research has received financial support from the following organisations to which I should like to express my gratitude and appreciation: The Kobayashi Setsutaro Fuji Xerox Foundation provided a generous grant in 1984 for the initial study and gave me further financial support for the follow-up study in 1988. Additional financial support was also generously provided by the Japan Foundation Endowment Committee and the Suntory Toyota International Centre for Economics and Related Disciplines (STICERD) of the London School of Economics.

I am also indebted to many people in Japan who have helped me a great deal with my field research. Tadashi Hanami gave me an introduction to Japan's Ministry of Labour and many other useful contacts. Ryoko Akamatsu, President of the Japan Institute of Women's Employment (former Director of the Women's Bureau of the Ministry of Labour), kindly gave an interview. Mitsuko

Horiuchi, Director of the Women's Bureau of the Prime Minister's Office and Kazuko Hitosugi, deputy chief of the Women's Bureau of the Ministry of Labour, provided me with very useful reference materials. I am also grateful to Tadashi Miura of the Japan Federation of Commercial Workers' Unions for helping me on many occasions. I am indebted to Shiraki Mitsuhide, Kazuhiko Nakao and many of my friends in Japan who have continuously sent me the latest publications and information.

Finally, special thanks to my husband David for his many very helpful comments and support throughout

The views expressed in this book are those of the author and engage neither the management of Seibu nor those who have provided funding for this research. Any errors remain the sole responsibility of the author.

Introduction

Chapter 1

Introduction and background

INTRODUCTION

It is often argued that the vitality of the Japanese employment system is sustained by personnel management rules and practices which make a clear distinction between the 'core' and the 'non-core' employees. The former, predominantly male, enjoy the privileges of long-term employment, wage increases and promotion based on age and length of service (*nenko*), and internal career progression through job rotation and in-company training; whereas the latter group is excluded (Galenson and Odaka 1976; Ishikawa 1980; Odaka 1984). Women workers constitute a high proportion of the latter category of employees. Their relatively low wages, high turnover and flexible entry and exit from the labour market play an especially important role in maintaining the flexibility of the employment system (Shinotsuka 1982; Kawashima 1987). Until very recently, direct exclusion and discrimination against women in all stages of employment was both legal and socially acceptable.

The picture began to shift from the mid-1970s. Social and economic changes gradually brought into question companies' discriminatory employment policies against women. The advent of the 'service economy' has expanded women's job opportunities and given them better access to the business world. Increased internationalisation of Japan also brought to the fore the low status of Japanese women in all aspects of the society, especially in the field of employment, compared with their counterparts in other advanced countries (*The Economist* 1988). Internal socio-economic changes, coupled with pressures from the international community, eventually led to the introduction of the Equal Employment Opportunity (EEO) Law in May 1985.

This law prohibits discrimination against women in vocational training, fringe benefits, retirement and dismissal. It also 'exhorts' ('morally obliges') employers to treat women equally to men with regard to recruitment, job assignment and promotion. The EEO Law marks an important turning point in the history of women's employment in Japan. For the first time in Japanese history, formal guarantees of equal treatment between women and men at all stages of employment are enshrined in a single piece of legislation. The enactment of the EEO Law has aroused much controversy and debate which is unprecedented in the history of labour legislation in Japan. The Japanese government described the passing of the new legislation as 'a great historical moment for all kinds of movements against discrimination in Japan' (MOL 1986). Despite its apparent lack of legal teeth, the legislation has important political and symbolic significance. The application of 'moral obligation' as a kind of indirect sanction puts the employers in a defensive position. Employment practices which were accepted as a 'natural' result of social customs would have to be put on the agenda for discussion and negotiation. Japanese companies, which have for a long time built their high performance upon an employment system which offers men 'lifetime' career jobs, are confronted with a fundamental dilemma of how to make greater use of women in key business positions without destroying the distinctive features of the employment system.

The central aim of this book is to examine the extent to which the growing pressures for equal opportunities between the sexes have caused Japanese companies to adapt and modify their employment and personnel management practices in recent years. It analyses the major social and economic factors prompting Japanese companies to adopt more open employment policies towards women since the mid-1970s and the programmes of change introduced by management. It looks especially at how companies have reacted to the 1985 EEO Law and, in the light of this, considers how far the present legislation will bring about fundamental changes in the Japanese employment system towards a more egalitarian treatment of women. A detailed case study was conducted at Seibu Department Stores Ltd, before and after the introduction of the EEO Law, as a critical test of the possibility of introducing equal opportunities for women in a large Japanese company (see p.21).

The theoretical approach of this study is located in the context of a major debate central to contemporary studies on the Japanese employment system: whether the drift away from the 'traditional' Japanese model of employment and personnel management as a result of socio-economic changes and external challenges is inevitable. This question has preoccupied many Japanese and foreign scholars. In the 1950s, when the 'Japanese employment system' was first perceived as distinctively different from the systems prevailing in western countries, it was seen as a hangover from the feudal past, destined to give way to more modern, 'rational' systems (Tsuda 1959). The continuous high performance of the Japanese economy led to a subsequent re-evaluation and to the recognition that the Japanese system has many merits, compared with those of the West (Nakayama 1975; OECD 1977). This positive re-evaluation has not eliminated recurrent prophecies about the inevitable change of the Japanese system in a 'western' direction. In the 1980s, the challenge of equal opportunities for women added extra impetus to the speculation about the eventual collapse of the Japanese employment system. How far and in what direction is the Japanese employment system changing? Is it changing in a direction which offers more egalitarian employment and career opportunities for women?

Equal employment for women is not an independent social or human rights issue. Companies' personnel policies for women constitute an integral part of the empoyment and labour market systems. Changes to women's labour market position would require major structural adjustments in the established employment system. The future of equal employment for women is greatly dependent on how far major Japanese companies are prepared to modify many of their core employment practices.

This book is a study of how Japanese companies have adapted their employment policies and practices in response to the growing pressures for more egalitarian treatment of women. It is also about the possibility of bringing about change in an employment system which has brought about the world's most closed and male-dominated internal labour markets.[1] From the theoretical and policy point of view, Japan provides a particularly interesting case study for examining the dynamics of change. There are three reasons for this.

First, internal labour market theorists argue that the rules and procedures which define the internal labour markets and govern their operation, once institutionalised, tend to be self-perpetuating and are difficult to change (Doeringer and Piore 1971). The Japanese employment system has been under increasing pressure for change as a result of many social and economic changes in recent years. Equal opportunities for women is one of the new challenges confronting Japanese management. The emerging situation in the 1980s provides an excellent opportunity to examine the interplay between social and economic forces in shaping employers' policies and practices – their strategies for change and adaptation in response to growing pressures for sexual equality. Japan, thus provides an interesting case for examining how an employment system with well-developed internal labour markets responds to the pressures for change.

Second, there are reasons to expect the process of change to be more complex in Japan. It is a country which is uniquely situated between the advanced industrial societies of the West and the less-developed countries. Japan emerged as a modern state after World War II. Economically, it is an advanced industrialised country. Socially, it shares many similar characteristics with other developing countries. Particularly illustrative is the position of women in the society. Further, the continued high performance of the economic system means that the desire among policy makers to maintain the present employment system is strong. This makes demands for equal employment a much more sensitive and complex issue than elsewhere.

Third, Japan also provides an excellent case to 'test' whether politics and policy intervention matter in equal employment issues. The struggle for equal employment for women in many western, advanced industrial societies has its base in economic and social changes, but the main force for propelling it to the level of state policies has been largely political. In the United States, the politics of the civil rights and women's movement have played an important role in transforming the demands for equal opportunities into public policies (Burstein 1985). In Japan, the economic conditions which are pushing Japanese companies to adopt more egalitarian employment policies for women are present. However, government intervention has been minimal; the EEO Law is an outgrowth of internal socio-economic changes and external pressures from the international community, not a result of an indigenous women's movement. Whether economic and commercial pressures alone can bring about changes in employment practices will reveal the degree to which equal opportunity strategies are needed.

The ultimate goals of equal opportunity policies involve normative choices which tend to vary from society to society. Moreover, the direction of change in the area of sexual equality also reflects the political strength and power balance of different social groups in a society and the demands of the economy. Despite the existence of many country-specific factors which may determine the ultimate shape of equal opportunity for women in different social systems, there are also many common fundamental issues facing all advanced industrialised countries. Japan, which is often regarded as representing an extreme case of sexual inequality and is often criticised as building its economic vitality upon the exploitation of women workers, provides a particularly interesting case for the examination of equal opportunity issues.

Before looking at the developments of recent years, a brief account is given of the origin and changing pattern of Japanese women's employment to set the scene.

A BRIEF HISTORICAL OVERVIEW OF WOMEN'S EMPLOYMENT IN JAPAN

Historically high participation but poor working conditions

Japanese women's entry into wage employment started in the early Meiji period and they constituted a much larger share of the industrial workforce than men during the first phase of industrialisation (1894–1913). The textile industry, the core industry in Japan during the first phase of industrialisation, employed a large number of women workers from the rural areas. In 1909, women comprised about 62 per cent of all factory workers and they comprised 86 per cent of the workforce in the textile industry (Takenaka 1983: 47). Female textile workers represented the first widespread category of wage employment in Japan, and they remained a major group in the industrial workforce until the 1930s. During the inter-war period (1914–37), some Japanese women began to enter clerical jobs but their number was rather small. In 1920, of the 4 million women in gainful employment, only 500,000 (12.5 per cent) were employed in offices. Males dominated clerical jobs, females accounted for a mere 6.5 per cent in 1930. Thus, the predominant form of female employment before World War II was in unskilled blue-collar jobs in the low-paying textile industry.

The majority of female workers in the textile mills were daughters of poor farming families who worked in the factories away from home for a few years before they returned to marry in their villages. Most of them were forced to work in the factories by their elders in the family in order to help the family finances. Okouchi (1959) described this type of worker as '*dekasegi gata chinrodo*' (household supplementary type labour migration). The working conditions of the female textile workers were extremely poor and wages exceedingly low.[2] The majority of the female workers were housed in dormitories and lived under the entire control of the factories. Women workers during this period had no independence. The working conditions were so poor that many girls quit by running away. The turnover rate of these workers was extremely high. Saxonhouse (1976: 100) described the Japanese textile industry's labour force as the 'most female and the most transient' in international comparisons.

Despite their high participation in industrial work in pre-World War II Japan, women workers were not able to gain economic independence. In both Britain and the United States, the experiences of the 'working girl' in the textile industry did eventually lead to the increasing economic independence of women and their freedom as individual wage earners (Matthaei 1983: 153; Pinchbeck 1930: 313). In the case of Japan, the women workers' strong ties with their rural families and their subservience to the patriarchal family system prevented them from establishing themselves as independent workers in the urban areas. Unlike the European countries where industrialisation led to the disintegration of patriarchy, the patriarchal family system in Japan, prescribed in the Meiji Civil Code (1898), persisted until the end of World War II.[3] The patriarchal family system supported the early formation of capitalism in Japan and women workers were exploited by both systems (Kobayashi 1976: 74).

World War II and the democratisation policies

As elsewhere, Japanese women were mobilised to take part in a wide range of economic activities during the war when men were recruited to the army. However, the impact of the war economy on the work experience of Japanese women was not as great as that in the European countries. This was partly because Japan did not have the history of relying on the female labour force during World War I, and partly because the government's effort in mobilising the female workforce was delayed during World War II. Despite the need to rely on the female workforce, the government's attitude towards mobilisation of women was rather ambivalent. There was strong concern that women's participation in the labour force might lead to a reduction of the population. The government issued a national mobilisation directive early in 1938, but the final decision to mobilise women did not come into effect until as late as the autumn of 1943. By that time, there was already a shortage of raw materials and the productive capacity of the economy was declining. During the brief period when women took part in the war economy, they continued to be treated as an auxiliary labour force. The policy statements issued by the government at that time specified that women were to be used only for 'simple and easy work', for 'light handwork calling for dexterity' and 'as semi-skilled or unskilled workers' (Akamatsu 1977: 33–5).

The greatest impact of the war on Japanese women came not so much through their direct work experience during the war but through the post-war reforms imposed by the Allied Occupation which lasted from 1945 until 1952. The sweeping reforms carried out by General MacArthur, as Supreme Commander for the Allied Powers (SCAP), brought about dramatic changes in the legal status of Japanese women. For the first time in history, women were granted equal rights with men under the new constitution of 1946. The constitution declared equality of all people before the law. Article 14 of the constitution prohibited discrimination in political, economic and social relations because of race, creed, sex, social status or family origin. Article 24 stipulated equality of the sexes in family life. Based on this principle of equality between the sexes, the Family Law of the pre-war period which was based on patriarchy was abolished. The new family law put an end, at least in formal legal terms, to women's centuries-old subjugation to the male head of the family. In the field of employment, the Labour Standards Law of 1947 provided for equal pay for equal work and granted women a series of protective measures in the areas of working hours, night work, underground work, menstruation leave, maternity leave, holidays and restrictions on dangerous work. The labour standards provided by the new legislation could be said to be one of the most advanced in the world at that time. In some instances, it was even said that the Occupation managed to inject more progressive provisions into the new Japanese system than existed in the United States. For example, equal pay for equal work legislation did not become law in the United States until 1963 (Robins-Mowry 1983: 100). Pharr (1981: 29) described the changes as the 'world's greatest experiment with feminism outside a revolutionary context'.

Post-war experience suggests that the externally imposed changes took longer to take root. It was not until the late 1960s that some women workers began to challenge their employers' discriminatory employment practices through the courts by using the equal rights provided for them in the constitution and the Labour Standards Law (see chapter 5).

Economic growth and changing patterns of women's employment in contemporary Japan

Rapid economic development over the last three-and-a-half decades has brought about dramatic changes in the role of women in the Japanese economy. One of the most significant has been the tremendous increase in the number of women working as paid employees (wage earners) – more than threefold from 5.3 million in 1955 to 18.3 million in 1990. In contrast to the upsurge in the number of women working as employees, those working as unpaid family workers reduced by more than half from 9 million in 1955 to 4.2 million in 1990, while the number of self-employed remains more or less stable (see table 1.1).

In 1955, women constituted 26 per cent of all paid employees; the figure rose to 37.9 per cent in 1990. The labour force participation rate of Japanese women had reached 50.1 per cent by 1990, a

Table 1.1 Number and proportion of women workers by work status, 1955–90 (all industries)

Year	Total		Self-employed		Unpaid family workers		Paid employees	
	No. (millions)	%	No. (millions)	%	No. (millions)	%	No. (millions)	%
1955	17.0	100.0	2.7	15.7	9.0	53.1	5.3	31.2
1960	18.1	100.0	2.9	15.8	7.8	43.4	7.4	40.8
1965	18.7	100.0	2.7	14.5	6.9	36.8	9.1	48.6
1970	20.0	100.0	2.9	14.2	6.2	30.9	10.9	54.7
1975	19.5	100.0	2.8	14.3	5.0	25.7	11.7	59.8
1980	21.3	100.0	2.9	13.7	4.9	23.0	13.5	63.2
1985	23.0	100.0	2.9	12.6	4.6	20.0	15.5	67.4
1990	25.2	100.0	2.7	10.7	4.2	16.7	18.3	72.6

Source: The Ministry of Labour, *Fujin Rodo No Jitsujo*, (Report on Female Workers).

Table 1.2 Distribution of the labour force by industrial sector, 1950–90

Year	Total labour force				Female labour force			
	Primary %	Secondary %	Tertiary %	Total No. (millions)	Primary %	Secondary %	Tertiary %	Total No. (millions)
1950	47.0	21.3	29.8	35.6	61.2	13.2	25.6	13.9
1960	32.6	29.2	38.2	43.7	43.1	20.2	36.7	17.1
1970	19.4	34.0	46.6	52.1	26.2	26.0	47.8	20.4
1975	13.9	34.0	51.9	53.0	18.4	25.7	55.7	19.6
1980	10.4	34.8	54.6	55.4	13.2	28.2	58.4	21.4
1985	8.8	34.3	56.5	58.1	10.6	28.3	60.8	23.0
1990	7.2	33.6	58.7	62.5	8.5	27.3	63.8	25.4

Source: For 1950–75, Kokusei Chosa (Population Census). For 1980–90, Rodoryoku Chosa (Labour Force Survey), Statistics Bureau, Management and Co-ordination Agency.

relatively high figure compared with many western European countries.[4]

Although Japanese women work in all economic sectors, the rapid expansion of the tertiary sector has absorbed a large proportion of them (see table 1.2). Female employment in the tertiary sector expanded especially rapidly after the 1970s. The changes in women's employment structure can also be indicated by the shift in their occupational distribution (see table 1.3). During the 1960s, when manufacturing industry was expanding rapidly, a high proportion of women worked as 'craft and production process' workers or labourers in the factories. After 1973, the increase of production

Table 1.3 Distribution of female employees by occupation, 1960–90

Occupation	Percentage distribution			Share of women in each category		
	1960	1975	1990	1960	1975	1990
Professional and technical workers	9.0	11.6	13.8	33.3	44.4	42.6
Managers and officials	0.3	0.9	1.0	2.5	5.4	7.7
Clerical and related workers	25.4	32.2	34.4	35.9	48.5	57.9
Sales workers	8.7	11.1	12.5	34.7	30.2	33.8
Farmers, lumbermen and fishermen	3.6	0.8	0.6	32.9	22.0	28.2
Mining and quarrying	0.3	0.0	0.0	5.7	0.0	0.0
Transport and communication	0.7	1.5	0.5	5.3	7.7	4.2
Craftsmen and production process workers	}35.9	24.6	20.6	}26.9	23.6	28.2
Labourers		3.7	5.6		32.6	41.6
Service workers	16.1	13.7	10.7	54.8	50.8	51.3
Total	100.0	100.0	100.0	31.1	32.0	37.9
(No. in millions)	(7.4)	(11.7)	(18.3)			

Source: The Ministry of Labour, *Fujin Rodo No Jitsujo* (Report on Female Workers).

process workers slowed down while clerical jobs expanded rapidly. In 1990, over one-third of women workers were in clerical jobs. This was followed by 'craft and production process' workers. The third largest category was professional and technical jobs. The increase in the number of women in professional and technical jobs has been re-markable since the 1970s, from 1 million in 1970 to 2.5 million in 1990. There has also been a marked increase in the number of sales workers as the Japanese economy entered a period of high con-sumption and the number of big stores increased dramatically.

The rapid expansion of women in white-collar jobs reflects both the change in the industrial structure as well as the rise in the educational level of women. Women's advancement rate to higher education (including two-year junior college and four-year university) rose from 17.7 per cent in 1970 to 37.4 per cent in 1990; while that of men from 29.3 per cent to 35.1 per cent. The edu-cational gap between men and women has narrowed considerably over the past two decades.[5] Another striking feature has been the rapid growth of married women's employment. Up to the mid-1960s, fresh school leavers and family workers were the major source of labour supply. With the rapid advancement of women to higher education and the absolute decline in the number of family workers, the increase in the female workforce after the mid–1960s came from housewives. The Japanese economy faced the problem of a severe shortage of labour after the mid-1960s. Economic necessity pushed companies to depart from the traditional practice of limiting their recruitment to fresh school leavers. Since the mid-1960s more and more companies started to recruit mid-career entrants, in particular, middle-aged women were encouraged to enter the labour force as part-time workers.

In 1965, the proportion of women employees who were married was 38.6 per cent, rising to 51.3 per cent in 1975 and further up to 58.4 per cent in 1990. If both the divorced and the widowed are included, the proportion reached 67.5 per cent in 1990, constituting about two-thirds of women employees. The average age of women employees also crept up from 26.3 years in 1960 to 35.7 in 1990, and their average length of service increased from 4.0 to 7.2 years over the same period. Thus, the dominant group of women employees shifted from the young unmarried to that of the middle-aged and married.

Although there has been a great increase in the participation of married women in employment, Japanese women's labour force participation by age groups still shows a bi-modal pattern ('M-shape') with two peaks, in the 20–24 and 45–49 age groups, and with the 25–34 age group at the bottom, indicating women's withdrawal from the labour market at their marriage and child-rearing ages. However, in recent years, a new trend is taking place: the great fall in the rate at age 25–34 is becoming smaller. The increase in the participation rate of those aged 25–29 has been especially remarkable (figure 1.1). This is related to the changes in women's attitudes to work as a result of increased higher education and the growing economic pressure for women to engage in wage employment in order to supplement the household income. Many analysts point out the involuntary character of the reduced participation rate of women in the marriage and child-rearing age groups (Yashiro 1983: 27; Takeishi 1987: 36–7). Survey evidence shows that a high proportion of the non-job holders in this age group wish to work (Somucho 1982). Thus, if more social services such as child-care facilities were available, more women in the 25–34 age group would go out to work.

AN EXTREME CASE OF UNEQUAL TREATMENT

Women's participation in the labour force in contemporary Japan shares many characteristics with that of western industrialised countries. Both social and economic changes are moving towards an increasing role of women in employment. However, compared to the western industrialised countries, Japan has been rather slow in granting women equal treatment in the workplace. Employment practices which were overtly discriminatory against women and were explicitly prohibited by legislation in most of the advanced industrialised countries by the mid-1970s were until recently still part of the norm of the employment system in Japan. A government survey in 1981 shows that many companies discriminated against women not only in recruitment but also in wages, job assignments, training, promotion and retirement age (MOL 1981a). For example, the survey found that 73 per cent of the firms restricted their recruitment of graduates to men only, 83 per cent of the firms had positions that were not open to women and 43 per cent gave women no opportunity for promotion. Until May 1985 when the EEO Law was passed, there was virtually no legal protection against discrimination of women in employment.

The labour market position of Japanese women appears to 'lag

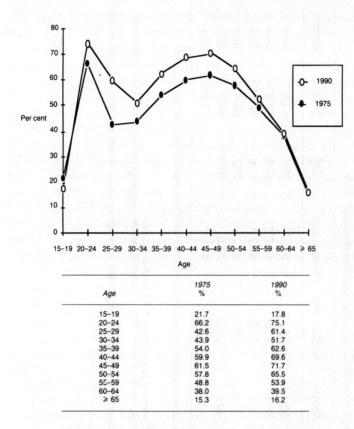

Age	1975 %	1990 %
15–19	21.7	17.8
20–24	66.2	75.1
25–29	42.6	61.4
30–34	43.9	51.7
35–39	54.0	62.6
40–44	59.9	69.6
45–49	61.5	71.7
50–54	57.8	65.5
55–59	48.8	53.9
60–64	38.0	39.5
⩾ 65	15.3	16.2

Figure 1.1 Women's labour force participation by age, 1975 and 1990
Source: Statistics Bureau, Management and Co-ordination Agency, *Rodoryoku Chosa* (Labour Force Survey).

behind' their counterparts in other advanced countries. Recent statistics and studies in several countries show that women's earnings have remained markedly lower than men's, but the wage gap in Japan is the greatest and has remained so over the past two decades (see table 1.4). Japanese women's share in managerial and administrative jobs is also remarkably small when compared to their counterparts in the West. They constitute only 8.8 per cent of all administrative and managerial posts as compared with 39.8 per cent in the United States, 18.4 per cent in the former West Germany and 21 per cent in Sweden (ILO 1990–1).

Table 1.4 Female earnings as a percentage of male earnings, selected countries and years

Year	Belgium	Denmark	France	W.Germany	Switzerland	UK	USA	Japan
1965	61.2	71.3	83.1	68.1	61.9**	59.5	59.6**	52.2
1970	66.7	73.6	86.9	69.2	62.8**	60.1	62.3**	56.4
1975	71.2	83.2	86.6	72.3	66.7**	67.6	62.0**	60.2
1980	69.4	84.5	87.4	72.4	67.3	69.7	63.4**	59.4
1985	74.6	83.8	88.5*	72.9	67.5	69.5*	68.2	56.5
1989	75.0**	82.7	–	73.5	67.4**	–	70.9**	57.6

Sources: ILO, *Year Book of Labour Statistics, Handbook of Labour Statistics, USA; Maitsuki Kinro Tokei Chosa* (Monthly Labour Survey). Ministry of Labour, Japan.

Notes: 1 The data refer to full-time year round workers or adults working normal hours.
2 The US data in 1965 is annual earnings, the data after 1970 are median weekly earnings; other countries are all hourly earnings.
3 The hourly earnings in Japan are calculated by dividing monthly cash earnings by actual hours worked during the month.
* 1984 data
** 1988 data

Table 1.5 A ten country comparison of women workers' responses to the statement 'I can use my abilities at work' (in electronic and electrical industries, 1984)

Country	Responses in percentage					
	Absolutely true	Fairly true	Unclear	Only slightly true	Not at all true	NA
France	21	16	8	24	12	20
Hong Kong	14	20	10	29	20	8
Hungary	35	15	25	9	4	12
Italy	30	31	8	13	9	10
Japan	3	30	39	19	8	2
Poland	21	16	37	7	4	16
Sweden	25	28	11	13	13	11
UK	22	23	13	15	23	5
W. Germany	16	22	19	27	16	0
Yugoslavia	31	32	1	14	5	17

Source: Compiled from *Denkiroren Chosa Jiho*, No. 204, 1985.

A ten country survey on the attitudes of workers in the electronic and electrical industries shows that Japan has a much lower proportion of women workers believing that they can use their abilities at work (see table 1.5). It also shows that Japanese women workers are least satisfied with their working conditions, pay and benefits, equal opportunities and various aspects of personnel policies such as training, job grading and promotion (*Denkiroren* 1985).

Nowhere in the industrialised world do women enjoy equal status with their male counterparts in the labour market. Sexual inequality in employment appears to be a universal phenomenon but evidence seems to indicate that Japan represents an extreme case among the advanced industrialised countries. Nobuko Takahashi, a prominent labour administrator and supporter of the women's cause in Japan, pointed out that women workers in Japan not only had to cope with problems common to women workers in all industrialised countries, but they were also confronted with some 'unique problems' which stem from the special features of the Japanese employment system, in particular, the practice of lifetime commitment and *nenko* wage and promotion system (Takahashi 1983: 4). From the viewpoint of the firms, employment of a permanent workforce and wage increments by age and length of service make the employment system extremely rigid. This inevitably means that the benefits of the practices can only be applied selectively: to the core workers. The majority of women workers, workers in small firms and a large number of part-time and temporary workers are excluded. Women play an especially important role as 'periphery' workers in maintaining the flexibility of the employment system.

The logic of the Japanese employment system is sustained by personnel management rules and practices which operate to exclude the majority of women from the core career jobs. Japanese companies are reluctant to invest in the long-term training of women because of their higher average turnover rate as compared to men's. In western countries, women can use external vocational or professional training as credentials for career development. In Japan the emphasis on long-term firm-specific training means that Japanese women tend to face greater institutional barriers to their career advancement and firms have a stronger discretionary power in allocating opportunities for career development. Occupational advancement depends much more on the allocative rules and procedures of the firms than elsewhere.

The importance of the seniority rule in job allocation, promotion and wage determination also operates to the serious disadvantage of women. Women retiring from the firm tend to lose all their accumulated seniority. When they re-enter the job market, they have to start again at the bottom of the job hierarchy. Career interruption is a disadvantage to women in any country, but it is much more of a handicap in Japan. Many firms, particularly the large ones, only recruit their regular workers from fresh school leavers. Job openings available for mid-career workers are limited; and for women they are often limited to jobs in the small firms or part-time jobs. Promotion and career development in Japanese firms also generally involve regular job-rotation which often requires geographical mobility. Firms do not expect women employees to be as mobile as their male counterparts. The immobility of women is often given as a reason for not promoting women and not assigning women to the mainstream career jobs.

The customary rules and practices in Japanese companies are based upon the traditional assumption that 'men's sphere is at work', therefore they are expected to be committed and loyal workers; whereas 'women's sphere is at home', therefore their role in the workplace can only be partial or marginal. This deep-rooted sex role distinction in Japanese society serves as an important ideological basis for justifying sexual inequality in the workplace. Sexual inequality in employment is very much related to the sexual division of labour in the family. This is true in Japan as well as in all other countries. However, what sets Japan apart from other advanced industrialised countries is that such an extreme sex role distinction has survived into a period of rapid and dramatic economic growth and that it has rarely been challenged until very recently.

THE FORCES FOR CHANGE

If unequal treatment of women workers constitutes part of the inherent logic of the employment system, then one might expect change in women's conditions to occur as a result of economic pressures on the employment system. Women's conditions might also improve if people start to question the morality of a system which continues to treat a growing proportion of the workforce in an unequal manner. In fact, since the mid-1970s, changes have been occurring – in the economic and industrial structure, in the employment system itself and, most important of all, in the legislative framework.

Since the mid-1970s, there has been a rapid growth of the service economy in Japan (Mizuno 1984). The shift of balance in the industrial structure from manufacturing to services has led to the rapid growth of new job opportunities. Women have entered jobs in the growing service sector at a much faster rate than men. In many industries, companies are finding it difficult to ignore the demands and needs of women whose performance and morale are becoming increasingly important for their competitiveness. The shortage of young qualified labour has pushed companies to recruit more female graduates, a category of women whom they used to shun before. The growing purchasing power of women and their dominance in the consumer market (Japanese women are almost in total control of the family budget) has made companies more aware of the need to utilise women's ideas in product development, marketing and sales. Some companies started to introduce special career development programmes for women after the mid-1970s.

The economic pressures for change culminated in the enactment of the EEO Law in May 1985. This new legislation was also partly a product of international pressures on Japan to bring her legislative framework on women into line with international standards. From the western perspective, the Japanese EEO Law may appear rather peculiar. It has granted women very few new rights and imposed only limited legal obligations on employers. The legislation makes a distinction between 'prohibition' and 'exhortation' in its provisions for ensuring equal treatment between men and women. Prohibition against discrimination applies to basic vocational training, fringe benefits, retirement and dismissal – areas in which substantial changes had already taken place before the law was introduced. With regard to the most important stages in employment including recruitment, job assignment and promotion, the law 'exhorts' employers to treat women as equally as men. The hortatory provisions appear to be highly ambiguous and their enforcement is dependent upon the administrative guidance (*gysoei-shido*) of the Ministry of Labour.

A detailed analysis of the contents of the law and the guidelines set by the Ministry of Labour suggests that the standard of equality as required by the Japanese legislation falls far short of the 'western norm'. The Japanese Ministry of Labour, however, points out that the EEO Law is a developing piece of legislation and that the requirements stipulated in the law represent no more than temporary minimum standards aimed at raising the average norm of equal opportunities in the Japanese enterprise community by reducing the number of bad practice companies. According to the Ministry, the spirit of the law goes beyond the requirements stipulated in the law. Good practice employers – those who have already satisfied the minimum requirements – are expected to fulfil their moral obligations by making 'further efforts' in providing equal opportunities for women, in respect of the spirit of the law. The EEO Law has two objectives. The first is to use the prohibitory provisions to remove the most blatant forms of direct discrimination; this first objective in effect aims at formally ratifying changes that have already occurred in the past and also to enforce changes in the worst practice companies. Its second, more important, objective is to use the hortatory provisions to exert 'moral pressure' on the good practice employers, to move beyond the minimum requirements enshrined in the law, and set the new norms and standards of equality. Thus, the real significance of the law lies not only in the extent to which companies in general are prepared to comply with the stipulated requirements but more importantly, in the extent to which it can act as a symbol of new moral standards to stimulate the good practice employers to set the pace for further change.

An important part of this book is to examine how Japanese companies have reacted and responded to the legislation and to see whether the model of change pursued by the companies, following the introduction of the EEO Law, is having a positive impact on the position and status of women workers. A detailed case study was conducted at Seibu as a critical test of how a large Japanese company, which already has strong commercial incentives to offer women better career opportunities and is regarded as a 'leading edge' company in personnel management reforms, might have taken the lead in responding positively to the spirit as well as the letter of the EEO Law. The Seibu case study is also used to test the outcomes of the equal opportunity policies on the position and status of women and to explore how far the equality debates have brought about a shift in women's work attitudes and career expectations.

A NOTE ON THE METHODOLOGICAL APPROACH

The choice of research methods is often determined by the type of problems one intends to pursue. For the purpose of understanding a complex and evolving situation, the case study method has many advantages. Information derived from representative questionnaire surveys would have been unlikely to yield the detailed and in-depth information that was obtained by establishing and maintaining a relationship with an organisation for over four years. Further, by having direct contact with the parties – both the managers and the employees – involved in the process of change, the author was able to gain a better and more precise understanding of the dynamics of the situation and how the actors actually perceived the process of change.

The Seibu data were obtained by using various research methods. These include in-depth interviews with personnel managers and individual women employees, a one-month period of participant observation (during which the author worked as a temporary shop assistant on the sales floor) and questionnaire surveys (see appendix A for details).

In addition to the Seibu case study, the author has collected information about a large number of cases from a great variety of sources such as management journals, government publications and newspapers. These empirical cases prvide invaluable information on the changes which have been going on in other Japanese companies in recent years and set Seibu in context. As the implementation of equal opportunity policies in Japanese companies is a very recent phenomenn, no previous study has been conducted in this area. It is therefore necessary to collect direct empirical evidence from as wide an angle as possible, piecing the information together in a systematic way and trying to arrive at some improved understanding of the complex and evolving situation.

The data and analysis introduced in this study represent a comprehensive and varied approach. The reader will be exposed to macro- and micro-analysis, a case study, analysis of secondary surveys and policy evaluations. Given the nature of the problems intended to be explored in this study, the adoption of a multi-method approach is necessary. It improves the validity of the interpretation and analysis. By examining the issues through a variety of data sources, one can gain a more balanced and in-depth understanding of the complex reality.

THE STRUCTURE OF THE BOOK

The main body of the book falls into three parts. Part I (chapters 2 to 4) deals with the theory and practice of labour market discrimination against women in Japan. Chapter 2 sets out the main theoretical approach and the key concepts used in the study. It argues that the institutional approach, especially internal labour market theory, provides a useful framework for analysing the process and mechanisms of labour market discrimination. Its greatest strength, in comparison with the neo-classical school, is that it examines in much greater detail the organisational rules and practices and explains how these rules operate to exclude certain groups of workers. Chapter 3 analyses the role of women workers in the Japanese employment system and examines the extent of labour market inequality. The main objective is to give a cross-sectional view of the role played by women workers in the employment system and to explain how the special nature of the Japanese employment system is supported by personnel practices which discriminate against the majority of women. Chapter 4 examines the changing situation after the mid-1970s, focusing on the ten years before the enactment of the EEO Law.

In May 1985, the Japanese government pased the EEO Law which came into force in April 1986. Part II of the book analyses the EEO legislation and examines the extent to which companies have

responded to it. In chapter 5, the nature and contents of the EEO
Law are discussed. The chapter examines why the EEO Law came
out the way it did and the extent to which it is meant to be 'an
instrument of social change'. Chapter 6 examines whether the
legislation has made any difference to companies' personnel policies
on women and whether there is any evidence that the shift in
personnel policies will bring about more egalitarian treatment of
women. The chapter presents an overall analysis and evaluation of
employers' policy responses, based on numerous surveys and reports.

Part III presents a detailed case study conducted at Seibu Department Stores on the changing position of women in the company.
Seibu is treated as a critical case. This is because it is a company in
which positive changes are more likely to occur than elsewhere
owing to the nature of its management philosophy, the type of
business and the importance of women to its successful operation.
The background of the case study is described in chapter 7. Chapter
8 examines the changes in the company's employment policies and
personnel practices on women. It looks at the situation both before
and after the introduction of the EEO Law. Chapter 9 examines the
shifts in the position and status of women by comparing their
situation in 1984 to that of 1988, and evaluates whether the policy
changes are leading to better career opportunities for women. It also
examines whether the equality debates and the enactment of the
EEO Law have raised women's career aspirations and expectations.
The study shows very limited improvement in terms of more women
gaining senior positions. There is no evidence of a reduction of
discrimination against women in promotion. There is also no
significant evidence that the expectations and aspirations of Seibu
women have gone up over the period observed.

The final chapter identifies the obstacles and constraints that limit
equal opportunities for women in Japanese companies. It argues that
management's continued attachment to the 'traditional' employment
practices, especially the 'lifetime commitment' practice, for their
core (predominantly male) employees, presents the greatest obstacle
to the introduction of more liberal, equal opportunities policies for
women. The present EEO Law has not undermined the mechanisms
which perpetuate sexual job segregation in the employment system.
The model of equal opportunity as enshrined in the law accepts the
persistence of the structural and institutional factors which
contribute to women's unequal position in the labour market. It

appears that any positive effects the recent changes in company policies might have on a small number of 'elite women' might, in the long run, be swamped by other opposing forces which are working against equal opportunities for women.

Part I

Discrimination against women in employment: theory and practice

Chapter 2

Internal labour markets and discrimination

This chapter sets out the main theoretical approach and the key concepts used in the study. The main focus is the internal labour market theory and its application to the problem of sexual inequality and discrimination. Although the original model underlying internal labour market theory does not apply explicitly to the specific situation of women, it provides a very useful framework for analysing the structural sources of labour market inequality and the mechanisms which perpetuate discrimination.

Another reason for turning to internal labour market theory is its relevance to Japan. Despite much debate about the 'cultural uniqueness' of the Japanese employment system, many Japanese and foreign scholars have increasingly come to accept the concept of an internal labour market as a useful approach for analysing the basis of the lifetime commitment practice and the *nenko* reward and promotion systems characterising large Japanese companies. Koike points out that the practice of internal promotion, though existing to some degree in other countries, appears to be much deeper and more widespread in Japan (Koike 1988: 280). Cole also concludes that large Japanese firms have much stronger internal labour markets than those in the United States, based on his comparative study of labour mobility practices in the two countries (Cole 1979: 100). Moreover, according to Cole, the dominant role played by individual characteristics such as age, education, seniority, ability and merit in pricing and allocating labour within Japanese firms, together with high job security, implies that the Japanese type of internal labour markets are more effective than western arrangements in defining the rights and privileges of those currently employed. In other words, the set of internal labour market rules in Japanese firms tends to be more exclusive and discriminatory.

Some scholars are critical of applying such universal concepts to Japan, pointing out that it disguises the distinctive structural characteristics of the Japanese type of internal labour markets. Dore uses the term 'internal redeployment' to describe the Japanese system, stressing the need to make a distinction between a competitive internal market and an internal 'personnel posting' system governed by administrative process (Dore *et al.* 1989: 12). These views, however, can be interpreted to mean not that the concept of internal labour market itself is inapplicable, but rather that we must allow for variations in the strength and bases of internal labour markets in different countries (Cole 1979: 44).

I would argue that in analysing the problem of employment discrimination against women in Japan, the internal labour market approach is particularly relevant. Many scholars noted that the prevalence of internal labour markets in Japan poses special problems for women (Takahashi 1983; Sano 1986; Yashiro 1983). This is not simply because internal labour markets are more established and widespread in Japan, but, more importantly, the nature of the rules and practices governing the Japanese internal labour markets are based more on personal characteristics than job classifications. Sex and age are often used as criteria for defining the rights and obligations of the employees. Discrimination against women constitutes an important basis for the employment practices characterising Japanese companies. We shall deal with the distinguishing characteristics of Japanese employment practices and the problem of discrimination against women in the next chapter.

The present chapter examines the problem of inequality and discrimination on the theoretical level. Before turning to internal labour market theory, the chapter first looks at the concept of 'discrimination' and explains why orthodox economic theories have provided only limited insights into the problem.

INEQUALITY AND DISCRIMINATION: LIMITATIONS OF THE CONVENTIONAL APPROACH

Labour market discrimination against women is manifested through different rates of pay and occupational and industrial segregation. The concept of 'discrimination' is rather complex. There is a lack of consensus among academics and policy makers as to what exactly constitutes discrimination. The following quotation from Kenneth

Boulding illustrates the difficulties involved in trying to come to grips with the concept of discrimination:

> Discrimination is a phenomenon which is so pervasive in all human societies that there is no doubt at all that it exists. It is not, however, a unitary phenomenon but a complex of a number of related forms of human behavior, and this makes it not only hard to define but frequently difficult to comprehend fully.
>
> (Boulding 1976)

Inequality is an outcome of discriminatory behaviour and it can be used as an index by which the presence of discrimination is assessed. But is an act or procedure to be regarded as 'discriminatory' simply because women are disproportionately affected? If labour market inequality is an outcome which appears to be caused by the fact that women are in a disadvantaged position before they enter the labour market, how far can one attribute such inequality to 'discrimination' in the labour market? Further, how can one evaluate a situation whereby current lower productivity is the cumulative effect of past discrimination? There are no easy answers to these questions.

An issue central to various theories attempting to explain the existence and persistence of labour market inequality is the debate on the extent to which such inequality is a result of differences on the supply side, e.g. differences in job choices, career aspirations or productivity between men and women, and how far it is a consequence of 'discrimination' on the demand side – 'discrimination' defined in simple economic terms as 'the receipt of lower pay for given productivity' or 'any form of unequal treatment of different groups of employees which does not directly result in cost minimisation in labour utilisation' (Jain and Sloane 1981: 26).

Many neo-classical economic theorists attempt to explain the problem of sexual inequality in employment. However, they have provided only a limited and simplistic explanation of the sources of inequality and offer little insight into why and how discrimination persists in the long run. Individuals and firms in neo-classical theory are assumed to exercise freedom of choice and behave rationally to maximise their utility. Human capital theorists hold that the amount of investment in human capital determines labour productivity, and consequently an individual's wage (Becker 1964). They assume a direct relation between the amount of investment in human capital, productivity and the wage level. Thus, women's lower earnings simply reflect their smaller investment in human capital and hence lower productivity. Productivity between men and women of the same age and level of education is said to differ for two reasons. First, women on average spend proportionately fewer years in the labour force than men. They interrupt their market work to bear and rear children. Second, when women are working, the jobs they choose provide them with fewer opportunities to enhance their skills. They therefore acquire less experience and on-the-job training than men; and their earnings reflect this (Mincer and Polachek 1974). Interruption of market work for child-rearing contributes to lower returns on the education and training of women, and hence makes investment less attractive.

There are several unresolved issues in the above argument. Human capital theorists cannot explain why women with the same education and productivity related characteristics as men still earn less. Many empirical studies indicate the persistence of a considerable degree of wage inequality between men and women despite controlling productivity related variables (OECD 1979). A second loose end in the human capital argument is its inability to explain the concentration of women in a small number of female occupations. Human capital theorists have to rely on women's 'tastes' in order to explain this phenomenon. Yet, it is not clear why only women should have such tastes nor is it clear why a large proportion of women should exhibit the same set of tastes – as demonstrated by their occupational distribution (Blau and Jusenius 1976: 187–8). Moreover, it is not clear in the human capital theorists' argument whether the low levels of human capital of women are the cause or effect of observed labour instability. Low wages due to discrimination in the labour market may discourage women from investing in human capital; and low investments in human capital perpetuate women's lower earnings. In response to these criticisms, some neoclassical theorists assume that discrimination in the labour market exists and they introduce new elements such as employers' tastes (Becker 1957), imperfect competition due to monopsony (Madden 1973) or the notion of imperfect information (Arrow 1973; Spence 1974) to explain the phenomenon of discrimination. However, within these models, the problem of discrimination is reduced to the pure economic question of whether and why wages are different among people with the same productivity. The existence of discrimination is deduced from labour market outcomes. Behavioural influences which are social, cultural or ideological are assumed to be stable and such extraneous influences are lumped together as 'tastes' which are outside their theoretical models. The greatest weakness of these theories is that they all fail to explain why discrimination persists in the long run. The processes and mechanisms which perpetuate discrimination at the firm level remain underdeveloped in the orthodox theories.

It is not our intention to provide a detailed review or critique of the neo-classical theories as these have already been dealt with by many other authors (Blau 1984; Blau and Jusenius 1976; O'Neill 1984). The crucial point to note is that for the purpose of understanding the nature of the processes which generate and perpetuate sexual inequality, neo-classical theorists do not provide much useful insight. In comparison, the institutional school, which explicitly takes into account the institutional and social origins of the divisions in the labour market, and stresses the effect of these processes on the rules governing the allocation of labour within the different segments, provides a more useful approach for analysing the problem of inequality and persistent discrimination. The particular institution model which is especially relevant to the analysis of the questions of job segregation by sex and women's low pay is the internal labour market theory developed by Doeringer and Piore (1971) and the related concept of the dual labour market (Piore 1971 and 1975).

INTERNAL LABOUR MARKET ANALYSIS

The concept of an internal labour market

Doeringer and Piore (1971) define the internal labour market as 'an administrative unit within which the pricing and allocation of labour is governed by a set of administrative rules and procedures'. This is distinguished from the external labour market where wages are more directly determined by market forces. The two markets are linked together mainly at entry-level jobs.

Doeringer and Piore attribute the origin of internal labour markets to the development of modern technologies, by which skills have become more firm specific, so that a worker's productivity increasingly becomes a function of on-the-job training and experience, and consequently of length of service. In such circumstances, it becomes particularly important for the employer to encourage stability and reduce turnover. This is done by providing wages, benefits and prospects better than those available in the external labour market. The internal labour market has a limited number of entry points, mainly at lower level jobs; higher level jobs are filled from internal sources through transfer and promotion of existing employees. The wage structure tends to reward length of service with the firm rather than general labour market experience.

Providing more favourable terms and conditions is costly and not all jobs are of the kind where technological change makes stability and on-the-job training important. Thus the labour market can be depicted as segmented into two sectors. The part of the economy characterised by internal labour markets is called the 'primary' sector where workers enjoy job security and are recruited internally through well-defined promotion ladders. The remaining jobs form the 'secondary' sector. The secondary sector includes many jobs requiring little job-specific skill and workers are generally low paid with a high turnover rate and limited promotion prospects. In many firms, the two types of jobs exist side by side. Between the two categories of jobs, mobility is limited.

Within the primary sector, Piore (1975) introduced a further division. He suggested an upper or 'primary independent' tier, composed of professional and managerial jobs. These were distinguished from the lower tier, 'subordinate primary' jobs, by their higher pay, higher mobility and turnover patterns which, in some ways, resembled those of the secondary sector.

The development of internal labour markets in the primary sector thus gives rise to an extreme form of labour market segmentation – the formation of a dual labour market (Piore 1971 and 1975). In the primary sector, jobs are characterised by high wages, good working conditions, employment stability and job security, equity and due process in the administration of work rules, and chances for advancement. By contrast, jobs in the secondary sector offer low wages, poor working conditions, considerable variability in employment, harsh and often arbitrary discipline, and little opportunity to advance. Mobility barriers prohibit the movement of workers from the secondary sector to the primary sector. Piore explains the allocation of workers between sectors in terms of the demands for different kinds of workers' behaviour, in particular, employment stability. The majority of women are excluded from jobs in the primary sector and become trapped in the secondary sector because of their lack of employment stability.

Employment stability is seen as particularly important in internal labour markets because of the importance of developing firm-specific skills on a long-term basis. Doeringer and Piore argue that there is a strong incentive for employers to emphasis on-the-job training as this is less costly. On-the-job training enables the training period to be spread over a whole succession of jobs, with the jobs arranged so that as people progress through them, each job provides some of the experience required for the next. Continuity of employment is essential as firms would want to capture the benefit of natural on-the-job training sequence. Given the sexual division of labour in society, women are seen as less desirable employees as they are less likely to be able to comply with the 'employment continuity' requirement for jobs in the internal labour market. Thus, the majority of them are trapped in the secondary sector. In the internal labour market model, discrimination against women is seen as an inevitable outcome deriving from the work norms that are required by modern technology and the need to conserve skilled labour. In other words, discrimination against women is an incidental by-product of work rules designed to achieve efficiency needs.

Although Doeringer and Piore's explanation of the origins of the internal labour market is criticised as being centred too much on the role of technology and neglecting the importance of employer strategy and social structure in shaping some of the internal labour market rules (Marsden 1986: 144), their model has provided very useful insights into the problem of discrimination. Their model not only recognises that discrimination plays an important part in the structuring of labour markets but that it also tends to persist, because it is in the interests of the employers and employees within the internal labour market to protect the structure.

Internal labour market rules and discrimination

The distinction between jobs in the internal labour market and those in the external labour market gives rise to discrimination in three ways.

First, discrimination occurs as a result of segmentation and direct exclusion: 'the privileges conferring upon the internal labour force are not available to those in the external labour market' (Doeringer and Piore 1971: 133). Current employees are likely to be given preferential treatment over outside job applicants on account of factors such as possession of specific skills and knowledge of the enterprise. Workers in the external labour market may not be aware of the existence of job opportunities in the internal labour market, even if they possess the requisite skills. Further, if they succeed in gaining entry to the internal labour market, such workers may remain disadvantaged because of their lack of seniority. Thus the crucial feature of the internal labour market is not just that 'the "ins" are treated under a different regime than the "outs" but that they attain markedly better outcomes than do their excluded counterparts' (Ryan 1981: 16). Discrimination is therefore an inevitable outcome of segmentation of workers into the 'ins' and the 'outs'.

Second, discrimination can also occur indirectly 'through the rules which define internal labour markets and govern their operation' (Doeringer and Piore 1971: 133). This involves two main aspects: discrimination through entry rules and discrimination through internal allocative rules. Entry discrimination can occur as a result of hiring standards, screening criteria or recruitment procedures. Doeringer and Piore refer to the entry rules as 'the most loosely constrained instruments of manpower adjustment available to management' in internal labour markets and point out that these rules 'depend for the most part upon the judgment of personnel managers and foremen' (ibid: 138). For example, hiring standards such as educational or testing standards, can be arbitrarily imposed in order to exclude certain workers yet practised under the guise of objective procedures to ensure a competent workforce or justified by reference to the requirements of jobs at the top of the promotion ladder or to forecasts of changing job requirements. Discrimination or more accurately, 'statistical discrimination' may also occur as a result of using cheap screening criteria such as sex to implement hiring standards. In the high-wage primary sector, given the investment made by the firm in training and the cost of defective hiring procedures, employers will attempt to increase the rate of return on their investment by selecting employees who are likely to prove stable. Since obtaining accurate information about each individual job applicant may be costly, it is common for employers to use group characteristics such as sex or education as a screening device. Following this explanation, if employers perceive women on average to be less stable workers, then individual women may be barred from primary jobs on a probabilistic basis. Further, the internal labour market tends to establish rather stable channels of recruitment, such as recruiting through a selected group of educational institutions and these are in part used as a kind of screening procedure. Once the channels of recruitment become well established, they tend to perpetuate and continue to reproduce the existing patterns of employment.

Discrimination within the internal labour market can also occur through internal allocative rules – through the design of job mobility clusters and the criteria used for movement between or within them. In internal labour markets, employers' interests are to minimise the cost of turnover and to capture natural on-the-job training sequence. Seniority combined with ability are the crucial criteria for moving along the line of progression within or between job clusters. From this perspective, women are seen by employers as less desirable employees because of their relative lack of employment stability. Exclusion of women can be effected by applying certain restrictive promotion criteria, for example, mobility requirements, or by restricting them to certain clusters of jobs which require less training. Another important point to note is that the vested interests of the employees tend to become a powerful force in deterring the adaptation of these rules to changing technological or economic circumstances. One good example is that seniority rules cannot be so easily disrupted as this might create frustration and resentment among older employees if younger members move above them in the line of progression. Similarly, employers might want to promote women to 'male' jobs but male resentment can deter employers from doing so.

Third, stable work groups in the internal labour market tend to develop certain customs based upon precedent and repeated practices; what Doeringer and Piore call the 'natural outgrowth of the psychological behavior of stable groups'. These customs and practices can come to acquire an ethical, or quasi-ethical, status within the work group, which can function socially and psychologically to reject groups which do not conform to the established customs. Custom also imparts a rigidity to the internal labour market rules and procedures and makes it difficult to change them in response to dynamic economic forces:

> Custom at the workplace is an unwritten set of rules based largely upon past practice and precedent . . . work rules appear to be an outgrowth of employment stability within internal labor markets. Such stability . . . is of value to both the employer and the workforce, and one of the factors producing internal labor market is the desire to effectuate stability.
>
> (Doeringer and Piore 1971: 23)

Internal labour market theory gives powerful insights into the persistence of discrimination and why change might not occur even

when the original market and technological factors which produce
the rules and practices cease to exist:

> Because one effect of custom is to inhibit change, it causes the
> allocative structure to reflect efficiency considerations, employees
> interests, and the balance of power prevailing at some time in the
> past.
>
> (Doeringer and Piore 1971: 61)

Internal labour market theory not only recognises that labour
market discrimination exists but also that it tends to perpetuate
because it has positive economic value for the groups in the
privileged sector. Hence, there are groups interested, not only in
resisting the elimination of discrimination, but in actively seeking its
perpetuation. Though inherently a static model, internal labour
market analysis illuminates the likely complexity of the adaptation
process when the internal labour market rules and practices are
challenged by external forces such as economic and technological
changes or equal employment opportunity pressures. Doeringer and
Piore (1971) point out that both the employers and the employees
are likely to resist rapid alteration of the internal labour market rules.
This is not only because the internal labour market arrangements are
seen as economically efficient by the employers and they guarantee
job security and stable career progression for the incumbent
employees, but also because customs and expectations tend to form
around the long-standing rules which become a strong deterrent to
adaptation within the internal labour market. Underlying internal
labour analysis is an assumption that the process for eliminating
discriminatory practices is bound to be highly complex. It requires a
resolution of the conflict between various social and economic goals
and an accommodation of conflict of interests among different
groups in the society. Thus internal labour market analysis gives
powerful insights for understanding the dynamics of the adjustment
process as it takes into consideration the socio-political forces underlying labour market discrimination.

THE SPECIFIC SITUATION OF WOMEN AND SEXUAL DIVISIONS IN THE HOUSEHOLD

Despite the usefulness of the internal labour market model in highlighting the crucial role of labour market rules and company
practices in sustaining and reproducing discrimination, the model is

nevertheless limited when applied to the special issue of discrimination against women. It fails to explain the specific situation of women and has treated sexual divisions in the household and society at large as exogenous factors.

Doeringer and Piore attribute the origin of labour market segmentation to developments within modern industry. They explain the development of internal labour markets in the high technology monopoly sector in terms of employers' initiatives with particular emphasis on the demand for a certain kind of work behaviour—employment stability. This demand, according to their model, is related to the need to minimise training cost. Implicit in their model is an assumption that work behaviour determines which workers fill which jobs. Men fill the primary jobs in the internal labour markets because they are in a position to comply with the demands of the internal labour markets rules; whereas the majority of women are said to be excluded from the primary jobs and remain trapped in the secondary sector because of their lack of employment stability.

This primary–secondary distinction, however, is too simplistic a view of sexual divisions in the labour market. Many analysts have noted that the division of labour by sex cuts across all segments of the labour market; sex divides internal labour markets in the primary sector, and even in the secondary sector men and women hold different jobs (Beechey and Whitelegg 1986; Hartman 1987).

Further, Doeringer and Piore's model assumes that skill content is a criterion determining whether certain jobs are to be located in the primary or secondary sectors. Many empirical studies show that the division of jobs into primary and secondary categories is not independent of characteristics of the workers who are employed. Craig *et al.* (1985) show that employers tend to classify women's jobs as low-skilled and assign them to low pay grades irrespective of job content and the workers' skills. Phillips and Taylor (1980) also point out that the very labelling of jobs as skilled or unskilled is an object of struggle and that social definitions and ideological constructions enter into the definitions of certain kinds of work as skilled:

the classification of women's jobs as unskilled and men's jobs as skilled or semi-skilled frequently bears little relation to the actual amount of training or ability required for them. Skill definitions are saturated with sexual bias. The work of women is often deemed inferior simply because it is women who do it. Women

workers carry into the workplace their status as subordinate
individuals and this status comes to define the value of work they
do. Far from being an objective economic fact, skill is often an
ideological category imposed on certain types of work by virtue
of the sex and power of the workers who perform it.

(Phillips and Taylor 1980: 79)

Discrimination against women cannot be interpreted merely as an
incidental by-product of labour market segmentation originated
from technological demands. Sexual divisions and power relationships have an independent role in shaping employers' segmentation
strategy and hence in the structuring of labour markets. As pointed
out by Ryan:

the racial and sexual variants of discrimination cannot be traced
entirely to prior conditions of segmentation. The availability of
racial and sexual differentiation can affect the extent of market
segmentation not just because of the opportunity provided to
employers to weaken the bargaining power of workers but also
because the repression of blacks and women, whether coercive or
cultural, makes it unlikely that they will exploit the opportunities
for bargaining presented by their working environment as
intensively as do their white male counterparts.

(Ryan 1981: 17)

Feminist analysts, such as Hartman (1976), introduce the concept of
patriarchy in their analysis of women's subordinate position in the
labour market. She identifies a number of factors which partly
account for segregation of women into low pay jobs. These include
the exclusionary power of male trade unions, the financial
responsibility of men for their families, the willingness of women to
work for less and women's lack of training. She emphasises the role
of trade unions in maintaining job segregation and excluding women
and sees this as an expression of men's desire to control and dominate
women. Hartman argues that job segregation creates a vicious circle
for women from which they cannot escape:

Job segregation . . . is the primary mechanism in capitalist society
that maintains the superiority of men over women, because it
enforces lower wages for women in the labour market. Low wages
keep women dependent on men because they encourage women
to marry. Married women must perform domestic chores for their
husbands. Men benefit, then, from both higher wages and the

domestic division of labour, in turn, acts to weaken women's position in the labour market. Thus, the hierarchical domestic division of labour is perpetuated by the labour market, and vice versa.

(Hartman 1976: 139)

Women's unequal position in the labour market cannot be understood solely in terms of an analysis of production and the labour market process. Sexual division of labour within the family plays an important role in determining the conditions in which women enter the labour market. It affects women's labour supply pattern and the type of work they do. Moreover, women's expectations are conditioned by their perception of employment opportunities and by their position in the family which determines their income needs and domestic responsibilities (Craig *et al.* 1985: 279). In the economic models, sexual division of labour in the family is treated as given. Many economic theorists fail to recognise that familial ideology and state family policies, which embody an assumption that women are mothers and housewives dependent upon men, imposes a powerful constraint on women's employment behaviour and expectations, and has an independent effect in shaping employers' labour force strategy.

In sum, central to feminist analyses of women's employment is the argument that 'women's unequal and inferior position within paid employment and their low pay has little to do with economic factors, for instance, that they are cheap labour, but is a consequence of gender relations and gendered assumptions which affect employers' hiring strategies, trade union practices, which relegate women to a subordinate position' (Beechey and Whitelegg 1986: 127). The feminist perspective provides important insights into sexual discrimination in the labour market: it cannot be seen merely as a consequence of economic forces, but that gender divisions, power, ideology and culture all have a role to play. This implies that strategies for dealing with inequality between men and women need to confront all these issues and devise ways to break the vicious circle.

INSTITUTIONAL DISCRIMINATION AND EQUAL OPPORTUNITY

The concept of institutional discrimination

Labour market discrimination is a multifaceted social, economic and political phenomenon. It cannot be reduced to the 'pure economic question of whether and why wages are different among people with the same productivity' (Schmid and Weitzel 1984: 265). Internal labour market theory, which stresses the significance of employment rules and practices in excluding certain groups of workers from the primary jobs, directs our attention to the structural and institutional factors in perpetuating labour market inequality.

The concept of 'institutional discrimination' originated in the study of race relations in the United States in the 1960s. Until the late 1950s the study of American and British race relations was dominated by the study of prejudice. By the late 1960s, the predominant approach in the United States changed to one which emphasised institutional and structural reasons for exclusion in addition to 'prejudiced discrimination' (McCrudden 1982). Early in 1968, Mayhew used the term 'structural discrimination' to describe the exclusion of the Negro community from employment in America. He pointed out two important aspects of discrimination: the normative patterns and the social structures which define and perpetuate discrimination. According to Mayhew, there are important connections between the two aspects and therefore the elimination of prejudice or social stereotyping will not eliminate discrimination because social forces maintain established structures despite changes in the attitudes of individuals: 'Inequalities in some institutional spheres are reproduced in others. An unprejudiced person can apply standards in a completely universalistic and equitable manner and still exclude Negroes' (Mayhew 1968: 57).

Knowles and Prewitt used the term 'institutional racism' to describe a situation where:

> behavior has become so well institutionalized that the individual generally does not have to exercise choice to operate in a racist manner. The rules and procedures of large organization have already prestructured the choice. The individual only has to conform to the operating norms of the organization and the institution will do the discriminating for the firm.
>
> (Knowles and Prewitt 1969: 143)

Discrimination against women in the internal labour market can well be described as a kind of 'institutional sexism'. To the extent that jobs in the primary sector are staffed by men and they provide the norms for work behaviour, women's work characteristics then come to be defined negatively as deviating from this norm. The requirement for employment continuity, the allocation of jobs and rewards according to seniority and the use of mobility rules as criteria for promotion are clearly 'male-oriented' practices which put women in a disadvantaged position. Discrimination against women, in such cases, is derived from the existence of work norms that are conventionally male (Kendrick 1981: 169). Under these circumstances, employers need not operate in a prejudiced manner in order to discriminate against women. By simply following the existing employment rules and workplace practices, they automatically exclude women from the primary jobs in the internal labour market.

The exclusion of women from primary jobs tends to reinforce the social perception that women are inferior workers only suitable for unskilled and low pay jobs. The confinement of women to inferior secondary jobs tends to reinforce their 'secondary worker traits' such as higher labour turnover and lower morale, it also lowers their career expectations and aspirations. This psychological effect thus creates a 'vicious circle' which reinforces the discriminatory power of the trait which was made the basis of selection criteria, and the labelling process becomes self-fulfilling (Barron and Norris 1976: 53)

Institutional discrimination cannot be eradicated by simply asking employers to adopt an attitude of 'non-discrimination' or by applying equal treatment policies. What needs to be scrutinised are the mechanisms of exclusion, the organisational rules and procedures which maintain and perpetuate inequality. The logic of the above analysis suggests that to reduce inequality in employment, changing the employment rules and practices is a critical priority. Removing employment discrimination therefore means breaking the vicious circle which perpetuates inequality.

Tackling institutional discrimination: from 'prejudiced treatment' to 'adverse impact'

Institutional discrimination is a universal phenomenon. Whether or not it is illegitimate depends on societal values and how the issue is brought into the political arena. The shifts in the legal definitions of discrimination and the differences in the ways it is being defined in the anti-discrimination policies of different countries signify not only the changes in societal values and perceptions of inequalities in the labour market, but also reflect the relative bargaining power of different interests groups in different societies.

In the United States, the concept of labour market discrimination has undergone three stages of development since the first days of explicit anti-discrimination policies. This change has been well summarised by Jain and Ledvinka (1975): initially, discrimination was defined as 'prejudiced treatment', i.e. harmful acts motivated by personal antipathy toward the group of which the target person was a member. However, since it is difficult to prove intent to harm, that first definition was ineffective as a means of solving the problems of labour market inequality.

Consequently, discrimination came to be defined in the courts as 'unequal treatment'. Under this second definition, the law was said to mean that the same standards be applied to all employees and applicants. In other words, the employer was allowed to impose any requirements, so long as they were imposed on all groups alike. Yet many of the most common requirements such as education and testing had unequal effects on various groups, even though they were imposed on all groups equally. This meant that employers were still allowed to ignore the inequalities built into the rest of society, especially into the processes by which people acquired credentials.

In recognition of such concerns, the US Supreme Court articulated the third definition of employment discrimination in *Griggs* v. *Duke Power Co* (Blumrosen 1972). There the court struck down employment tests and educational requirements that screened out a greater percentage of blacks than whites. Those practices were prohibited simply because they had the consequence of excluding blacks disproportionately, and because they bore no relationship to the jobs in question. Thus, the concept of labour market discrimination shifted from a concept of intent to a concept of 'adverse impact'; and consequently, the focus shifted from individuals to groups. According to this approach, the problem of labour market inequality is to be solved by eliminating those employment practices that had unequal impact on the groups covered by equal employment law, independent of whether there was conscious discrimination or not. What matters are consequences and not intentions.

The development of the legal concept of labour market discrimination in the United States is also mirrored in the Sex

Discrimination Act (1975) in Britain which covers both direct and indirect discrimination (O'Donovan and Szyszczak 1988). The concept of indirect discrimination is intended to deal with effects of seemingly neutral conditions which have a disproportionate impact upon one sex. As in the United States, the extension of the scope of legislation from tackling direct discrimination to indirect discrimination, that is, from an idea of intention-based discrimination to one that focuses on 'disparate impact', was the result of a recognition of the structural sources of unequal opportunity and in particular an acceptance of what has become known as 'institutional discrimination' in Britain (McCrudden 1982).

The extension of the scope of legislation to cover indirect discrimination has great potential in identifying and attacking exclusionary employment practices, and in urging employers to find alternative, non-discriminatory ways of implementing employment policies. Nevertheless, the technicalities involved in proving and measuring 'disparate impact' remains highly complex and controversial (Smith 1980).

CONCLUSIONS

This chapter has reviewed some major theories and concepts in an attempt to understand the nature of discrimination against women in employment. The institutional approach, especially the internal labour market theory, provides a useful framework for analysing the process and mechanism which produce and perpetuate inequality between men and women. The greatest strength of the internal labour market model is that it examines in great detail how the rules and practices governing internal labour markets operate to exclude certain groups of workers and how the established rules and practices are maintained and supported by the employers and employees within the internal labour market. These rules tend to reinforce and reproduce discrimination. By emphasising the role of socio-political forces in sustaining the established labour market rules and workplace customs, internal labour market theory provides powerful insights for addressing the issue of persistent discrimination. Though inherently a static model, internal labour market theory illuminates the likely complexity of the adaptation process when the internal labour market rules and practices are challenged by external forces such as economic and technological changes or equal employment opportunity pressures. Doeringer and Piore (1971) point out that both the employers and the employees are likely to resist rapid alteration of the internal labour market rules. This is not only because the internal labour market arrangements are seen as economically efficient by the employers and they guarantee job security and stable career progression for the incumbent employees, but also because customs and expectations tend to form around the long-standing rules which become a strong deterrent to adaptation within the internal labour market.

Despite the usefulness of the internal labour market model in highlighting the crucial role of labour market rules and company practices in sustaining and reproducing discrimination, the model is nevertheless limited when applied to the special issue of discrimination against women. The brief discussion of some of the contemporary feminist analyses is provided to overcome the limitations of the economic models in dealing with the specificity of women's situation. The feminist perspective sheds light on how gendered assumptions and sex role ideology help to shape employers' labour market policies and manpower strategies which in turn reproduce the hierarchical relationship between the sexes in society.

To summarise, internal labour market theory emphasises how the maintenance of the established rules, supported by the dominant parties, can reinforce and sustain discrimination. This, combined with insights from the feminist analyses, provides a useful framework for examining the dynamic relationship between labour market structure, company rules and practices and the nature of discrimination against women. The study uses this framework to examine the case of Japan. The Japanese case is theoretically relevant and significant because it has developed one of the world's most closed internal labour markets and historically operated on the basis of discrimination against women. This study therefore explores a particular and extreme case of internal labour markets and how they apply to the special issue of discrimination against women.

Chapter 3

Sexual inequality in the Japanese employment system: discriminatory company practices

Having looked at various theories explaining sexual inequality and discrimination in employment, the focus now turns on the situation in Japan. The present chapter examines how the special features of the Japanese employment system are sustained by company practices which operate to exclude the majority of women from having equal opportunities with men. The chapter first presents some empirical evidence showing the nature and extent of sexual inequality in the Japanese labour market. It then examines the main characteristic features of the Japanese employment system, the role of women workers and the discriminatory employment practices. Finally, the chapter discusses the role of culture and ideology in sustaining the structure of sexual inequality in the Japanese employment system.

LABOUR MARKET INEQUALITY: SOME EMPIRICAL EVIDENCE

The wage gap

Nothing better illustrates women's unequal status than their wages. In 1989, adult full-time women earned on average only 57 per cent of men's gross monthly cash earnings. Table 3.1 shows the changes in the male–female earnings gap from 1960 to 1989. The rise in women's pay relative to men's between 1960 and 1975 was due to the effect of the labour shortage during the period of high economic growth in the 1960s and the rapid decline of employment in the low-paying industries such as textiles and electrical machinery where many women were employed (Kawahashi 1983: 132–5). However, since the economic recession in the mid-1970s, women's earnings have shown little sign of improvement despite the continued expansion of their labour market activities and the improvement of their education. In fact, the wage differential has widened slightly after the mid-1970s. The rapid expansion of jobs in the female-intensive service sector which contains a large proportion of low-paying small firms, since the mid-1970s has lowered women's average wage level, although there are some recent signs of gradual improvement.

Many factors contribute to the unequal earnings between men and women. Human capital theorists explain women's lower earnings in terms of their lesser investment in education and training. Segmented labour market theorists argue that women earn lower wages because of their position in the labour market – women tend to be segregated in low-paying sectors and low-paying jobs. The existence of labour market barriers means that equally productive workers may not be rewarded equally. Segmented labour market theorists suggest that employment discrimination plays an important role in contributing to women's unequal earnings. Empirical studies indicate that human capital factors explain only part of the earnings gap (Yashiro, N.

Table 3.1 Monthly earnings of male and female full-time regular employees, 1960–89 (all occupations and all industries)

Year	Total cash earnings [1]			Regular cash earnings [2]		
	Female	Male	Differentials (Male=100)	Female	Male	Differentials (Male=100)
	(in 1'000s yen)		%	(in 1'000s yen)		%
1960	9.9	22.0	45.0	–	–	–
1965	18.2	35.5	51.3	17.5	31.6	55.4
1970	35.2	68.4	51.5	33.7	60.1	56.1
1975	88.5	150.2	58.9	85.7	139.6	61.4
1980	122.5	221.7	55.3	116.9	198.6	58.9
1985	153.6	274.0	56.1	145.8	244.6	59.6
1989	176.7	310.0	57.0	166.3	276.1	60.2

Source: Ministry of Labour, *Chingin Kozo Kihon Tokei Chosa* (Basic Survey of Wage Structure), various years.

Notes: [1] Total cash earnings include overtime pay.
         [2] Regular cash earnings exclude overtime pay.

1980; Kawashima 1983). Table 3.2 shows that a substantial wage gap between men and women still remains after controlling for age, education and length of service, which are the three most important factors in wage determination in Japanese firms. Yashiro (1980) estimates that length of service accounted for 46.8 per cent of the total wage differential between men and women; while education accounted for 7.2 per cent and firm size accounted for a mere 2.4 per cent. There still remains 43.6 per cent (34.3 per cent in the case of standard workers) of the wage differential that is not accounted for in his equation.

Neo-classical economists would argue that the remaining wage gap does not solely reflect wage discrimination as one needs to look for compositional factors such as industrial and occupational distribution and other productivity-related factors such as qualitative differences in education and training that are not measured statistically. However, one should be cautious about controlling too many variables in measuring discrimination. If it were possible to control virtually all sources of variation in wages, one could pretty well eliminate labour market discrimination as a significant factor

Table 3.2 Wage differentials between male and female standard employees,[1] with senior high school education, by age and length of service (all occupations and all industries), 1989

Age	Years of service	Monthly contract earnings (in 1,000s yen) Female	Male	Differentials (Male = 100) %
18–19	0	126.5	136.6	92.6
20–24	3–4	144.3	160.7	89.8
25–29	5–9	170.9	199.8	85.5
30–34	10–14	205.4	254.1	80.8
35–39	15–19	231.9	305.0	76.0
40–44	20–24	264.0	367.2	71.9
45–49	25–29	309.8	430.7	71.9
50–54	30 or above	320.1	471.1	67.9

Source: Ministry of Labour, *Chingin Kozo Kihon Tokei Chosa* (Basic Survey of Wage Structure), 1989.

Note: [1]Standard employees refer to those who work continuously for the same companies since they left school.

LIVERPOOL JOHN MOORES UNIVERSITY
LEARNING SERVICES

contributing to wage differentials by sex. It is not our objective here to determine the extent of 'pure' wage discrimination as such. The uneven distribution of women in low-paying jobs and, the productivity differences between men and women may well be a consequence of labour market discrimination as well as factors contributing to wage differentials.

As in most industrialised countries, Japanese law (Article 4 of the Labour Standards Law, 1947) prohibits paying women unequal wages for equal work. It is thus very rare, at least on the formal level, that women receive a different rate of pay for doing the same job within the same establishment.[1] A survey by the Ministry of Labour in 1981, however, indicated that 65 per cent of the companies offered women lower starting wages. The major reasons given were that women were assigned to different jobs (71 per cent) or that they were assigned to the same type of job but with some differences in job content (33 per cent) (MOL 1981a: 8–9). This indicates that an important mechanism for paying women lower wages is through job segregation. The concept of 'job' in Japanese companies is extremely vague and diffuse; this gives employers a wide margin within which to manipulate the differences in 'job content' and justify paying different categories of employees different wages.

Another crucial phenomenon in Japan is that the wage differences between men and women are rather small when they are young, but the differences increase with age, peaking when they reach middle age. This is a common phenomenon in most countries, but much more accentuated in Japan (see figure 3.1). The prevalence of the

Fig. 3.1 Women's average earnings as a percentage of those of men, by age group, in selected countries, various years

Sources: United Nations, *The Economic Role of Women in the ECE Region*, 1985, p.82; Japan, Ministry of Labour, *Chingin Kozo Kihon Tokei Chosa* (Basic Survey of Wage Structure).

Notes: [1] Annual average earnings of full-time workers; youngest age group refers to 19 and under.
[2] Net yearly earnings of full-time workers and employees in the private and semi-public sector. Age groups are: under 18; 18–20; 21–25; 26–30; 31–40; 41–50; 51–60; 61–65; 65+.
[3] Average monthly full-time earnings in establishments affiliated to the Norwegian Employers' Confederation (mostly manufacturing); the last age group refers to 60–66 years of age.
[4] Monthly earnings of full-time employees in industry (ISIC 2+3).
[5] Average gross weekly earnings of all adult full-time workers. First age group: under 18; second age group: 18–20.
[6] Average monthly regular earnings (excluding overtime pay) of full-time workers in non-agricultural activities. First age group: under 17.

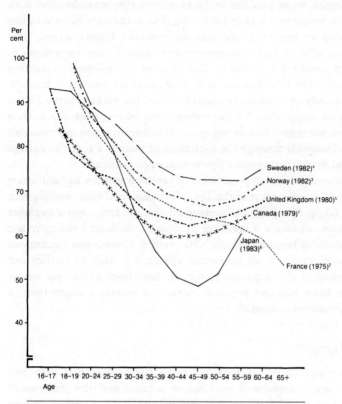

Age groups	Canada[1]	France[2] 1975	Norway[3] 1975	Sweden[4] 1982	United[5] Kingdom 1980		Japan[6] 1983
16–17...........	} 83.7	119.6	—	—	93.0		93.2
18–19...........		94.6	99.7	99.5	79.1		92.3
20–24...........	75.4	84.4	86.9	89.3	75.0		87.7
25–29...........	} 66.9	78.7	81.6	85.8	72.8		79.1
30–34...........		} 69.9	74.9	81.2	} 65.9		66.0
35–39...........	} 59.6		76.2			56.8
40–44...........		} 65.0	} 69.4	73.5	} 62.4		50.4
45–49...........	} 60.2		72.6			48.5
50–54...........		} 63.0	} 66.9	72.5	} 64.9		51.6
55–59...........	} 65.1		68.9	72.6			60.4
60–64...........		59.4	72.1	75.2	67.9		—
65+............	—	53.6	—	—	—		—

nenko-based wage practice in Japan means that workers start with very low wages when they are young, but as they get older they are promoted to higher grade jobs and receive higher wages. The principal way of skill formation, particularly in the large firms is through on-the-job training. The chances for on-the-job training and promotion for Japanese women workers are extremely limited. The majority of women are excluded from the *nenko* system. This is one factor responsible for the enlargement of the wage gap as they reach middle age. Thus an important mechanism justifying women's unequal wages is through the limitation of women's access to certain jobs and by restricting their promotion opportunities.

Furthermore, a high proportion of Japanese women still withdraw from the labour market at the age of marriage and child-rearing (see figure 1.1, p.15). Such an interrupted career pattern has a negative impact on women's wages and promotion in most countries, but particularly in Japan where the *nenko* system prevails and continuous long-term service is an important criterion in skill formation and promotion in the large firms, the discontinuous career pattern of women has a stronger negative impact on women's wages than in other industrial countries.

Job Segregation

The concept of job segregation refers to the fact that men and women are concentrated in different occupations (the 'horizontal' component of occupational segregation) and that even when women occupy the same occupation they are often employed at different levels of responsibility and allocated to different tasks from men (the 'vertical' component). It is, however, difficult to obtain statistical evidence of the latter unless one can have access to firm-level data.

Table 3.3 shows the occupational distribution of male and female employees. The sexual imbalance is striking. Over one-third of women work as clerical workers, and another quarter work as production process workers or labourers, only 1 per cent of them work as managers and administrators. The concentration of women in some occupations is obvious if we look at women's share relative to that of men: women constitute 51.3 per cent of service workers, 58 per cent of clerical workers and 41.6 per cent of unskilled labourers. They are severely under-represented in administrative and managerial jobs, constituting a mere 7.7 per cent of the total. It is often pointed out that women's occupational status has improved

Table 3.3 Occupational distribution of male and female
employees, 1990

Occupation	Male No. ('000s)	%	Female No. ('000s)	%	Women's percentage share of each category
Professional and technical workers	3,400	11.3	2,530	13.8	42.6
Managers and officials	2,150	7.2	180	1.0	7.7
Clerical workers	4,570	15.2	6,310	34.4	58.0
Sales workers	4,500	15.0	2,300	12.5	33.8
Farmers, lumbermen and fishermen	280	0.9	110	0.6	28.2
Mining and quarrying	20	0.1	0	0.0	0.0
Transport and communication	2,070	6.9	90	0.5	4.2
Craftsmen and production process workers	9,650	32.2	3,780	20.6	28.2
Labourers	1,440	4.8	1,020	5.6	41.6
Service workers	1,870	6.2	1,970	10.7	51.3
Total	30,010	100.0	18,340	100.0	37.9

Source: Statistics Bureau, Management and Co-ordination Agency, *Rodoryoku Chosa* (Labour Force Survey), 1990.

tremendously as indicated by their large share in professional and
technical jobs (42.6 per cent). A closer look reveals that the majority
of professional women are concentrated in sectors such as health
service and teaching. These two occupations together constitute 75
per cent of all women in the professional and technical category.

Statistical evidence from the Basic Survey of Wage Structure
(1983) shows that within each of the occupations for which data are
available, women still earn much less than their male counterparts.[2]
For example, female shop assistants in department stores earned only
70.5 per cent of men's wages, and female radio and TV assembly line
workers earned only 62.4 per cent of men's wages. This implies that
within each occupation, women tend to be employed at lower grades
and/or they are employed in smaller firms which pay lower wages.

The above data on occupational distribution provide only an extremely limited view of the extent of male–female labour market segregation according to job status. The Japanese labour market is not occupationally based. The labour market status and earnings of an employee are mainly determined by educational attainment, the size of the firm and the rank and position within the firm. However, in the case of women, there exists only a very 'weak link' between their educational attainment and labour market status. The Ministry of Labour's survey in 1981 shows that among those firms which recruited university graduates, 73 per cent did not recruit female graduates. Among those which recruited female graduates, only 19 per cent placed them in the same jobs as their male counterparts, 41 per cent of the firms placed female graduates in clerical support jobs, similar to that offered to junior college graduates (MOL 1981a). This 'weak link' between women's educational attainment and labour market status was confirmed by Kawashima's study which showed that women with university education were almost excluded from the large firms with well-developed internal labour markets; only 18.7 per cent of them work in these firms compared to 60.5 per cent of male graduates (Kawashima 1983).[3] Until very recently, the majority of large firms which had a well-developed internal job hierarchy, avoided hiring female graduates for jobs connected to higher positions on the promotion ladder. They hired a small number of women with junior college education for clerical or specialised jobs with little chance for promotion.

Women's concentration in small firms

As already mentioned, in the Japanese labour market, the company one works for is more influential than the occupation in determining one's status, position and more importantly, earnings. Clark (1979: 53) describes company membership as 'the prime attribute' defining the worker's position in the world of work.

The persistence of duality in the structure of production has been one of the conspicuous features of the post-war Japanese economic structure and labour market. This duality is focused on differences between big firms and small firms. The large firms, and also to some extent the medium-sized firms, have well developed internal labour markets. They hire school leavers for entry jobs; higher positions are filled through internal promotion. They pay higher wages and offer good working conditions. *Nenko* wages and lifelong commitment are common practices. Small firms, in contrast, have many entry points and a higher labour turnover rate. Labour mobility from small firms to large firms is not very common. Wages in the small firms are more exposed to the operation of the competitive labour market. Many small firms are, in fact, sub-contractors for the large firms and they are under their domination.

There is an obvious imbalance in the distribution of the male and female workforce by firm size: 54 per cent of women work in firms with 99 employees or less, and one-fifth work in firms with 500 or more employees. In the case of the male workforce, 46 per cent is found in firms with 99 employees or less and over a quarter of them work in firms with 500 or more employees (see table 3.4). The proportion of women working in the public sector is also lower than that of men. More striking is that a high proportion of young women work for large firms, whereas middle-aged women are highly concentrated in small firms (see table 3.5).

The fact that large firms only recruit school leavers for permanent jobs means that their doors are closed to many of the middle-aged women re-entering the labour market as mid-career entrants. Many of them can only find employment in small firms under poor working conditions.

Women's concentration in small firms has remained unchanged over the last two decades. The proportion of women employed in

Table 3.4 Distribution of male and female employees by firm size, 1990 (non-agricultural sector)

Firm size (no. of employees)	Male %	Female %	Women's share of total %
1–29	30.1	37.0	42.4
30–99	15.6	16.7	39.6
100–499	16.2	15.9	37.4
500 or more	26.0	20.5	32.4
Public sector	11.2	9.5	34.3
Total	100.0	100.0	37.9
(Number in millions)	(29.8)	(18.2)	

Source: Statistics Bureau, Management and Co-ordination Agency, *Rodoryoku Chosa* (Labour Force Survey), 1990.

Table 3.5 Distribution of male and female employees by firm size and age groups, 1990 in percentages, (non-agricultural sector)

Age groups		*1–29*	*30–99*	*100–499*	*500 +*	*Public sector*	*Total*
20–24	F	25.9	15.9	19.3	32.6	6.0	100.0
	M	30.5	16.6	18.6	25.8	7.8	100.0
25–29	F	28.0	14.2	16.6	28.4	12.0	100.0
	M	24.7	14.6	18.2	30.8	11.5	100.0
35–39	F	39.0	15.3	15.3	17.2	12.8	100.0
	M	28.3	14.1	16.3	27.7	13.3	100.0
40–54	F	40.9	18.5	15.2	15.9	9.4	100.0
	M	29.6	15.1	15.3	28.2	11.5	100.0

Source: Statistics Bureau, Management and Co-ordination Agency, *Rodoryoku Chosa* (Labour Force Survey), 1990.

firms with 99 employees or less has in fact increased slightly from 52.4 per cent in 1970 to 53.7 per cent in 1990. This has been due to the increase in the number of women working in the service sector which constitutes a large number of small firms.

Women as part-time workers

Part-time jobs have accounted for a large proportion of the increase in female employment since the 1960s. The number of female part-time workers (defined as those working less than 35 hours per week in the Labour Force Survey) increased by over eight times from 0.6 million in 1960 to 5.0 million in 1990 (see table 3.6). In 1960, part-time employment accounted for only 8.9 per cent of the total number of women employed; by 1990 they constituted 27.9 per cent. The growth of part-time employment has been largely a female phenomenon. In 1960, women accounted for 43 per cent of the total number of part-time workers, the proportion rose to 69 per cent in 1990. Part-time jobs are also predominantly 'middle-aged women's jobs', women in their late thirties and forties constituting about 60 per cent of the total number of female part-time workers.

Many factors accounted for women's increased engagement in part-time employment. On the supply side, the extra income to

Table 3.6 Number and proportion of part-time employees,[1] 1960–90
(non-agricultural sector)

	Total			Women		
	All employees	Part-time		All employees	Part-time	
Year	No. (millions)	No. (millions)	As % of total employed	No. (millions)	No. (millions)	As % of total employed
1960	21.1	1.3	6.3	6.4	0.6	8.9
1965	27.1	1.7	6.2	8.5	0.8	9.6
1970	32.2	2.2	6.7	10.7	1.3	12.2
1975	35.6	3.5	9.9	11.4	2.0	17.4
1980	38.9	3.9	10.0	13.2	2.6	19.3
1985	42.3	4.7	11.1	15.2	3.3	22.0
1987	43.5	5.1	11.6	15.8	3.7	23.1
1990	47.5	7.2	15.2	17.9	5.0	27.9

Source: Statistics Bureau, Management and Co-ordination Agency, *Rodoryoku Chosa* (Labour Force Survey), various years.

Note: [1]Part-time employees defined as those working less than 35 hours per week

supplement the household expenditure has been one of the most important factors pushing more housewives into the labour market. This trend became more visible after the first oil crisis in 1973 (Yashiro, N. 1983: 50). According to a survey by the Ministry of Labour in 1979, 57 per cent of those aged 35–54 replied that the major reason for their engagement in employment was the need for extra income to maintain or improve their standard of living (MOL 1981b: 187). The Japanese labour market for full-time regular jobs is rather closed. For many of the middle-aged women entering or re-entering the labour market part-time employment is the only option open. Many married women also regard part-time employment as a possible compromise with their domestic responsibilities.

On the demand side, the primary motive for creating part-time jobs has shifted over time. During the period of high economic growth, it was mainly prompted by labour shortages; part-time jobs were created to encourage more housewives to enter the labour market. Since the mid-1970s, reduction of labour cost and the increasing need for a flexible workforce have been the primary reasons for employing more women as part-time workers.

The term 'part-timer' has a rather special meaning in Japan. It is an ambiguous term. The Labour Force Survey's (*Rodoryoku Chosa*) statistics grossly underestimate in reality the number of women employed as 'part-timers' as defined by their employers. Many employers simply use the term 'part-timer' to distinguish a worker's employment status (as a non-regular employee) from that of the permanent regular employees, whatever their working hours. According to the Employment Status Survey (*Shugyo Kozo Kihon Chosa*), which defines 'part-timers' as those so called by their employers, the total number of 'part-timers' was 4.67 million in 1987, among whom 4.46 million were women, constituting 95.4 per cent of total part-time employment (the number of female part-timers reported in the Labour Force Survey for the same year was 3.65 million, constituting 72.1 per cent of total part-time employment) (MOL 1989: 216–8). Takanashi (1988) estimates that about one-third of the so-called 'part-timers' actually work exactly the same hours as full-time regular workers, these are described as 'pseudo-part-time workers'. They are, like the 'proper' part-time workers, excluded from the wage structure, long-term employment security and benefits applied to the full-time regular workers.

In addition to part-time employment, there has been a rapid growth of various forms of *arubaito* workers (temporary and casual workers) in the Japanese labour market in recent years. A high proportion of these are women and they share the common characteristics of low wages and lack of employment stability.

A wide discrepancy exists between the relative position of men and women in the Japanese labour market. It is difficult to assess the extent to which this discrepancy can be attributed to 'pure discrimination' in the labour market as such. However, to attribute women's unequal position solely to 'quality differences' between male and female workers cannot explain why women as a group are systematically located in a disadvantaged position. At the same time, it is important to note that 'quality differences' between men and women can be both the result of pre-market discrimination as well as discrimination in the labour market. Certain institutional forces appear to be at work in the Japanese labour market which bias the distribution of the male and female workforces. It is therefore essential to know what these institutional forces are.

THE NATURE OF THE JAPANESE EMPLOYMENT SYSTEM AND THE ROLE OF WOMEN WORKERS

The subject of the 'Japanese employment system' is a large and complex one. For anything like a complete description and analysis the readers will have to refer elsewhere (Clark 1979; Cole 1971 and 1979; Dore 1973; Dore *et al.* 1989). The objective here is to highlight the characteristic features of the system with a view to understanding the role of women workers.

A most popular version of the Japanese employment system is that it consists of three institutional components, described in a much quoted OECD report (1977) as the 'three sacred treasures': the lifetime commitment practice, the *nenko* wage system and enterprise unionism. Lifetime commitment refers to a practice whereby an employee enters a company after school graduation, receives in-company training, and remains an employee of the same enterprise or enterprise group until the retirement age of 55 or 60. This practice is supported and reinforced by the *nenko* wage and promotion system, whereby wage increase is not so much based on job performance as on personal characteristics such as age, length of service, education and sex. The *nenko* system reinforces high commitment because leaving the company means giving up all the accumulated seniority and promotion chances. Enterprise unionism is based on a type of unionism which organises employees of the same firm irrespective of whether they are blue- or white-collar workers. It is a normal practice that union membership is restricted to the regular employees. Despite repeated prophecies of the inevitable dissolution of the traditional model, the practice of long-term commitment is still a dominant feature of the employment system in Japan in the 1990s. Up to the present, there is little evidence showing that job mobility between the large firms has increased (JPC 1987). Indeed, recent statistical evidence shows that, far from disappearing, the lifetime commitment practice retains its centrality and that it appears to be diffusing down the firm-size hierarchy (Dore *et al.* 1989). Mutual commitment on both the employer and employee side on a long-term basis still constitutes the most important aspect of the employment system in the large firms and, to some extent also, in the medium-sized firms in Japan.

From the viewpoint of the company, guaranteeing lifetime employment and linking wage increases to age makes the employment system very rigid, both in terms of the size of employment and labour costs. This inevitably means that the benefits of the practices can only be applied selectively: to the core workers. Several measures are adopted by the firms to adjust employment and labour costs to business fluctuations.

The employment of non-regular workers, including temporary workers (*rinjiko*) and casual day workers (*hiyatoi*), is common. These workers are hired during a business boom and may be fired when it comes to an end. Many non-regular workers may be doing the same job as the regular workers but are paid less and they are not entitled to various kinds of fringe benefits. They do not belong to the enterprise union. The use of non-regular workers started at the time when the lifetime employment practice took root after World War I (Sumiya 1979). It functions as a safety valve for the system. According to the Labour Force Survey (1990), 94.6 per cent of male employees were regular workers against 5.4 per cent non-regular workers; whereas only 80.9 per cent of female employees were regular workers against 19.1 per cent non-regular workers. The trend since the 1960s is that female non-regular workers have increased while male non-regular workers have decreased slightly.

Women workers play an important role in maintaining the flexibility of the employment system. It has long been a customary practice that women worked only for a few years between the end of schooling and marriage. They are encouraged by the companies to quit before they benefit from wage increases under the *nenko* system. Before the mid-1970s, many companies actually forced women to retire under the compulsory early retirement system. As the system is now ruled illegal by the courts, many companies have changed to an informal system by encouraging women to retire at marriage or childbirth through offering them special allowances. Since the majority of women are assigned to unskilled or assistant type of jobs, the replacement of senior women by young school leavers serves the purpose of reducing labour costs. Even in the 1990s, many employers still regard it as a rational practice to encourage high turnover among women workers as a means to reduce the rigidity of the employment system.

The employment of a large number of female part-time workers is another important means for adjusting to business fluctuations and reducing labour costs. The majority of the part-time workers are middle-aged women who move in and out of the labour market as demand fluctuates, as a type of marginal workforce. Among the permanent regular workers, women's employment fluctuates more than men's, and part-time female employment fluctuates much more than that of the permanent regular workers (Kawashima, Y. 1983: 153–4).

Another mechanism for maintaining the flexibility of the employment system is the use of sub-contracting. Large firms sub-contract work to medium-and small-sized firms to adjust production levels to the fluctuation in demand and also to take advantage of a cheap labour force. As already mentioned, a higher proportion of women work in the medium- and small-sized firms.

It is no exaggeration to say that the employment security and favourable working conditions enjoyed by the permanent regular employees are based upon an exploitative system which excludes a large number of women workers, part-time, temporary workers and workers in small firms from enjoying the benefits of the system. Unequal treatment of workers outside the framework of lifetime employment is thus an inevitable outcome of a system strategically designed to sustain the employment stability of the permanent workforce. As pointed out by Galenson and Odaka:

> The Japanese system of lifetime employment guarantee, as practised by virtually all large corporations and many medium-sized ones as well, is a noteworthy aspect of the country's labor market organization. Although limited in scope to a minority of the labor force, where it applies, it has provided firms with major benefits at relatively small cost. In our own view, its economic rationality is beyond question. Japanese customs and tradition may have contributed to its adoption and to its continuing ideological strength, but the profitability criteria alone would be sufficient to sustain its popularity in business circles, whether it has served the workers equally well is a different question.
>
> (Galenson and Odaka 1976: 626)

The utilisation of women as a group of low cost peripheral workers has served the Japanese economic system well. Personnel management practices carried out by the majority of Japanese companies present strong barriers to women's participation in the work organisations on an equal basis to men. These barriers are sometimes created by direct exclusion of women in different stages of employment, i.e. direct discrimination, or generated by the customary rules and practices of Japanese management which operate to the disadvantage of the majority of women, i.e. indirect discrimination.

DISCRIMINATORY COMPANY PRACTICES

Direct discrimination

Until the introduction of the EEO Law in 1985, blatant discrimination against women in all stages of employment was widespread, according to a nationwide survey conducted by the government (MOL 1981a).

Recruitment

It is a common practice for large firms in Japan to recruit directly from school leavers. Each year, they decide in advance the number and educational qualifications of the new recruits they need. Many firms in western countries tend to recruit whenever new vacancies arise and individuals with suitable qualifications are sought to fit the job. Japanese firms tend to recruit the individuals into the organisation first before assigning them to specific jobs. In most cases, personal criteria and formal school education are more important than job qualifications in the firms' recruitment and hiring decisions. Sex constitutes an important personal criterion in the firms' recruitment policy. The Ministry of Labour survey shows that among those firms which recruited high school leavers, 62 per cent recruited both men and women and 22 per cent recruited men only. The picture was worse in the case of university graduates with 73 per cent of the firms limiting their recruitment to male graduates and only 26 per cent recruiting both male and female graduates. The reasons given by the companies for not recruiting female graduates were that 'female high school leavers and junior college graduates were sufficiently well qualified for the jobs' (55 per cent), 'jobs for university graduates were limited to men only' (25 per cent) and that 'female university graduates quit too soon' (16 per cent). These are obvious examples of direct discrimination against women at the point of entry.

Conditions of hiring

Among the firms surveyed, 25 per cent replied that they set different hiring conditions for male and female high school leavers and 38 per cent of the firms set different hiring conditions for male and female university graduates. The common differences were to require different qualifications or fields of study, to hire men as nationally mobile employees and women as local employees or to restrict the employment of women to local branch offices.

Job assignment

The survey shows that 83 per cent of the firms had jobs to which they did not assign women. The reasons given for not assigning women were: 'requirement of physical strength' (51 per cent), 'requirement of high qualifications' (36 per cent), 'frequent assignment outside the office' (27 per cent) and 'need to make external contacts' (23 per cent).

Job rotation and promotion

Job rotation constitutes the most important part of the training and skill formation process in Japanese firms. Among those firms which carried out regular job rotation, 50 per cent did not offer women the opportunity. The reasons being that 'the assistant nature of women's jobs makes job rotation unnecessary' (66 per cent), 'women do not want job rotation' (31 per cent) and that 'women are only employed on a short-term basis' (11 per cent). A direct result of limiting women's job assignment and training opportunities is their poor chances for promotion: 45 per cent of the firms replied that they did not offer women any chance for promotion to supervisory positions. Among those firms which offered women some promotion opportunities, 36 per cent limited promotion up to the level of first line supervisor (*kakaricho*), 25 per cent limited to sub-section chief (*kacho*) and only 14 per cent offered women promotion up to the level of section chief (*bucho*).

Retirement

In those firms where there was a formal retirement system, 19 per cent set different retirement ages for men and women. Compulsory retirement at the time of marriage, pregnancy or childbirth was official policy in 2 per cent of the firms surveyed, although it was believed that the practice existed more extensively in an informal manner than the official figures indicated. Discriminatory retirement rules were challenged by many court cases from the early 1970s (see chapter 5). Many companies had eliminated their discriminatory policies, at least on the formal level, by the late 1970s. This is an area where companies are least resistant to change as it only affects employees who are leaving the company rather than the entire personnel management system.

Indirect discrimination

Even if employers do not discriminate intentionally, many of the customary rules and practices which characterise Japanese management will still operate to the disadvantage of the majority of women. As Doeringer and Piore (1971) point out, the rules and practices which define the internal labour markets and govern their practice will result in indirect discrimination and perpetuate the advantages of the core workers.

In the large firms where lifetime employment exists, personnel policies are built upon the assumption that workers will commit themselves to the firms long-term. Japanese firms tend to invest heavily in the training of their workers, much more so than companies in western countries. There is a strong emphasis on the development of firm-specific skills which include both technical and organisational skills. Long-term, on-the-job-training and regular job rotation are regarded as essential for the development of both types of skills. Training incurs heavy costs and firms will only invest if they expect that such costs can be recouped in the future. Investment in the training of women is regarded as 'risky' because of their high average turnover rate. Even for those women who work for many years, firms still hesitate to invest in their training because the expected risk of not being able to recoup the cost is higher. This type of discrimination has been described as 'statistical discrimination' (Phelps 1972; Arrow 1973). However, this is appropriately defined as a form of discrimination even if employers' perceptions of the average sex differential are correct, since it is a manifestation of stereotyping, the treatment of each individual member of a group as if he/she possessed the average characteristics of the group (Blau and Jusenius 1976: 194).

In recent years, there is evidence that some Japanese firms will start to invest in the training of their female employees and offer them job rotation opportunities around the age of 30 when the probability of their quitting the job is reduced (Ishida 1985). However, women's chances for developing a career often start five or even ten years later than their male counterparts. In western countries, women can use external occupational or professional training as credentials to career development; in Japan the emphasis on firm-specific training means that Japanese women tend to face greater institutional barriers to their career advancement because firms have a stronger discretionary power in allocating the chances for career development. Occupational advancement depends much more on the allocative rules and procedures of the firms.

The importance of the seniority rule in the allocation of jobs, promotion and wage determination also operates to the serious disadvantage of women. Women leaving the firm lose all their accumulated seniority. When they re-enter the job market, they have to start again at the bottom of the job hierarchy. Wage data show that female mid-career entrants earn the same wages as 18- or 19-year-old school leavers, disregarding their age or previous work experience (Shinotsuka 1982: 175).

Promotion in Japanese firms often means moving up the standard rank hierarchy according to one's age, length of service and performance. Since the mid-1960s, many firms started to stress the importance of 'merit' and 'job performance' in their promotion system, but the idea of 'job evaluation' or 'job appraisal' is not well developed in Japanese work organisations. One of the characteristics of Japanese work organisations is the lack of clear definition of jobs. On the formal level, firms do have clear-cut definition of jobs, but in actual operation the idea of individual job responsibility is usually quite blurred. There is a tendency for the actual performance of any job to be really the joint effort of a work group, thus the objective evaluation of any individual based on ability or performance becomes difficult. This is often pointed out as one advantage of Japanese work organisation because the lack of a clear definition of individual job responsibility enhances flexibility and facilitates job transfer. However, when it comes to evaluation of job performance, there is always a tendency that it becomes an evaluation of the person rather than the person's job performance. Discrimination is more likely to occur under this situation yet more difficult to detect.

Up to the present day, age and length of service are still the two most important criteria in the determination of promotion in Japanese firms. In Britain, promotion based on seniority is regarded as indirectly discriminatory because it has a disproportionate impact on women.[4] The tendency of Japanese firms to use the seniority criterion as a basis for evaluation and promotion will continue to operate to the disadvantage of women.

Promotion and career development in Japanese firms often involves regular job rotation and job transfer. Regular job rotation is used as a means for the development of multi-skill, and the enhancement of a worker's organisational skill. It is also implemented for increasing organisational flexibility. Compliance with the mobility requirement is important for promotion to managerial positions. Firms do not expect women to be as mobile as their male colleagues. The immobility of women is often used as an excuse for not promoting women and not assigning women to the mainstream jobs. Their role in the family is seen as a barrier to their mobility but the mobility requirement itself is rarely questioned or challenged.

The exclusion of women from the mainstream career jobs is further reinforced by many informal, yet deep-rooted workplace customs and social practices which are part of normal corporate life in Japan. Japanese companies are commonly characterised as social communities, where the members share a strong sense of group identity. Commitment and loyalty to the work group and to the corporate community is crucial for career success. Working long hours, intense involvement in extra-work activities and socialising with co-workers outside working hours are all part of the obligations of a committed member of the work group. The domination of corporate life over private life means that women with family obligations are seen as marginal members. *Tsukiai* (after work socialising), such as going to bars and playing mahjong, plays an important role in the cultivation of the informal clique network (Izumi 1989: 25). The importance of informal clique networks and male patronage in promotion is another aspect of company life which puts women at a disadvantage (Osako 1982: 130). Entry to the clique normally starts at the time when the new recruits joined the company. It is very rare for women to join the clique networks as they are not expected to be permanent members of the corporate community. Finding patrons among the senior staff, who are invariably men, is even more difficult for women. The dominance of such 'male enterprise culture' creates strong barriers to women's acceptance as full members of the corporate community. The intensity of Japanese corporate life makes the combination of a career with family life extremely difficult for the majority of women.

THE ROLE OF CULTURE AND FAMILIAL IDEOLOGY

The exclusion of women from the core of corporate life in turn reinforces the centrality of the household in their lives. The social norm of sex role distinction remains more marked in Japan than in other industrial countries. An international attitude survey in 1983 showed that 71 per cent of Japanese women agreed with the statement that 'men's sphere is at work and women's sphere is at home', as compared to 34 per cent in the United States, 32 per cent in West Germany, 26 per cent in the United Kingdom and 14 per cent in Sweden (PMO 1983).

One question which puzzles many foreign observers and western scholars is why more than three decades of rapid economic development have not eroded the traditional strict distinction between sex roles in Japanese society? Why is it that discriminatory treatment of women in employment has rarely been seriously challenged?

The 'cultural persistence' hypothesis is popular among many scholars: as relative 'latecomers' to the industrial world, Japanese women are still inhibited by many traditional values and norms and are slow in developing their occupational consciousness. The persistence of traditional cultural values which emphasise the importance of women's role as mother and wife in the family is often pursued as an explanation for the lack of equality consciousness among Japanese women. Lebra *et al.* (1976: 297), in a study on the lives of Japanese women in various occupations in the mid-1970s, concluded that 'the fabric of feminine tradition in Japan has remained unchanged despite the growth in economic strength of individual women'. They observed that the majority of women in Japan, whether married or single, clung to the traditional definition of women's role as 'good wife and wise mother' and that there had been no fundamental questioning of that role. According to Susan Pharr (1977: 251), 'Japanese society still judges the adult women primarily on the basis of her performance in the wife–mother role. The major forces impeding the improvement of women's position in society derive from Japan's cultural tradition.'

These observations of the attitudes of Japanese women still hold true today. However, one should be cautious in interpreting the situation of women in contemporary Japan simply as 'cultural lag'. According to Cole, when interpreting how the past influences the present, one should distinguish between 'tradition based on a carry-over of habitual attitudes and behavior from preindustrial society' and 'tradition based on conscious manipulation of the past to devise new solutions to emergent problems' (Cole 1979: 24). The unequal position of Japanese women in contemporary industrial organisations is not simply a phenomenon of 'cultural lag' which will gradually fade away as Japan becomes more 'modernised'. This is because unequal treatment of women has been a major factor contributing to the development and smooth functioning of the Japanese employment system. Discrimination against women has been built into companies' personnel management practices which perpetuates the extreme sexual division of labour in society. Discrimination has been justified by a deeply-rooted familial ideology, the epitome of Japanese uniqueness.

To understand this, it is necessary to look at the ideological basis of the Japanese employment practices and how this was historically related to the feudalistic view of women's role in the family and society.

The origin of the peculiar lifetime employment practice has attracted a great deal of scholarly debate. Many Japanese scholars have concluded that the practice developed around World War I, resulting from a desire of employers to stabilise labour relations in large firms by cutting high labour turnover, especially male skilled workers and technicians in the expanding heavy industries. During that period, employers were also confronted with the problem of an emerging labour movement. They were thus forced to develop new practices and ideas to support their position and justify their authority. The ideology of 'managerial familism' which emphasised the intimate relationship between employers and employees, the ideal of harmony and co-operation, pervaded the development of personnel practices during that period. At a time when the traditional *ie* (household) system was regarded as the ideal of the whole society, it was natural that employers should look to this traditional ideal as a model for employment relationships.

The historical context against which lifetime employment practice was formed and the prevailing ideology of familism has had two important implications for the position of women. First, the original model of Japanese employment practices was developed at a time when the Meiji government was making attempts to resuscitate the older, elite models of family and gender roles. The Meiji Civil Code of 1898 raised to the level of national law a subordinate status for women and it legitimated a male-centred household (Kondo 1990: 265–6). Second, the traditional *ie* model was based on a gender ideology which emphasised women's secondary status and domesticity. Thus, with the traditional principles of the *ie* system serving as a model for the firm, it was a normal situation that only men were treated as permanent members. The original model of lifetime employment was essentially a male-centred system.

Although Japan's defeat in World War II led to the defeat of feudal society, and the democratisation reforms of the Occupation dismantled the legal strictures of family embodied in the Meiji Civil Code, this did not have dramatic effects on women's social position. On the contrary, post-war economic development and the consolidation of Japanese employment practices in the post-war years further strengthened and reinforced the traditional familial and gender ideology. The social conditions of women have provided resources for employers in their institutionalisation of employment practices and labour force strategies in the post-war years. The employment system has reinforced and perpetuated women's inferior social status.

The traditional familial and sex role ideology has also been sustained by deliberately formulated government policies. Throughout the post-war period up until the present day, the government's family and education policies have consistently stressed the importance of motherhood as a sacred mission and continue to emphasise the rearing of the next generation as the sole responsibility of women (Meguro 1980: 161–200). Early in the 1960s, rapid industrialisation, urbanisation and the increased participation of married women in employment led to a growing concern about the disintegration of the family system. In 1963, the government issued a report on 'The Proper Way of Child Caring' which stressed the importance of child care within the family and the prime responsibility of the mother in the rearing of the second generation. The report stated that 'it is to an individual adult's free choice to arrange for the appropriate way to rear their children but it is the children's right to be reared by their mothers' (Yamate 1972: 84–5).

The success of the Japanese employment system is highly dependent on the willingness of the majority of women to accept their primary role in the household and their secondary role in the labour market. In the 1980s and 1990s, when commercial, legal and social forces are pushing Japanese companies to make more use of women in key business positions, management is extremely cautious not to introduce drastic personnel reforms which might disrupt the fabric of gender roles – the social basis which has for a long time sustained the stability of the male-dominated internal labour markets.

Chapter 4

The emerging situation: changing company practice in response to market pressures

From the mid-1970s, some changes began to appear in Japanese companies' policies towards their female employees. Many companies started to talk about 'utilisation of women power' (*josei no katsuyo*) or 'revitalisation of the female workforce' (*joshi rodoryoku no kasseika*). Some companies began to introduce new personnel practices and design special project teams or career development programmes for their women employees. These were all new events in Japan as Japanese companies were traditionally indifferent to the 'women's issue'. Why did the 'women's issue' become a problem of concern for Japanese companies and what prompted some major companies to introduce personnel management reforms to utilise better the abilities of their female employees after the mid-1970s?

This chapter examines the background factors leading to the shift in company policies on women. It also looks at the new personnel practices introduced and evaluates their implications for the position of women, and particularly focuses on the ten years between 1975 and 1985. There are two reasons for this.

The first is that the oil crisis in 1973 marked an end to the period of rapid economic growth. After the mid-1970s, the Japanese economy entered a new phase of development. The economic growth rate started to slow down and the industrial structure was undergoing rapid transformation. Beginning in 1975, the proportion of the labour force working in manufacturing industries remained stagnant while those working in the tertiary industries rose rapidly (see table 1.2 on p. 11). The 'service economy' has grown rapidly in Japan since the mid-1970s (Mizuno 1984). It is generally believed that the growth of the service economy tends to open up more job opportunities for women and enhances their status in the labour market. Early in 1968, Victor Fuchs, based on his observation of the changes in the American economy, pointed out that 'the advent of the service economy should make for greater equality between the sexes' (Fuchs 1968: 11). Moses Abramovitz (1972) has also observed that the transformation in employment, which has characterised our time, is largely a shift from 'hard handed' to 'soft handed' work – from jobs calling for relatively low inputs of human capital which were filled largely by men, to jobs with higher demands on education and training, which can be filled by both men and women. Generally, service jobs are seen as more suitable for the abilities of women than were the old industrial jobs. Stanback, *et al.* (1981: 60) argue that 'women, perhaps, gradually, but nevertheless inevitably, will be substantial beneficiaries'.

This chapter asks whether the changes in the industrial structure and the new demands of the economy have brought about improved job opportunities for Japanese women, and looks at how Japanese companies have sought to modify the traditional employment practices in order to accommodate the evolving new situation.

The second reason for focusing on the ten years between 1975 and 1985 is to see where matters stood before the EEO Law came into effect. The Japanese government passed the new legislation in May 1985 and it came into effect in April 1986. Part II of the book will examine the nature of the legislation and how companies have responded to it. The main objective of the present chapter is to examine changes in company practices in response to market pressures, assuming that the 'legal compulsion factor' was non-existent before 1985. In practice one can never isolate the effects of the legislation from the processes leading to changes in company practices even before the legislation came into force. Some companies might have taken steps to initiate changes in anticipation of the legislation, and the debates on the enactment of the legislation might have an educative effect on the attitudes of some employers. It is nevertheless essential to have a picture of the situation before the law was introduced in order to understand the background context.

SOURCES OF MANAGERIAL REFORM

Changes occurring both on the demand side and the supply side of the labour market have exerted pressures on Japanese companies to initiate changes in their employment policies for women.

Demand side: changes in the economic and labour market environment

There are three major factors relating to the changes in the economic and labour market environment which have pushed Japanese companies to pay more attention to the 'women's issue' and to initiate programmes better to utilise their abilities. First, the rapid expansion of the service economy since the mid-1970s has greatly transformed the employment structure and led to increased demand for more female labour. Between 1975 and 1985, the total employed labour force increased by 18 per cent; among these male employment increased by 11.5 per cent and female employment increased by 32.6 per cent. Of the 3.8 million increase in the number of employees between 1975 and 1985, service industries contributed 40 per cent, and wholesale and retail industries contributed to 30 per cent of the increase. These are all traditionally female-intensive sectors, their rapid expansion has led to a growing demand for more female labour. Although the increase in the number of female employees has been continuous since the 1950s, there are significant differences between the major factors leading to the increase in recent years as compared with the period of rapid economic growth before 1973. The Labour White Paper of 1981 noted that between 1965 and 1971, female employees increased by 2.5 million, and 80 per cent of the increase was due to the growth in the aggregate demand for all types of labour; whereas between 1974 and 1979, female employees increased by 1.8 million, with only 63 per cent of the increase due to general economic growth, 20 per cent to the structural shift of the economy and a further 12 per cent to the increase in the proportion of female labour in each industrial sector (MOL 1981b). This indicates that the expansion of the female labour in recent years has resulted partly from the growth in demand for more labour in general and partly from the rapid growth in the demand for specifically female labour.

The sectoral shift of the economy has altered the occupational distribution of the labour force. In particular, there has been an expansion of white-collar jobs and knowledge-intensive occupations into which more women have entered (see table 4.1). The proportion of women engaged in clerical, professional and managerial occupations increased from 11.0 per cent in 1955 to 24.4 per cent in 1970 and up further to 34.6 per cent in 1980. This increase has been most remarkable in the tertiary sector where the proportion of women engaged in clerical, professional and managerial occupations surpassed that of their male counterparts in 1975. In 1980, 46.3 per cent of women working in the tertiary sector were engaged in clerical, professional or managerial jobs as compared with 37.3 per cent of their male counterparts. The rapid growth of the services, finance, banking and retail distribution industries has prompted companies to recruit more highly educated women and train them as specialists and experts in various fields. There has been not only a demand for more female labour but more importantly there has been a demand for better quality female labour. Many companies which had previously closed their doors to female university graduates changed their recruitment policies after the mid-1970s.

A second factor, not unrelated to the first, has been the shortage of skilled labour, particularly in the rapidly expanding high-technology industries which has caused companies to look for ways of using more women. The shortage of skilled labour has been particularly acute in information technology, especially software engineers. Early in the 1980s, the Ministry of International Trade and Industry warned that there would be a shortage of 600,000 software engineers if companies did not seek an additional source of supply. Major electronic firms such as Fujitsu, NEC, Toshiba and Matsushita started to recruit female university graduates and train them as software engineers in the early 1980s. For the first time in the history of the company, Fujitsu recruited 100 female university

Table 4.1 Male and female employees in clerical, professional and managerial occupations as a percentage of all employees in the sector, 1955–80

Year	All industries			Manufacturing			Tertiary		
	Total	Male	Female	Total	Male	Female	Total	Male	Female
1955	15.1	17.8	11.0	15.4	17.0	14.1	33.8	36.6	29.0
1960	17.4	19.3	14.5	16.7	17.8	14.6	34.3	36.1	31.2
1965	21.5	22.2	20.3	18.4	18.7	17.7	36.3	36.7	35.6
1970	24.5	24.5	24.4	19.9	20.6	18.7	38.1	37.4	39.3
1975	28.6	26.7	31.8	21.4	21.3	21.5	40.9	38.4	44.8
1980	29.7	26.8	34.6	20.8	21.1	20.3	41.0	37.3	46.3

Source: The Prime Minister's Office, *Kokusei Chosa* (Population Census), 1980.

graduates in 1980, with the number more than doubling to 230 in 1985. NEC adopted the policy in 1981. Labour market pressures have prompted these companies to look towards women as an un-tapped human resource.

A third factor motivating Japanese companies to utilise women more fully has been the growing importance of women in the consumer market. Paradoxically, the extreme sex role segregation in Japanese society, which is often deemed the source of sexual dis-crimination in the workplace, has led to expanding job opportunities for women. Japanese women are almost in total control of the consumer market because they control the family budget. Increased market competition has made more and more companies realise that in order to remain competitive, they need to bring in more women and utilise their ideas in product development, marketing and sales. This phenomenon is not limited to the retail distribution and financial sectors, but is also present in manufacturing companies such as electrical appliance makers, automobile and office automation machinery manufacturers. Many companies in these sectors set up special women project teams to plan and develop products to suit 'women's tastes' and to market the products to women consumers. The advent of the service economy and the growing dominance of the consumer market has expanded women's job opportunities and given them improved access to the business world.

Changes in the industrial structure and the shifting characteristics of the economy implied that a growing number of Japanese compan-ies could no longer afford to treat all their women employees as a single group of marginal or temporary workers. For the first time in history, Japanese companies have had to consider finding a way to integrate women into the traditionally male-dominated work organisations.

Demand side: internal organisational changes

The onset of slower growth in the mid-1970s brought to the fore organisational problems created by the *nenko* reward and promotion system. Previously, when the economy was expanding rapidly, promotion and reward based on *nenko* did not cause many organisational problems. Up to the early 1970s, about 70 per cent of the male graduates working in large firms could expect promotion at least up to section chief (*kacho*) or department head (*bucho*) by the time they reached retirement age (Yoshikawa 1980: 45). This could be easily accomplished when the scale of the business was expanding which helped to create a large number of positions at the top of an organisation's hierarchy. The system was also sustained by the continual recruitment of a large number of young school leavers every year maintaining the pyramidal shape of the age structure in the organisation. However, the onset of slower economic growth after the mid-1970s implies that the capacity of the company to expand and create more positions at the top has been reduced. The ageing of the population means that there is a shortage of young workers and an excess of older ones. This imposes tremendous pressures on the companies both in terms of labour cost and organisational rigidity. Since the mid-1970s, many companies have sought ways to reduce labour cost on the one hand and to introduce more flexible personnel systems on the other. This has affected their employment and utilisation policies on women. Many companies actually saw it as a 'safer' policy to recruit more women, not only as part-time or temporary employees to take up bottom-level and peripheral jobs, but also to recruit more highly qualified women to take up specialist jobs, as companies assumed that the majority of women did not expect *nenko* promotion and a high proportion of them would retire at some stage in their careers to have families. From the company's point of view, it is beneficial to use more women because this not only reduces labour cost and increases organisational flexibility but also helps to maintain the pyramidal shape of the age structure which ensures the possibility of maintaining the lifetime employment and *nenko* system for the 'elite' (predominantly male) employees. Thus internal organisational dynamics are one major factor explaining why many companies started to adopt more open employment policies towards women and an increasing number of companies which had formerly closed their doors to female university graduates changed their policies after the mid-1970s.

Supply side: a highly-educated female workforce

Changes on the demand side explain only part of the shift in companies' employment policies on women. The rapid rise in the educational level of women has been one of the most important changes on the supply side which has brought about the changes in companies' recruitment policy after the mid-1970s. In 1965, only 6.0 per cent of women entering the job market were graduates from two-year junior colleges or four-year universities; the figure rose to 26.8 per cent in 1975 and crept up further to over 40 per cent after the mid-1980s (see table 4.2). If we look at the actual changes in the number of male and female four-year university graduates between 1965 and 1989 (see table 4.3), the reasons for companies' move to employ more women graduates can be easily understood. In 1965, women constituted 12.9 per cent of the total number of graduates; the proportion rose to 22.3 per cent in 1975 and up further to 26.3 per cent in 1989. Between 1975 and 1980, the total number of graduates entering the job market increased by 52,446; female graduates contributed to 36 per cent of the total increase. Between 1980 and 1985, while the number of male graduates declined by 2,118, the number of female graduates increased by 5,332. The greatest increase in the absolute number of female graduates occurred between 1970 and 1980. Given the shift in the industrial structure and the growing need for more highly qualified labour, Japanese companies could no longer afford to close their doors to female university graduates.

According to annual surveys carried out by the *Monbusho* (Ministry of Education), the job placement ratio of female university graduates increased by 10.6 percentage points between 1975 and 1985, rising from 62.8 per cent in 1975 to 73.4 per cent in 1985; whereas the job placement ratio of male graduates increased only slightly from 77.5 per cent to 79.8 per cent during the same period.

Table 4.2 Educational composition of women entering employment, 1960–89 (in percentages)

Year	Middle school	High school	Junior college	Four-year university	Total
1960	54.4	42.1	1.7	1.8	100.0
1965	43.2	50.8	3.5	2.5	100.0
1970	20.2	64.8	10.5	4.5	100.0
1975	9.2	64.0	18.3	8.5	100.0
1980	5.2	60.6	22.5	11.7	100.0
1985	5.1	57.0	25.1	12.7	100.0
1989	3.4	54.6	28.4	13.7	100.0

Source: Ministry of Education, *Gakko Kihon Chosa* (Basic Survey on Education).

Table 4.3 Number of male and female university graduates entering employment, 1960–89

Year	Male	Female	Women's share of total %
1960	89,166	10,540	10.5
1965	117,891	17,528	12.9
1970	159,037	29,190	15.5
1975	190,246	42,437	18.2
1980	223,671	61,558	21.5
1985	221,453	66,890	23.2
1989	221,036	78,983	26.3

Source: see table 4.2

A survey conducted by the Tokyo Metropolitan Labour Office also indicates that the majority of the companies which recruited female graduates started to do so after the mid-1970s (TMLO 1983: 69).

Women graduates not only have been entering the job market in greater number but the type of occupations they enter has also changed significantly. The most significant change in recent years has been the increase in the number and proportion of those engaged in specialist and technical jobs other than the traditional field of teaching (see figure 4.1). In 1965, over half of female university graduates went into teaching. At that time, job opportunities for female graduates in the corporate sector were extremely limited. However, by 1989, only 20 per cent of them became teachers: the majority went into specialist, technical and clerical jobs in the corporate sector. The expansion of specialist and technical jobs has been particularly dramatic after the mid-1970s. In 1975, 14.6 per cent of women graduates went into specialist and technical jobs, increasing to 25.1 per cent in 1989. This is consistent with our earlier argument that the increasing need for more specialist and technical experts has prompted companies to open their doors to female university graduates.

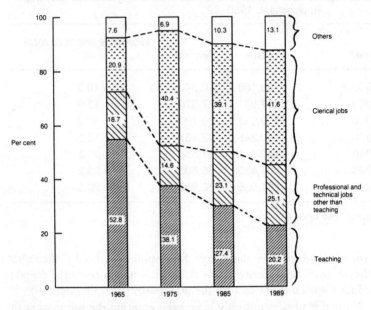

Figure 4.1 Changes in the occupational distribution of female
    university graduates, 1965–89
Source: Ministry of Education, *Gakko Kihon Chosa* (Basic Survey on
    Education).

'CAREER DEVELOPMENT PROGRAMMES' FOR WOMEN

The growth of the service economy and the increase in specialist and
technical jobs has expanded job opportunities for women,
particularly for the highly-educated. Some companies began to
introduce new policies in an attempt to open up promotion
opportunities for women and to improve their morale, particularly
for those who have stayed with the companies for a reasonable
number of years. The average length of service of women workers
increased from 4.5 years in 1970 to 6.8 years in 1985, according to
the Ministry of Labour. Companies employing a large number of
women began to show concern about the low morale of their female
workforce. Special career development programmes were
introduced to 'revitalise' the female workforce. The pages that
follow examine these programmes. There have been few statistics
available to illustrate the extent of coverage of the new practices. In

some cases we are looking at pioneering examples. Such cases should not be ignored simply because they were not representative of the overall picture as they may illustrate a new trend.

Creation of women's project teams

This has been the most common approach adopted by some major companies as a first step to 'revitalise' the female workforce. The original purpose had very little to do with promoting equal opportunities between men and women. Some companies started to organise women's project teams purely out of business needs but in some cases it represented a deliberate attempt to provide an opportunity for women to demonstrate their ability and to enhance their sense of participation through involvement in team work (Mokushi 1980). Most companies, however, have tried to integrate the former objective with the latter (GR 1980).

Women's project teams have been most widely adopted by department stores and supermarkets where women are organised into small groups to improve productivity and customer services, to organise special bargain sales and to make suggestions to the management regarding improvement of the working environment and welfare for women. These women's project teams often represent part of the companies' wider attempts to develop small group activities for productivity improvement and to enhance a sense of participation in management (GR 1979; Komatsu 1980). More recently, similar project teams have been taken up by manufacturers in the consumer electronics industries to promote product development and marketing by utilising 'women's ideas'. Some recent examples include electrical appliance manufacturers such as Sony, Matsushita Electric and Hitachi where women were specially assigned to project teams to plan and develop products. These companies believed that products made using men's ideas were failing to penetrate the market (*The Japan Times*, 25 July 1985). Another example is Toshiba where a 'women's marketing group' was set up in 1984 to promote the sales, development and marketing of household appliances. The company also established a 'Toshiba Lady Headquarter' in 1986 to promote the sale of word processors. According to the company, the major reason for organising women in project teams was increased market competition in office automation machinery. The women's project teams were part of the company's marketing strategy (*Koyo Shinko Kyokai* 1986: 92–6; *Nikkei Shimbun*, 1 March 1986).

These are typical examples of how some companies have been integrating their policies of 'revitalisation of women' with their productivity improvement activities and marketing strategies. These cases are often dramatically taken up by the mass media to portray an image of 'progressive' company policies for women. However, these policies are aimed at effectively 'utilising women', not for promoting equal opportunities between men and women. The project teams are often established on an *ad hoc* and informal basis. They are not part of the formal organisational structure and there is no formal link between these project teams and formal career progression in the company. However, 'female group leaders' do sometimes emerge through these informal work groups. In some cases these special project teams have led to a second stage in women's career development programmes with the training of 'female group leaders'.

The 'female group leader' system

The creation of the role of 'female group leader' has been most commonly found in the female-intensive industries such as banking, insurance and retail distribution. Surveys carried out by Noriko Inagei (1983), an expert on female leadership training in Japan, found that the group leader system was quite widely practised and had been gaining popularity in recent years. Table 4.4 shows the percentage of companies reported to have introduced the female group leader system, both formally and informally, in 1968 and 1982. For all industries, the proportion of companies which had introduced the system on a formal basis increased from 42 per cent in 1968 to 57 per cent in 1982, and those adopting it on an informal basis was as high as 84 per cent in 1982. The system was most widely adopted in department stores, supermarkets and the financial sector.

The group leader role is created in order to provide a training ground for women with supervisory potential. This is partly because some women are staying longer with companies, which then start to feel that there is a need to provide a career route for them to avoid demoralisation. It also stems from the belief that women are better qualified to train women. In most cases the female group leader system has been introduced in sections or departments with a high concentration of women. Generally the first-level supervisor (*kakaricho*) will be a man and a female group leader will be appointed to play the role of 'go-between' between the *kakaricho* and the female members of the work group. The 'female group leader' system is a

Table 4.4 Percentage of companies with the female group leader
system, 1968 and 1982

	Formal		Informal	
Industries	*1968*	*1982*	*1968*	*1982*
All industries	42.0	56.6	57.5	84.2
Textile	52.4	25.0	66.7	100.0
Pulp, leather, iron and steel, oil	20.0	66.7	60.0	66.7
Chemical and food	52.8	53.3	41.7	86.7
Metal and electrical machinery	36.8	43.5	61.4	78.3
Insurance and finance	40.0	83.3	60.0	100.0
Department stores	75.0	100.0	75.0	100.0
Supermarkets	–	75.0	–	100.0
Commerce and hotels	21.4	40.0	57.1	80.0
Transport and gas	–	50.0	25.0	66.7
(Sample no.)	(174)	(76)	(174)	(76)

Source: Inagei (1983: 15).

unique Japanese adaptation in two ways. First, it manifests extreme
sex role segregation in Japanese companies – the belief that women
are better at training women and that a woman is needed to play the
role of 'go-between' between the male supervisor and the female
group members. Second, the 'female group leader' is a specially
created work role outside the formal organisational chart. It provides
an opportunity for women to demonstrate their supervisory abilities
but it does not threaten the role of the male supervisor.

Female group leaders are generally assigned to the following four
types of job functions (see figure 4.2)

1 As a 'senior' (*senpai*) to provide individual on-the-job-training
   and day-to-day instruction for the new recruits.
2 As a first-level group leader, that is, leader of the female work
   group.
3 As a second-level group leader, that is, a leader of the first-level
   female group leaders, playing the 'go-between' role between
   the supervisor and female group members.
4 As a supervisor (*kakaricho*) of the work unit.

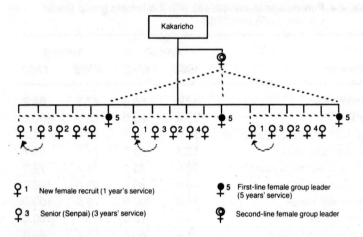

Figure 4.2 A model of the female group leader system
Source: Adapted from Inagel (1983:9).

In most cases, 1 and 2 are informal work roles not appearing on the formal organization chart; 3 is a formal staff function but not a supervisory function. There is no clear career connection between 3 and 4 although in practice women who eventually do gain promotion to first-level supervisor have mostly gone through the experience of being female group leaders. In this sense, the female group leader system provides a special training ground for women and it functions as a 'screening' process to select women with outstanding supervisory potential. Personnel experts in Japan point out that such a system is a necessary 'transitional stage' for opening up supervisory opportunities for women in Japanese companies (Inagei 1983: 10). As the system involves very low training costs and causes little disruption to the formal organisation, companies are quite willing to 'try it out'. However, the female group leader system is usually not uniformly applied throughout the company but mainly introduced in sections or departments with a high concentration of women or where the nature of the tasks requires a female group leader. Though in most cases established on an informal basis, the female group leader role does occasionally provide a stepping stone for some women to pursue a career in management. Many companies, however, simply stop at the stage of training women as group leaders, with no further step taken to provide these women with formal promotion opportunities.

The career conversion system

In the early 1980s, some major companies in the banking and financial sectors took new steps to open up formal promotion chances for women by introducing a 'career conversion system' (*shokumu tenkan seido*). This is a system by which women in clerical positions are given an opportunity, at a certain stage in their careers, to apply for conversion to the managerial career route. The conversion procedures would normally include written tests and interviews with top management. This has been a rather peculiar adaptation introduced by some major banks, insurance and securities companies. Previously, women employed in the banking and securities fields were assigned to clerical positions where they remained throughout their careers. Men, on the other hand, joined the companies as prospective managers, gained work experience in different sections to eventually assume managerial positions (see figure 4.3). The major criterion for making a strict distinction between the two separate career routes is the mobility requirement. Jobs in the clerical stream involve mostly routine work which does not need widespread training or job rotation. There is no requirement for job transfer involving geographical mobility. Promotion is limited to a lower managerial grade. The managerial stream involves broad training in different kinds of jobs and experience. There will be frequent job rotation which may involve geographical mobility. Promotion up to top management is possible. Women who apply for conversion to the managerial career route will need to make a commitment to the mobility requirement.

In these companies, the new system has not dramatically increased women's promotion chances. In practice very few women have applied for conversion and even fewer passed the 'conversion exam'. The mobility requirement presents the greatest barrier. Nevertheless, the introduction of this new system is regarded as an important breakthrough in the traditionally male-dominated fields where before women were virtually shut out from the mainstream career route. More recently, some companies have extended the system to the new recruits by offering both men and women a choice of career routes at the point of entry – referred to as the 'two-track employment system' (see chapter 6).

The nature of the career conversion system is illustrated by looking at two actual examples, one adopted by a bank (company A) and the other by a trading company (company B).

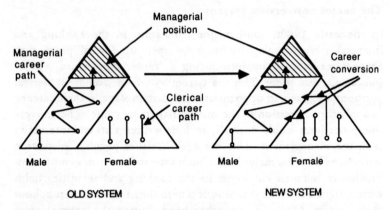

Figure 4.3 The career conversion system
Source: Adapted from Yashiro (1986: 230).

Company A introduced the two-track personnel system in 1982. All the jobs in the company were divided into two streams; the clerical stream and the generalist (or managerial) stream. Each stream has its own grading and promotion system as shown in figure 4.4. As may be expected, all women joined the clerical stream and all the men took the generalist stream. At the time when the two-track personnel system was adopted, the company also introduced the career conversion system to give a chance to those women who intend to pursue a career in management. For women who have reached clerical grade 1 and are above 30 years of age, an opportunity for converting their careers to the generalist stream would be offered. As can be seen in figure 4.4 the conversion would take a woman of clerical grade 1, 2 or 3 to manager grade 2 which would normally take a male university graduate eight years to reach (about 30 years of age). That is to say, no matter how many years of work experience the woman has with the company, success in conversion implies that she has to start again at the junior supervisory level. From the company's point of view this is rational because former clerical job experience does not offer women any training in supervisory skills.

Within three years of the introduction of the conversion system, thirteen women in company A succeeded in converting from the clerical to the generalist career route. This was a small minority taking into consideration that the company employed several thousand women.

In company B, men and women join the company on different

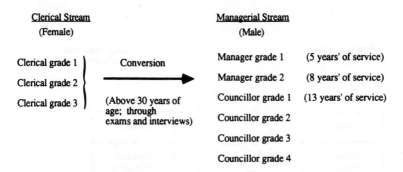

Figure 4.4 Career conversion in company A
Source: Adapted from Yashiro (1986:227)
Note: The minimum ages for women to enter clerical grades 1, 2 and 3 are
25, 35 and 40 respectively.

status and totally different career routes. Men are recruited as regular employees whereas women are recruited as 'local employees'. Regular employees are required to be nationally and internationally mobile; local employees are recruited to work at the local branch offices only. Formerly, local employees were not offered any promotion opportunity, and the grading system applied only to the regular employees. Recently, the company has introduced a new grading system for the local employees, with two separate career courses: career course A has prospects for promotion up to top management; whereas career course B consists mainly of routine clerical work with no prospect of promotion to management positions (see figure 4.5). This is a modified form of career conversion as the female career route (as local employees) is still different from the male career route (as regular employees). Even if a woman chooses career course A, her status will still be that of a local employee and her wage rate will still be lower than a male regular employee of the same grade.

From the viewpoint of the company, the 'career conversion system', as a way of utilising women, has a double advantage. First, by providing a chance for the career-oriented women to join the mainstream career route, the system improves the morale of the female workforce and they work better during their earlier years. Second, it permits better screening by giving the company a chance to 'screen out' those women who are capable of pursuing the male career pattern and are prepared to commit themselves to the company long term. This explains why most companies set the minimum

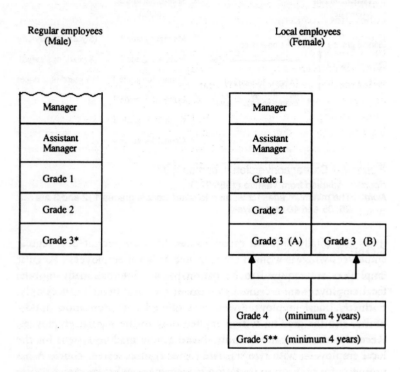

Regular employees
(Male)

Local employees
(Female)

Figure 4.5 Grading system in company B
Source: Adopted from Takizawa (1985:43).
Notes: * Male university graduates start at grade 3; a minimum of two years
           before being upgraded to grade 2.
          ** Female university graduates and junior college graduates both start at
             grade 5; a minimum of four years before being upgraded to grade 4.

conversion age at around 30 – the risk of women leaving to establish
a family is much reduced around that age. That means the risk of not
being able to recoup the training cost is greatly reduced, thus companies are more willing to offer them promotion to more responsible
positions.

Under this system only a selected minority of women can comply
with the mobility requirements and gain entry to the managerial
career route. Moreover, it is hardly a means of providing women
with equal opportunity because those women who are converted to
the male career route did not previously receive the same amount of

training and experience as their male colleagues, and it is very unlikely that they would be able to compete with their male colleagues on an equal basis. For example, in the case of company B, it takes a male employee a minimum of nine years to be promoted to the position of assistant manager, whereas in the case of a woman who has converted to the managerial career route at the age of 30, it will take her at least eighteen years to reach the same position. The conversion system hardly offers women equal opportunities with men. Instead, the separation of the two career routes formally legitimises total segregation of men and women. The conversion system also implies that unless a woman can satisfy all the requirements of the male career route, she is unlikely to be offered promotion to managerial positions. It further rationalises and justifies a system which is both directly and indirectly discriminatory against women.

CONCLUSIONS

This chapter has highlighted the major market and organisational forces pushing major Japanese companies to initiate changes in their traditional employment and utilisation policies on women. The positive shifts have been towards employing more highly-educated women and utilising them in specialist work roles. Many companies have set up special project teams or small group activities to provide women with an opportunity to utilise certain specific skills or abilities, to promote productivity and enhance their sense of participation in the work organisations. In companies which employ a high proportion of women, female group leader systems have been introduced to provide training opportunities for women with supervisory potential. More recently, some companies have formally opened up promotion chances for selected groups of women through career conversion.

Companies' moves to adopt more positive utilisation policies on women started before the introduction of the EEO Law. One cannot eliminate the possibility that some of the policy initiatives might have resulted from a general shift in company attitudes as a result of the equal opportunity debates before the EEO Law was enacted, or that companies might have taken steps to initiate policy changes in anticipation of the legislation. However, the nature of the change programmes introduced suggests that the primary motives behind the policy initiatives were either out of business needs or in response to labour market and organisational pressures. None of the programmes was aimed at promoting equal opportunities between men and women as such. The majority of the companies used the term 'utilisation of women' (*josei no katsuyo*) not 'equal opportunity', although positive utilisation of women might eventually lead to the improvement of women's position relative to that of men.

Our analysis of the initiatives introduced by management, however, suggests only very limited development towards greater equality between men and women. There are several reasons for this. First, most of the special 'career development programmes' for women were introduced on an *ad hoc* basis and their implementation was often restricted to certain sections or departments of the organisations rather than on a company-wide basis. Second, project teams or special work roles created for women were mostly informal, lying outside the formal organisational structure and there was very little formal link between these special work roles and the formal career structure. The informality of these policy attempts means that disruption to the formal organisation and career structure was only minimal. Third, in the case of formally opening up promotion chances for women through career conversion, a screening procedure was introduced to ensure that only those women who could comply with all the requirements imposed by the company, which virtually meant adopting the 'male career pattern', would be offered some chances. The conversion system actually justified promotion practices which were both directly and indirectly discriminatory against women.

To summarise, companies have sought to use women to overcome skill shortages and organisational manpower problems without altering the fundamental organisational rules and procedures which operate to allocate men and women separate career tracks.

Part II

Legislation and reform

Chapter 5

Legislating for change?
The Equal Employment
Opportunity Law

In May 1985, the Japanese government passed the Equal Employment Opportunity Law (hereafter referred to as the EEO Law) which took effect from April 1986. This law prohibits discrimination against women in vocational training, fringe benefits, retirement and dismissal. It also urges employers to 'endeavour' to treat women equally with men with regard to recruitment, job assignment and promotion. At the same time that the EEO Law was passed, the special protective measures for women provided in the Labour Standards Law of 1947 were amended. The purpose of this chapter is to examine the historical background leading to the enactment of the EEO Law, to describe and analyse its contents and to assess its potential impact on the elimination of discrimination against women.

HISTORICAL BACKGROUND

International influence

The international trend towards sex equality in recent years has strongly influenced the Japanese government's policy for women. The increased internationalisation of Japan on the economic and political front means that neither the business community nor the government can turn a blind eye to the latest moves and actions taken by their western counterparts. One important event which triggered off the debate on the issue of sexual equality in Japan was the launching of the 'women's decade' (1975–85) by the United Nations in 1975. This prompted the Japanese government to undertake concrete policy measures to promote the position of women. In 1975, the headquarters for the planning and promoting of policies relating to women was established in the Prime Minister's Office. In 1980, Japan participated in the world conference of the United Nations' decade for women and agreed to ratify the convention of the elimination of all forms of discrimination against women by 1985. The provisions of article II of the convention call for the removal of all forms of discrimination, not only wages but also the broader aspects of employment such as recruitment, training and promotion. In order to meet this requirement, the introduction of a law providing for equal employment opportunity and equal treatment between the sexes became an imperative task for the Japanese government. Under the then existing Labour Standards Law, the only requirement was for equal pay for equal work stated as a general rule. There was no stipulation against discrimination between the sexes in other aspects of employment. Thus in May 1981, the Japanese government officially reiterated that the foremost priority for the second half of the United Nations' women's decade was to review existing legislation and to formulate appropriate measures, including legislation, to ensure equality for women in employment (PMO 1981).

The United Nations convention was an immediate pressure on the Japanese government to pass the new legislation by the end of 1985. However, the enactment of the EEO Law was not merely a response on the part of the government to external pressures, it was also very much a product of internal social, economic and legal developments.

Increasing sex discrimination litigation cases and the growing awareness of the 'blind spot' in the Labour Standards Law

Rapid economic growth since the 1960s had expanded women's employment opportunities and led to some improvement in their general working conditions. However, blatant discrimination against women in wages and all stages of employment was widespread. Although article 14 of the Japanese constitution calls for equal rights of men and women before the law, no mention was made anywhere in the labour legislation of equal opportunity in recruitment, training, job assignment or promotion. The Labour Standards Law, the most important piece of legislation for women workers, enacted during the early post-war years, was mainly aimed at protecting women from the hazards of poor working conditions. It mentions sex equality only in respect of wages. One section of the law speaks of equality in conditions of work but limits it to creed, national origin and special status, omitting sex.

Despite the legal difficulties in bringing discrimination cases to court, by the late 1960s an increasing number of women were suing their employers for discriminatory practices (Cook and Hayashi 1980; Michida 1984). Many of these cases resulted in settlements favourable to women. The majority of the cases that were brought to the courts concerned pay or retirement practices. Procedures for dealing with pay discrimination cases were comparatively straight-forward since they were the subject of a section of the Labour Standards Law. Complainants could go to the Labour Inspectorate, which was set up to enforce the Labour Standards Law. Discrimination concerning working conditions other than pay was more complicated. First, a complainant had to bring the case to the ordinary court, the procedures for which were cumbersome and time consuming. Second, lawyers bringing such discrimination cases to court had to appeal to the extremely general terms provided for in article 14 of the Japanese constitution which states that 'All of the people are equal under the law and there shall be no discrimination in political, economic, or social relations because of race, creed, sex, social status, or family origin'. However, there are technical difficulties in applying article 14 in employment discrimination cases. It is a matter of controversy among Japanese lawyers whether article 14 can be construed to cover contracts between individuals or private organisations. In practice, judges dealing with cases brought under the article that involved women's labour contracts had, on the whole, been liberal in their judgements: the constitution was applicable only indirectly to such cases but women were entitled to equal treatment with men in respect of their working conditions. In several instances, lawyers had to appeal to a paragraph in the Civil Code in order to bring women's discrimination cases to the court. Article 90 of the Civil Code requires that 'good law and order are to be maintained' and judges have frequently found that working agree-ments condoning discriminatory conditions for women are contrary to the good intention and meaning of this article (Cook and Hayashi 1980: 22).

The increasing number of discrimination cases since the late 1960s has had two important results. First, the large number of cases involving discrimination against women in retirement practices, in particular, the traditional practice of compelling women to retire upon marriage, had formally disappeared by the late 1970s as a result of the repeated uniform rulings of the high courts.

Secondly, the growing number of discrimination cases involving working conditions other than pay brought to the fore the limitations of the Labour Standards Law. As no mention was made anywhere in the law regarding equal job opportunity between the sexes, cases concerning job opportunity had to be raised in constitutional or Civil Code terms that were extremely general. It was rather peculiar that in ruling that the compulsory retirement upon marriage practice was discriminatory and unlawful, the Tokyo District Court had to go round in circles by saying that the practice 'limits freedom of selection of a spouse' and that 'family is an important unit of society and an important part of the public order under law and should be respected as a part of the basic human rights'. In the course of the decision, the court referred to article 13 of the constitution, which protects an individual's right to life, freedom and happiness, and to three other articles of the constitution: article 24 guaranteeing equality and respect of the individual's home life, article 25 protecting the individual's right to exist and article 27 covering the individual's right to work (Cook and Hayashi 1980: 49). Such a decision indicates the great technical difficulty faced by the courts in judging discrimination cases because of the lack of a law guaranteeing equal job opportunity between the sexes. A Japanese labour lawyer referred to the lack of provision guaranteeing equal job opportunity between men and women as a 'blind spot' of the Labour Standards Law and urged the government to introduce a law providing for equal employment opportunity (Michida 1984: 129–31).

Demands from employers for repealing the protective provisions in the Labour Standards Law

The debates on women's job equality were closely related to the question of whether protection was an obstacle to equality. Early in the 1950s, employers started to lobby for the removal of the special protective measures for women, especially those which restricted women's working hours and night work. In 1955, *Nikkeiren* (Japan Federation of Employers' Associations) formed a research committee on the Labour Standards Law and proposed revisions of all aspects of the law in order to adapt to employment conditions in the medium- and small-sized firms. Their proposals specifically required the government to relax overtime restrictions on women from 150 hours to 200 hours a year. They also demanded that the government abolish the ban on holiday working and remove the provision for menstruation leave. During this period, the employers' argument was not that the Labour Standards Law had become obsolete but rather it set unrealistically high standards for the medium- and small-sized firms. Employers' lobbying during this period did not result in immediate government action.

The situation began to change in the mid-1960s when the Japanese economy was expanding rapidly. High economic growth, technological change and labour shortage led to a substantial improvement of working conditions. The argument against the Labour Standards Law shifted: there was a general feeling among the employers and the government that some of the protective measures, rather than protecting women, were becoming obsolete and would restrict the supply of female labour. It was felt that a review of the legislation was necessary in order to bring it into line with the new circumstances. In September 1969, the government set up a Labour Standards Law study group to engage in research and study on issues related to women workers with a view to revising the Labour Standards Law.

At the same time, employers' moves in demanding the repeal of the protective measures grew stronger. In 1970, the Tokyo Chamber of Commerce and Industry (TCCI) submitted proposals to the government asking for the revision of the Labour Standards Law and branded the special protective measures for women as 'overprotection'. The TCCI's proposals triggered off debates among labour lawyers, trade unions and women's groups about the question of whether protection was an obstacle to equality.

The Working Women's Welfare Law (1972)

The Working Women's Welfare Law, adopted by the Diet in 1972, bears an important relationship with the EEO Law. It manifests the government's fundamental attitude and policy on women workers which has remained unchanged until the present day.

The Welfare Law was enacted against the background of high economic growth with increased demand for additional labour. In November 1969, the Labour Force Research Committee of the government's Economic Council issued a report on 'The Future Prospect and Policy on Labour Force Supply'. The report stated that an additional eight million workers would be needed and this was to be supplemented by drawing the hitherto under-utilised middle-aged women into the labour market (Keizai Shingikai 1969). The Welfare Law was enacted with an aim 'to further the welfare and improve the status of working women by taking appropriate actions to help them reconcile their dual responsibilities of work and home or to enable them to develop and make use of their abilities' (ILO 1972). The law, however, was recommendatory, not mandatory, and left it to the Women's Bureau of the Ministry of Labour to persuade employers to accept its standards voluntarily. Practical measures the law proposed included provision by employers of any necessary childcare facilities for the women they employed, including the approval of childcare leave.[1] The law also envisaged improved vocational guidance and vocational training systems offered by central and local government through welfare centres for working women.

The fundamental concern of the Working Women's Welfare Law, as indicated by its title, was to improve the 'welfare' of women workers and to help them balance the demands of work and family; the idea of equal treatment of men and women was not mentioned.

One practical result of the government's labour policy was the upsurge in the number of middle-aged women entering the labour market. The majority of them were employed as part-time workers. The number of part-time female workers increased dramatically, from 0.8 million in 1965 to 2.6 million in 1980. The government's policy has been criticised on the grounds that it encourages more women to work part-time and attempts to preserve the traditional family system by stressing the importance of women's role as mothers and wives (Takenaka 1983: 255). This basic policy orientation remains unchanged in the EEO Law.

The proposals of the Labour Standards Law study group

Formal policy debates regarding the enactment of new legislation guaranteeing equal employment opportunity began in late 1978 following the report of the Labour Standards Law study group.

The study group submitted a report to the Minister of Labour in November 1978. It represented the most influential statement that could be made for the reassessment of the existing labour legislation for women (Nakanishi 1983). Most important of all, the study group proposed a new law prohibiting sex discrimination. The report specifically proposed that such legislation should cover all aspects of employment, from recruitment and hiring to retirement and dismissals. As regards enforcement procedures, it proposed a flexible approach by using such procedures as administrative guidance, conciliation and recommendations and that the responsible agency should have the final authority in issuing administrative orders for the elimination of discriminatory action. At the same time, it also proposed that those statutory protective measures exclusively applicable to women workers should be reviewed, so as to limit them to the necessary and reasonable limit required for the protection of the maternal functions of women. This report raised the most important issues which were to become the major subjects of debate in the later years when the government started to draft the EEO bill.

DRAFTING THE EEO BILL: PROBLEMS AND CONTROVERSY

The idea for introducing a law providing for equal employment for women was first proposed in 1978 but the law was not passed until May 1985. The debate lasted for a period of more than seven years. The long years of debate and controversy not only indicate the great difficulties the Japanese government encountered in drafting the bill because of the conflicting viewpoints between different interest groups, especially that of management and labour union; it also reveals the great sensitivity of the issue of sex equality in Japanese society.

Early in December 1979, the Tripartite Advisory Council on Women's and Young Workers' Problems (*Seishonen Mondai Shingikai*), a statutory advisory body to the Minister of Labour, appointed a committee of experts to study the 'substance of sexual equality in employment' and to develop standards for future legislation. The committee was composed of fifteen members, including representatives from labour and management and neutral members chosen among women's groups, university professors and lawyers. Over the seven-year period, it attempted repeatedly to draw up concrete guidelines for the legislation but because of conflicting views among the committee members it proved extremely difficult to reach a consensus. The main controversy centred around two areas: First, whether the protective measures provided in the Labour Standards Law were an obstacle to equality and second, the scope and measures for ensuring equality in employment.

With regard to the protective measures provided in the Labour Standards Law, employers insisted that if women workers claimed equality, they should renounce special protective measures in exchange; they argued that to offer women special 'privileges' other than maternity protection would be a form of discrimination against men and was inconsistent with the call for equality. Labour unions and women's groups argued that the pursuit of equality should be combined with the retention of protection. They were concerned that its removal, especially that related to working hours, would lead to a serious deterioration of the general working conditions for both men and women.

When it came to the concrete measures for ensuring equality, the members representing labour, management and the 'public interest' (the neutral members) held completely different views. The labour side and most neutral members wanted discrimination in all stages of employment to be legally prohibited and punitive measures to be taken against violations. The labour side proposed introducing 'discrimination on grounds of sex' to section 3 of the Labour Standards Law.

Management opposed the idea that companies should be legally bound to offer women equal treatment. They argued that while legal prohibition of discrimination with regard to age limits, retirement and dismissal would be inevitable (as these were ruled illegal by the courts in the past), other personnel procedures such as recruitment, job assignment and promotion were directly related to companies' assessment systems which should not be subjected to legal intervention. Hiroshi Kitamura, the representative from *Nikkeiren*, made the following argument:

> The current employment systems in Japanese business have been structured on the social custom of life-long employment . . . the labour [representatives'] demand will create a grave but meaningless confusion on the current corporate management system and will eventually destroy the 'vital force' of our economy.
>
> (JT 1984a)

The basis of management's argument centred on the issue of the difference in the average length of service between men and women and the 'logic' of lifetime employment practice. Representatives from small firms employed the same line of argument. Mitsugu Yamamoto, a senior official of the National Federation of Small Business Associations, made the following remark:

a great number of women still choose marriage rather than a career, although this is changing. Even so, it is inevitable that Japanese employers want to avoid the risks of making long-term commitments to female workers in business. We don't have an established sense of what employment equality is all about in society yet. So if these provisions become compulsory, it will only bring chaos to the business community.

(JT 1984a)

The management side recommended that the proposed law should 'morally oblige' ('*doryoku-gimu*') employers not to discriminate against women with regard to recruitment, job assignment, training and promotion. Labour representatives had strong misgivings about the effectiveness of 'moral obligation' and insisted on the need for more effective legal enforcement procedures. Members representing the public interest attempted to reach a compromise but apparently without much success.

It was not until May 1982 that the committee of experts issued a report representing an effort to reach a compromise between the conflicting views on the issue of protection. However, it avoided giving concrete guidelines with regard to the proposed legislation for guaranteeing equality. Apparently, the committee had failed to find a compromise solution.

The task of achieving a consensus on the proposed legislation then fell to the standing Tripartite Advisory Council, which also consisted of labour, management and neutral representatives. In December 1983, the Ministry of Labour published a progress report of the discussions of the council. It indicated that all three parties had basically reached a consensual opinion that new legislation was needed to ensure sex equality in employment and that the special protective measures for women, except maternity provision, needed to be reviewed. However, with regard to the concrete measures to be introduced in the new legislation, their opinions were split along labour–management lines. The report merely stated the different views held by members representing labour, management and the public interest.

In view of the approaching deadline for ratifying the UN convention, the neutral members came out with a 'compromise plan' in February 1984. After a long and heated discussion, the Tripartite Advisory Council finally submitted a recommendation to the

government in March 1984. However, opinions were still divided on
the concrete measures to be taken. Some parts of the recommendation actually referred to the different opinions of the three
parties of the council. It made no attempt to disguise the differences.

As a result, a final decision on how to reconcile the conflicting
views between management and labour was left in the hands of the
Ministry of Labour. At that time there were doubts among the parties
concerned whether the ministry would be able to produce a bill
acceptable to both labour and management. It was predicted that
even if such a bill were submitted, there was a strong possibility that
it would be shelved because of strong opposition from both sides (JT
1984b). However, at the last minute, the Ministry of Labour took a
strong administrative initiative, declared the council's recommendation as a reasonable compromise, drafted a bill based on the neutral
members' position and submitted it to the Diet in May 1984. It
passed the Diet a year later, in time for Japan to ratify the UN
convention that summer, marking the end of the UN decade for
women.

The final version of the law that emerged from the Ministry of
Labour in May 1984 and was eventually enacted in May 1985,
nevertheless, turns out to be very much a product of compromise
with the management's position. It prohibits discrimination in basic
training, fringe benefits, retirement and dismissal; but with regard to
recruitment, job assignment and promotion, it urges employers to
'endeavour' to treat women equally with men. In a strict technical
sense, one can say that the new legislation granted women no new
rights that they had not already gained through litigation in the 1970s
and early 1980s, except for prohibiting discrimination in basic
training. In terms of the relaxation of statutory protections for
women workers in the Labour Standards Law, it also largely reflects
the interests of management. Restrictions on overtime, holiday work
or late-night work were abolished for women in supervisory or
managerial posts, or jobs requiring expertise, specialist or technical
knowledge.[2] The maximum number of hours of overtime for
women in non-manufacturing industries was doubled from 6 per
week and 150 per year to 12 and 300 respectively. Prohibition of
late-night work was repealed for women working in a special
category of industries such as food processing and taxi driving. Other
minor privileges such as guaranteed menstrual leave were repealed;
in return, statutory maternity leave was lengthened from six to eight
weeks.

During the final Diet debate on the legislation, the Minister of Labour was challenged by a member of the opposition party on whether the proposed legislation was lacking in a human rights perspective. Ryoko Akamatsu, then Director of the Women's Bureau of the Ministry of Labour, made the following reply:

> In Japan, the existence of lifetime employment practice means that the length of service of employees is crucially important. Although equality means one should not use average criteria to evaluate individuals, the controversy with regard to the issue of length of service and lifetime employment could not be overcome even in the expert committee.
>
> (quoted in Ouwaki 1987: 11)

The Minister of Labour further reinforced her point:

> It is generally agreed that the entry point to the companies is important. Until the present day lifetime employment has been a 'male-centred' system. The individual is of course important but one cannot ignore the average difference between men and women. Companies' personnel management systems have been operating on this assumption. Up to the present, women's length of service has been relatively short, and one cannot say for sure that their length of service will increase. The future improvement of this will have to rely mainly on administrative guidance.
>
> (quoted in Ouwaki 1987: 12)

The above statements made by the government clearly revealed that management had won a major victory in the EEO Law controversy. The hidden message seems to be that the UN convention is too idealistic for Japan to implement it as it is. The Japanese government seems to prefer a step-by-step approach, taking into account the employment practice peculiar to the country. The Tripartite Advisory Council on Women and Young Workers, in submitting the final recommendation to the government, made the following suggestion:

> in considering the legislative framework for promoting equality between men and women, it is necessary to adopt a long-term perspective with a view of future development rather than fixing the viewpoint on the present situation. In principle, the legislation should aim at eliminating discriminatory treatment of women in all stages of employment from recruitment, hiring to retirement

and dismissal. However, in formulating or amending legislation, the contents of the legislation should not be isolated from the present reality of our society.

(MOL 1986: 28–9)

It took the Japanese government over seven years to consider and study the issue. The process of drafting the bill was fraught with difficulties and tensions. On the surface, it appears as if the conflict of interests between management and labour both inside and outside the committees was the fundamental obstacle; underneath this facade, the real tension was experienced by all the parties concerned, including the government, management, labour unions and the general public. The tension stems from the general anxiety that change with regard to women's position in the society was necessary, yet there was a lack of consensus regarding how to go about it and what needed to be done in order to bring it about. Employers feared that equal employment for women would destroy the main pillars of the employment system and weaken the country's economic foundation. Some public commentators argued that equal opportunity for women would destroy the Japanese family and the country's cultural heritage (Hasegawa 1984; Yayama 1984). These commentators contended that the sex role distinction was not only necessary for the economic system but also central to Japan's uniquely successful culture. Other critics attributed the government's move to enact the law to international pressure and saw the legislation as yet another example of the imposition of foreign norms on Japan. Apparently, in the process of drafting the bill the government not only had to reconcile the conflict of interests between labour and management; added to this, there was the problem of trying to 'bridge the gap' between the 'Japanese reality' and the 'western norm' of equality. Whatever position the government took, it was bound to be criticised.

Although the content of the law appears to represent a general victory for management, this need not mean the end of equality for Japanese women. The present legislation is not only highly ambiguous, it also leaves plenty of room for manoeuvre and interpretation by the government.

THE EEO LAW: MAIN PROVISIONS AND CHARACTERISTIC FEATURES

The main provisions of the EEO Law are summarised in figure 5.1. The actual title of the law is 'Law Concerning Promotion of Equal Opportunity and Treatment Between Men and Women in Employment and Other Welfare Measures For Women Workers'.[3]

In reality, the EEO Law was not an independent new law, but basically a revision of the Working Women's Welfare Law (1972) with a number of new measures introduced to eliminate discrimination.[4] In many respects, the EEO Law is still based on the concept of the earlier law, the fundamental purpose of which was to improve working women's welfare and to promote measures to enable them to harmonise work and family roles.

Section 1 of the EEO Law states that the purpose of the law is 'to promote equal opportunity and treatment between men and women in employment in accordance with the principle contained in the constitution of Japan ensuring equality under the law; to foster measures for women workers, including the development and improvement of their vocational abilities, the provision of assistance for their re-employment, and attempts to harmonise their working life with family life; and thereby to further the welfare and improve the status of women workers'. According to the interpretation of the Ministry of Labour, the ultimate objective of the law is to improve women's welfare which is the 'main pillar' for guaranteeing equal opportunity and treatment of men and women. The ministry stated that the word 'welfare' should be interpreted in a broad sense which includes the meaning of promotion of status (MOL 1986: 34–5). Equality thus is defined as 'welfare' handed down from the state to women workers, not to be interpreted as 'individual right' as such.

With regard to provisions for securing equal opportunity and treatment, the EEO Law distinguishes two different types of sanction: 'prohibition' ('employers shall not discriminate against a woman . . . ') and 'exhortation' ('employers shall endeavour to treat women equally as men . . . '). The former, applied to training, fringe benefits, retirement age, resignation and dismissal, means that discriminatory behaviour is legally prohibited and if cases are brought to the courts, rulings are to be made from a legal perspective. The latter, applied to the most important stages in employment including recruitment, hiring, job assignment and promotion, is a rather peculiar Japanese innovation. Basically, the hortatory provisions have

(1) New measures for securing equal opportunity and treatment

Types of sanction	<ul><li>Basic training</li><li>Welfare benefits</li><li>Mandatory retirement age, retirement, dismissal</li></ul>	Prohibition without penalty (*Kinshi Kitei*)
	<ul><li>Recruitment, hiring</li><li>Job assignment, promotion</li></ul>	Exhortation (*Doryoku-gimu Kitei*)
Enforcement methods	<ul><li>Ministry of Labour issues guidelines for items under 'exhortation'</li><li>Voluntary settlement by grievance procedures within the enterprise</li><li>The director of prefectural Women's and Young Workers' Office is empowered to give necessary advice, guidance or recommendations</li><li>Mediation by an equal opportunity mediation commission</li></ul>	

(2) Assistance measures concerning employment of women

Methods to facilitate re-employment	Employers should endeavour to take special re-employment measures for their former female employees who have retired for reasons of pregnancy, childbirth or childcare
Childcare leave	The state should endeavour to give employers necessary advice, guidance and other forms of assistance, in order to promote the spread of childcare leave

Figure 5.1 Outline of the EEO Law
Source: Ministry of Labour

no legal effect. Enforcement of the hortatory provisions is not within the scope of the judiciary; the major responsibility for interpretation and implementation of these provisions lies with the Ministry of Labour. Section 12 of the EEO Law empowers the Minister of Labour to issue guidelines with regard to the implementation of the hortatory provisions.

The EEO Law also establishes methods for settling disputes that arise between employers and employees. The primary emphasis is on voluntary settlement within the enterprise. If no settlement results, the director of the local Women's and Young Workers' Office (a division of the Ministry of Labour) is empowered to give the parties advice or to offer recommendations, or, at their request, to settle the grievance. In addition, each local government should set up an equal opportunity mediation commission within the Women's and Young Workers' Office, to provide remedies and settle disputes. Each commission should be composed of three commissioners appointed from among persons of learning and experience. When a dispute arises, if either or both of the parties concerned apply for mediation, and the other party's consent is obtained, the Director of the Prefectural Women's and Young Workers' Office shall refer the dispute for mediation to the equal opportunity mediation commission, if the Director deems it necessary. Acceptance of the mediation plan will be voluntary.

The EEO Law empowers the Director of the Women's and Young Workers' Office to give necessary advice, guidance or recommendations when discrimination cases arise. However, the Director has neither enforcement authority nor the right to carry out investigation although he or she has the right to refer the case to the equal opportunity mediation commission. Again, the power of the commission is extremely limited; it cannot force the parties to accept the mediation plan. Moreover, neither the Women's and Young Workers' Office nor the mediation commission has the power to initiate mediation proceedings because the law requires that mediation should only be carried out when either or both of the parties concerned apply for mediation and, more importantly, when the other party's consent is obtained. That is to say, if the victim applies for mediation and the employer refuses, the mediation procedure cannot be carried out.

The Japanese EEO Law may have adopted the right approach by emphasising administrative mechanisms rather than litigation procedures which tend to result in rigidity and excessive legalism.

However, it is important that the administrative agency should have extensive powers in investigation, to initiate proceedings in its own right and to assist and act on behalf of the complainants to bring the case to the courts when necessary. Neither the Ministry of Labour nor the equal opportunity mediation commission has these powers.

Nevertheless, the greatest controversy over the EEO Law is not so much about its lack of effective enforcement procedures, but more about the way the law is written with regard to the measures for the elimination of discrimination.

ELIMINATION OF DISCRIMINATION: 'PROHIBITION' VS. 'EXHORTATION'

Prohibitory provisions (*kinshi kitei*)

With regard to basic training, provision of fringe benefits, retirement age and dismissal, sections 9, 10 and 11 of the law prohibit discriminatory treatment of women: 'an employer shall not discriminate against a woman worker as compared with a man by reason of her being a woman'. There are three reasons why elimination of discrimination in these areas appears to be relatively straightforward and caused much less controversy during the bill's drafting stage. First, with regard to retirement and dismissal, substantial changes had already occurred as a result of litigation in the 1970s and early 1980s. The present law therefore merely ratifies the changes and attempts to eliminate discrimination which still remains in the 'worst practice' companies. Second, in the area of basic training and provision of fringe benefits, the elimination of discrimination against women might impose additional costs on the companies, but they are least likely to cause major disruption to the companies' core personnel management systems. Third, in the area of training, prohibition of discriminatory treatment is limited to 'the acquisition of basic skills necessary for workers to perform their duties' (section 9, EEO Law). The most controversial point of this provision is the meaning of 'basic skills'. The Ministry of Labour interprets this as basic training at the point of entry to the company, i.e. 'freshmen training' which is widely practised by Japanese companies, and basic training necessary for taking up a new job or position in the company.

The main intention of the law is to eliminate overt discrimination in basic education or training for the new recruits such as differences in the training curriculum or the duration of training. (A survey by the Ministry of Labour in 1981 showed that 78 per cent of companies provided basic entry training for both men and women; among these 53 per cent replied that the contents of training courses were different (MOL 1981a).) The likely effect of the law on training in the later stages of the employee's career, however, can only be very limited, unless women are assigned or promoted to the same jobs as men. As regards the meaning of 'training', the ministry states that it does not include on-the-job training, because that is being carried out in day-to-day work and it is not possible for the law to intervene. As on-the-job training is the dominant form of training in Japanese companies, its elimination from the scope of the law means that only a small part of the training undertaken in companies is within the law's jurisdiction. The scope of the prohibitory provision with regard to vocational training is further limited by several exceptions which include training that has to be carried out late at night or on holidays, or to be conducted in distant places to which it is difficult to commute, and where company-provided accommodation facilities are for men only and employers cannot find alternative accommodation for women. Under these circumstances, according to the Ministry of Labour, different treatment of women does not constitute discrimination. It is quite common for Japanese companies to carry out training, particularly managerial training, which would require staying overnight in distant places. It is also common for company-provided accommodation to be available for men only – a traditional practice which is overtly discriminatory against women. The present law regards all these as 'reasonable' exceptions. Thus, prohibition of discrimination in training is, in effect, limited to basic training at the point of entry to the company.

Hortatory provisions (*doryoku-gimu kitei*)

With regard to recruitment, hiring, assignment and promotion, sections 7 and 8 of the law state that 'employers shall endeavour to give women equal opportunity with men' (*tsutome-nakereba-naranai*). These are the areas governing entry to the company and job allocation within the company over which employers resisted strongly any form of legal intervention. These provisions clearly represent an adaptation to and compromise within the existing employment system. The Ministry of Labour made the following explanation:

In the area of recruitment and hiring, the law *exhorts* employers to treat women equally with men rather than imposing a clear-cut prohibition of discriminatory behaviour. This is based on the consideration that there is an average difference in the length of service between men and women. Companies in our country generally operate their personnel management systems on the assumption of lifetime commitment, and expectation of long-term service is important. In recruiting new employees, companies simply cannot ignore the differences in the work attitudes and the conditions of employment between men and women. To prohibit discriminatory treatment will not only cause chaos in companies' personnel systems but also in the labour market. Therefore, at the present point, it is considered as more appropriate to adopt a step-by-step approach in promoting equal treatment between men and women . . . . Similarly, with regard to assignment and promotion, companies not only consider past and present performance but put strong emphasis on expectation of future performance. The differences in the length of service between men and women cannot be ignored. The present law therefore *exhorts* employers to move gradually towards equal treatment.

(MOL 1986: 40 and 69)

There are debates among Japanese labour lawyers whether such 'hortatory provisions' will have any effect in private law and whether it will affect the judgement of the courts. The general interpretation is that it has no legal effect and its enforcement and implementation will rely largely on the guidelines (*shishin*) provided by the Ministry of Labour (Hanami 1986: 225). Section 12 of the EEO Law empowers the Minister of Labour to issue guidelines setting forth measures that 'should be taken by employers' (*kozuru yo ni tsiutomeru beki*) in regard to the matters stipulated in sections 7 and 8 of the law. The use of such guidelines to achieve a government or regulatory objective is not unusual in Japan. Young (1984) describes this type of administrative guidance (*gyosei-shido*) as the principal bureaucratic behaviour in Japan. During the final session of the Diet debate on the EEO Bill, Ryoko Akamatsu, then Director of the Women's Bureau of the Ministry of Labour, pointed out the significance of the guidelines:

The guidelines will provide practical behavioural guidance to employers. As the guidelines spread and take root in society, such process itself represents the formation of new social order and public norms.

(quoted in Ouwaki 1987: 29)

In January 1986, eight months after the law had been enacted, the Ministry of Labour announced the guidelines, which apparently did not arouse much controversy. According to the ministry, the guidelines were formulated after a long process of consultation with the relevant committees, taking into consideration opinions put forward by the labour unions and numerous visits made by staff of the Women's Bureau to the major firms (MOL 1986). The guidelines therefore can be seen as a product of negotiation between these parties. A close examination of the guidelines reveal that the way 'equal opportunity' is being defined appears to be rather narrow and is subject to several exceptions in favour of managerial prerogatives.[5]

With regard to recruitment, hiring, assignment and promotion, sections 7 and 8 of the law state that 'employers shall endeavour to give women equal opportunity with men'. According to the interpretation of the Ministry of Labour, this means 'not to exclude women and not to treat women unfavourably'. 'To exclude women' means not offering women any opportunity; 'not to exclude women' means offering women some opportunity. For instance, in recruitment, employers are not allowed to advertise jobs for men only although they can specify the number of employees they intend to recruit by sex, such as '70 males required' and '30 females required'. This is not against the requirements of the guidelines because the employers do not exclude women.

Similarly, with regard to assignment and promotion, employers are asked 'not to exclude women', for instance, companies which do not offer women any job rotation opportunities or promotion to managerial jobs will be required to 'make efforts' to offer women some opportunity. However, in the case where the frequency of job rotation for women is less than for men or where assignment to certain jobs is limited to women workers with certain qualifications, these do not constitute exclusion of women. The guidelines make it clear that it is acceptable for employers, like those in the banking or insurance sectors, to classify jobs into different streams such as 'managerial' and 'clerical', provided that employers do not restrict women exclusively to the clerical stream but offer them opportunities to be assigned to managerial jobs (see chapter 4). Further, according to the interpretation of the Ministry of Labour, to exclude men from certain jobs or certain forms of employment does not constitute discrimination because the aim of the law is to promote equal opportunity for women and to expand their job opportunities, not the other way round. Following this interpretation, it is also acceptable to specify in job advertisements that women only are required for part-time jobs or clerical jobs. This is criticised by many Japanese labour lawyers as creating a potential loophole for employers to create more part-time or low-paid clerical jobs for women. Also, if employers are to interpret the guidelines in a narrow technical sense, they can assign one or two token women to managerial jobs but keep the rest in clerical jobs; this can be said to have fulfilled the requirement that 'women are not excluded'. The Ministry of Labour pointed out that the objective of the law was to open up job opportunities to women which were formerly closed to them; not to restrict their employment options. Employers are expected to 'make efforts' in respect of the 'spirit' of the law and not to interpret the guidelines in a narrow sense.

A second meaning of 'equal opportunity' means 'not to treat women unfavourably'. According to the guidelines, to treat women unfavourably means to set different qualifications or conditions of employment for men and women. Discrimination in this sense means unequal treatment; non-discrimination means equal treatment. The guideline specifies that if as a result less women than men are able to comply with such terms and conditions, it does not constitute 'unfavourable treatment'. For example, according to the guidelines, in the case of promotion tests, 'unfavourable treatment' means not to offer women the opportunity to take the test or to impose qualification requirements on women different from that of men, such as requiring longer years of service. If the results of the tests turn out to be that less women than men are qualified for promotion, this does not constitute 'unfavourable treatment'. Clearly, the Ministry of Labour's interpretation does not embody the concept of 'indirect discrimination'.

Taking the above interpretation literally, one can say that the guidelines are aimed at no more than removing the most blatant forms of direct discrimination against women. 'Equal opportunity' is interpreted as 'equal treatment of women to that of men'. On the whole, the Ministry of Labour seems to have compromised to the *status quo* and makes little attempt to tackle the problem of institutional discrimination.

The Ministry of Labour, however, pointed out that the guidelines were no more than 'tentative measures':

> The guidelines do not represent the 'ideal norms' for achieving equal opportunities between men and women. They are no more than tentative measures, formulated on the basis of the present social and economic conditions, which employers are expected to 'make efforts' to follow at this point of time. Employers are, therefore, expected to take practical steps to follow these measures. Nevertheless, even if they implement their personnel management systems in line with the guidelines, it does not necessarily mean that they have fulfilled the 'moral obligation' enshrined in sections 7 and 8 of the EEO Law. *Employers are expected to make further efforts to provide equal opportunities and equal treatment to women as that of men by taking measures which are not stipulated in the guidelines and adjust their personnel systems accordingly in respect of the spirit of the EEO Law.*
>
> (MOL 1986: 44; italics added)

The above statement contains two important messages for interpreting the underlying assumptions of the EEO Law. First, the guidelines are no more than temporary minimum requirements at the present point of time. As they are the product of consultation and negotiation, they represent a kind of average standard of behaviour which employers in general have agreed to observe. Employers will be held responsible if they violate this minimum standard. In this sense, the nature of sanction of the guidelines is not so different from the prohibitory provisions. From the 'western norm' of equal opportunity, the standard of behaviour can be said to be very low. Nevertheless, a government survey showed that blatant direct discrimination and exclusion of women were still quite common in Japan in the early 1980s (see chapter 3). The intention of the guidelines is targeted mainly at the bad practice employers, urging them to raise their standard of behaviour to the 'average norm'. However, the statement made by the Ministry of Labour indicates that the spirit of the law goes beyond the requirements stipulated in the guidelines.

A more important second message is that, the 'ideal norm' of equal opportunity as enshrined in the spirit of the law is of a much higher moral standard which employers are expected to 'make efforts' to achieve. This higher moral standard is not a fixed target, but it is something above the standard set in the guidelines. As it is indeterminate and not well defined, it embodies an element of constant improvement and progress. Good practice employers who have already satisfied the guidelines will still be expected to 'make further efforts' in order to fulfil their moral obligation.

If this interpretation is correct, then the emphasis on informal sanction and the ambiguity of the hortatory provisions do not mean that the law is practically irrelevant or socially insignificant. On the contrary, by manipulating the ambiguity and indeterminateness of the hortatory provisions, the Ministry of Labour has allowed itself plenty of scope for manoeuvring the scope of influence of the provisions. Underlying the hortatory provisions, there is an assumption that in attempting to introduce changes in the most sensitive areas of the employment system, the way forward is to use a step-by-step approach to push forward changes through administrative guidance.

Figure 5.2 shows the model of change underlying the Japanese EEO Law. The axis represents the spectrum of achievement of equal opportunity standards from the 'worst practice' companies (XYZ) to the ideal of 'equal employment opportunity' (true EEO). 'S' represents the position of the current 'good practice' employers (like our case company Seibu which had taken initiatives in removing the most blatant forms of direct discrimination and had attempted to adopt more positive utilisation policies on women before the enactment of the law), and 'G' indicates the position of the guidelines. Since the 'ideal norm' of equal opportunity as enshrined in the 'spirit' of the law is a much higher moral standard beyond that required in the guidelines, the intended 'spectrum of achievement' of the present EEO Law is represented by the 'Ls', a moving target which is oriented towards the ideal norm of 'true EEO'.

A UNIQUE JAPANESE APPROACH TO SOCIAL CHANGE?

Does the Japanese government genuinely believe that this model will work? Or, is it no more than a superficial political gesture to pay lip service to the value of equality?

To many westerners, particularly those who are trained in law, they are bound to view the Japanese EEO Law with a good deal of

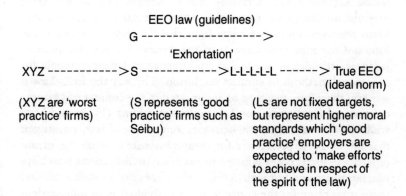

EEO law (guidelines)

G -------------------->

'Exhortation'

XYZ ----------->S ------------->L-L-L-L-L ------> True EEO
                                                             (ideal norm)

(XYZ are 'worst   (S represents 'good   (Ls are not fixed targets,
practice' firms)   practice' firms such as but represent higher moral
                            Seibu)   standards which 'good
                                                    practice' employers are
                                                    expected to 'make efforts'
                                                    to achieve in respect of
                                                    the spirit of the law)

Figure 5.2 Model of change underlying the Japanese EEO Law

scepticism. First, provisions like those in sections 7 and 8 are highly ambiguous. Offering women equality is interpreted as a kind of moral obligation on the side of the employers. Equality as an individual right simply does not exist in those provisions. Second, there is a total absence of any legally recognised sanction. Employers will not be penalised even if they do not 'make efforts' to fulfil their moral obligations. Third, litigation is discouraged and mediation is put forward as an alternative avenue for resolving disputes. The replacement of legal sanctions with moral suasion suits the interests of management. The hortatory provisions have removed the threat of litigation – a chief method which some determined women had used, indeed quite successfully in many cases, in the 1970s and early 1980s in their fight against discriminatory company practices. By removing the tool of litigation, women are deprived of an important avenue for setting the pace of change. Thus the form and the content of the legislation represents no more than a political compromise with Japanese management. By appealing to the 'good will' and 'moral obligation' of the employers, the enactment of the law has done no more than reasserting management control over the agenda of change. This interpretation of the EEO Law as a product of political compromise is not wrong and indeed, it is necessary for a complete understanding of the political significance of the EEO Law; but it only captures part of the meaning and the relevance of the law.

There are reasons to assume that the Japanese government is taking the EEO Law seriously and to believe that it will exert pressure on employers to provide equal opportunities for women. Many observers on Japanese law argue that the emphasis on informalism and the indeterminateness of the statutes is a manifestation of Japanese attitudes to law and the preference of Japanese people for consensual methods of conflict resolution. The way the EEO Law is written, therefore, needs to be interpreted in the context of Japanese culture and legal tradition. Takeyoshi Kawashima (1967a and b), a well-known sociologist on Japanese conception of law, points out that the Japanese preference for compromise stems from the nature of Japanese social order which consists of social obligations which are indeterminate and not well defined. He argues that in such a culture, there is no place for the concept of the individual as an independent entity equal to other individuals; the indeterminateness of social obligations does not allow the existence of the concept of 'right' as the counterpart of social obligation. In a society like Japan, therefore, according to Kawashima, 'the indeterminateness of the meaning of the statutes is taken for granted, and so scope for widening and narrowing the meaning of the statutes has been almost limitless' (Kawashima 1967b: 271). Many other Japanese legal scholars also emphasise that Japanese law has to be understood in the context of the legal consciousness of the Japanese people (*Nihonjin No Ho Ishiki*) (Hideo 1976; Noda 1976). They argue that the Japanese philosophy of law and their mental attitudes to litigation are fundamentally different from that of western countries:

> The Japanese manner of thinking clearly favours neither the formation nor the functioning of law as a conceptually arranged system of rights and duties. This does not, however, mean that there is no rule of conduct which functions for the maintenance of social order. Before the modern system of state law was established, a system of social rules of a non-legal nature directed the lives of Japanese, and that system continues to operate today, side by side with the more clearly defined system of state law. Whether this system be called 'custom' or 'non-law' its rules play a very important part in Japanese social life . . . . The traditional rules that the Japanese obey are called the rules of *giri*. They are rules of conduct, and do not presuppose the existence of any

relationship of clearly defined and quantitatively delimitable right and duties between the subjects whose conduct they regulate . . . . *Giri* is a duty or the state of a person who is bound to behave in a prescribed way toward a certain other person . . . . The person toward whom the duty is owed has no right to demand its fulfilment from the subject of duty. He must wait for the latter to fulfil it voluntarily.

(Noda 1976: 174–5)

In the Japanese cultural context, according to this view, compromise is a kind of social virtue and litigation which demands clear-cut decisions based on universal standards is simply not preferred by the Japanese. Thus, the peculiarity of the EEO Law is a manifestation of this specific 'Japanese way' of resolving social conflict. The use of informal moral sanctions for obliging employers to observe the spirit of the law and the emphasis on mediation are methods frequently employed by the Japanese for reaching social consensus. In dealing with the women's equality issues, the Japanese government has appealed to this time honoured 'consensus formation model'. This type of 'cultural explanation' or even '*nihon jin ron*' assumption is relevant if one is to understand why the EEO Law is written in the way it is. However, such 'cultural' interpretation should not be taken in a simplistic way as the 'natural' result of the continued strength of traditional values or culture. It is the consequence of a conscious political choice.

A crucial aspect of which one needs to take account is that the EEO Law is also a product of deliberate political decisions made by the governing bureaucracy. It represents an attempt on the part of the government to step in to maintain control and steer the direction of change in an area which has important implications for the economic and social order. The Japanese government was determined to enact the law, despite strong opposition from management. This was not purely out of a need to fulfil an international obligation, but was also a consequence of many internal social and economic changes which, as we have discussed, made the government realise that equal opportunity for women needed to be taken seriously and dealt with on the public policy level. The increased number of employment discrimination cases in the late 1970s was perceived as a threat to the social order; equality for women in employment would mean a substantial restructuring, not only of the employment system but the basis of Japanese society. In other words, equal employment issues were seen as becoming too important to be left to the courts or to the entire discretion of management.

Frank Upham, in his book on *Law and Social Change in Japan* (1987), argues that contrary to the stereotyped cultural assumption that litigation is insignificant in Japanese society, it is in fact politically highly significant. It is a tactic used by many suppressed groups in Japanese society like the *Burakumin*, the anti-pollution groups and women to shock society and challenge the establishment. In all cases, the government has reacted to the challenge by asserting its primacy in the resolution of individual cases through administrative guidance and mediation, thereby maintaining control over the issue. Upham uses the term 'bureaucratic informalism' to describe the Japanese model of law which, according to him, is fundamentally different from the rule-centred or judge-centred models prevalent in the West.[6] In the Japanese model, the governing bureaucracy plays a central role in the formulation of new rules and social norms. Both the rule-centred and the judge-centred models, according to Upham, are seen as socially and politically threatening because the litigation process is insulated from the state. The Japanese ruling bureaucracy has historically always played a prominent role in social change, thus the creation of a private domain of dispute resolution that is completely beyond its influence can be socially and politically threatening. As a consequence, the form and role of law in Japan, according to Upham, can be quite different from that of western countries:

> Central to the Japanese model of law generally and litigation in particular is the elite's attempt to retain some measure of control over the processes of social conflict and changes. The vehicle for that control is a skilled and dedicated bureaucracy, itself one branch of Japan's tripartite elite coalition, which has a long history of active intervention in Japanese society.
>
> (Upham 1987: 17)

The EEO Law is drafted in such a way that it leaves the definition and enforcement of equality up to the Ministry of Labour. The ambiguity of the hortatory provisions and the emphasis on informal methods of dispute resolution serves two important political functions. On the one hand, it is seen as less threatening by the employers. The informal methods of administrative guidance which allows for negotiation and compromise is regarded as more tolerable, and even welcomed at times. On the other hand, it has the advantage of allowing the governing bureaucracy to expand the areas into which it may intrude because it is highly flexible and allows for possibilities of unchecked administrative action.

The realisation of the norm of sex equality will require substantial restructuring of Japanese enterprise organisations and many other aspects of the society. In dealing with this issue, the Japanese government is taking a cautious stance. By asserting its role as a 'consensus maker' and by emphasising the role of administrative guidance in charting the future course of change, the government is trying to maintain control of the social agenda. The objective of the EEO Law is not to prevent women's equality but to ensure that equality will occur within the framework desired by the ruling bureaucracy after informal consultation and negotiation with business and organised labour.

CONCLUSIONS

If law is to be regarded as a tool to be used by women in challenging the established social order through the courts, the content of the Japanese EEO Law is clearly a political compromise. It has granted women very few new rights and imposed limited legal obligations on employers. However, if law in Japanese society is no more than a *denka no hoto* (a sword handed down from ancestors as a family treasure), which means that it is not for actual use, but for the 'symbolic manifestation of the prestige of the family' (Kawashima 1967b: 118), then no matter how conservative the actual content of the law is, one can still expect it to exert some influence on people's attitudes and behaviour. Law is acting as a symbol of a new moral standard.

If one takes the Japanese government's argument that the present EEO Law is a developing process of legislation – that the goals set in the guidelines are 'tentative measures' rather than ideal norms, then one need not be too critical of the letter of the law. In making the statement that 'employers are expected to make further efforts . . . by taking measures which are not stipulated in the guidelines and implement their personnel management systems accordingly in respect of the spirit of the law', the Ministry of Labour is clearly taking the rhetoric of the law seriously and appears genuinely to believe that it is possible to bring about change by relying on the 'good faith' and 'voluntary co-operation' of the employers. The

Ministry of Labour will urge the bad practice employers to follow the guidelines with good faith, and make attempts to promote further improvement among the good practice employers. Clearly, the Ministry of Labour is not simply relying on employers' 'goodwill' as such; the potential threat of future revision of the law is real to many employers. In view of the fact that it is a developing piece of legislation and its actual content is far from ideal as compared with the norm of equality in more advanced countries, pressures for more drastic revision remain.[7] The fear of further legislation might add extra pressure on employers to take some action.

Further, the enactment of the EEO Law itself has created a 'new environment'. It has important political and symbolic significance in the sense that employment practices which were taken for granted and accepted as a natural result of custom before will have to be put on the policy agenda for discussion and negotiation. The application of 'moral obligation' as a kind of indirect sanction puts employers in a defensive position. Bad practice employers will be challenged according to the criteria set out in the guidelines. Non-compliance can be directly questioned and disputes will be resolved according to those criteria. But even good practice employers, like our case company Seibu, may be challenged by the question 'whether enough efforts are being made' to promote equal opportunities for women.

The future outcome, however, is uncertain. The effectiveness of the model of change underlying the present EEO Law will have to be evaluated not only in terms of whether and how companies have responded to the legislation but also the extent to which the policy changes will actually benefit women in terms of their job status and career opportunities. Moreover, the attitudes and responses of women to the new situation will also be a crucial factor in determining the future outcome.

The next chapter analyses the responses and reactions of companies by looking at macro-level survey data. Part III of the book looks at a detailed case study conducted at Seibu, both before and after the introduction of the EEO Law, as a critical test of how much 'further efforts' a good practice company have made in response to the spirit of the law and whether the changes are having a positive impact on women's position and status.

Chapter 6

The management response

The analysis in chapter 4 shows how economic and market forces have pushed some major companies to initiate changes in their personnel management practices in order to improve the morale of their female workforces and better utilise their abilities. Most of the changes introduced, however, have been *ad hoc* and partial and could, at best, open up limited career opportunities for a small number of women. The policy adaptations introduced have not sought to bring about significant changes in the rules and practices governing job assignment and promotion, which operate to exclude the majority of women from the mainstream career jobs. If economic and market forces can only have limited effects in bringing about equal opportunities for women, will the EEO Law, as an external 'legal' and 'moral' force, make any difference? This is one major question to be answered in this chapter.

In the implementation of the EEO Law, the Japanese government put heavy emphasis on 'administrative guidance' (*gyosei-shido*) – a common Japanese regulatory technique which, although generally non-binding, seeks to make the behaviour of regulated parties conform to broad administrative goals. All compliance with administrative guidance is voluntary: an agency cannot employ the legal system or an administrative enforcement body to compel a regulated party to obey the government's directive. In some situations, government agencies tend to use a broad array of devices to accomplish their goals such as threatening to withhold services or encourage compliance by rewarding those who do (Young 1984). Some Japanese scholars point out that this type of administrative guidance can sometimes be quite effective (JERC 1987: 61–2). One of the most important means for assuring voluntary compliance is to encourage 'party input' – to undertake extensive consultation with regulated parties in order to build a consensus and, on occasion, to elicit the co-operation of the regulated parties. Thus, bargaining and negotiation are enshrined in the process of administrative guidance. It took the Japanese government more than seven years to draft the EEO Law; the long process of consultation and negotiation with employers and unions through their involvement in a number of committees (*shingikai*) was itself an administrative guidance process. The guidelines which explain the practical requirements of the EEO Law were issued by the Ministry of Labour after a long process of consultation with the related committees and numerous private visits made by members of the Women's Bureau to the major firms. Administrative guidance itself is a process of moral suasion to elicit the goodwill of the regulated parties and assures voluntary compliance once the law is passed.

So far the EEO Law has given rise to few legal disputes. Grievances brought to the Women's and Young Workers' Offices were small in number and were accordingly resolved through the advice and guidance of the offices. Up until July 1990 no case had been referred to the mediation commission. The major role of the Ministry of Labour has been concentrated in the more general areas of 'enlightenment guidance', for example, conducting seminars to explain the guidelines to job advertising firms, employment agencies within universities and schools, and running public conferences, aiming at raising the equality consciousness of employers and enhancing the public's general understanding of the law. More recently, the ministry has been encouraging firms to appoint equal opportunities officers to monitor the progress of equal opportunities within their companies.

Given the nature of the law, it would make sense to assess its impact by looking at how companies have been responding to it. The present chapter examines management responses to the legislation at two levels. First, the direct impact of the legislation on employer policies as reported in a number of major nationwide surveys. It looks specifically at the extent to which companies have (or more precisely, reported that they had) introduced changes in personnel policies and practices in order to comply with the 'practical requirements' of the law, including the prohibitory provisions in basic training, benefits and retirement and more importantly, the requirements stipulated in the guidelines with regard to the hortatory provisions in recruitment, job assignment and promotion. Second, it looks in greater detail at the type of personnel policy changes and evaluates how far companies have moved beyond the letter of the law in the promotion of equal opportunities for women.

Referring to the model of change underlying the Japanese EEO Law as shown in figure 5.2, the objectives of this chapter are twofold: (1) to examine how far the 'bad practice' companies (XYZ) have moved towards point 'G' on the spectrum of achievement of equal opportunity standards and, (2) to see whether there is evidence or an indication that they are attempting to move beyond 'G'.

The analysis is based on the following three major surveys. First, the 'survey on employment and management of women workers' (*Joshi rodosha no koyo kanri ni kansuru chosa*) carried out by the Ministry of Labour in February 1987 (hereafter referred to as the Rodosho survey) (MOL 1987b).[1] Second, the report published by the Japan Economic Research Centre in October 1987, which is the result of a one year monitoring of the implementation of the EEO Law by a group of academics and personnel management practitioners (hereafter referred to as the JERC study) (JERC 1987). The qualitative research methods used in this study, including in-depth interviews and discussions with the personnel managers of major companies, complements the more superficial questionnaire survey method of the Rodosho survey. Third, the 'survey on the utilisation of women workers' (*Kigyo ni okeru joshi no senryoka ni kansuru chosa*) carried out by the National Institute of Employment and Vocational Research in October 1986 (hereafter referred to as the NIVER survey) (NIVER 1987).[2] Additional data were also obtained from a great variety of sources including reports in newspapers and numerous surveys and studies reported in various journals since the implementation of the EEO Law.

The nature of the survey data used in this chapter restricts a full test of the second objective. An in-depth case study at a good practice company proves to be necessary. Hence the present chapter provides a background context for the detailed case study presented in part III.

ACTIONS AND REACTIONS OF FIRMS

Shift in policy orientations on women

There appears to have been a general, positive shift in management attitudes and policy orientations on women employees (NIVER 1987). The proportion of companies claiming to adopt 'a positive utilisation policy based on individual ability disregarded of sex' had increased from 39.6 per cent before 1985 to 54.8 per cent after 1985; at the same time those saying that their main policy orientation was 'to utilise women in assistant type of jobs' had declined from 33.9 per cent to 15.3 per cent (see table 6.1). Nevertheless, these were policy statements made by the management of the companies, which did not necessarily mean that there had been an actual shift in the companies' policies. Further, a part of the survey results was based on retrospective questions. The dividing line of before and after the year 1985 is arbitrary rather than real. In the survey, companies were asked to indicate their policies on women employees roughly during the three-year period before 1985 and their policies for the three-year period after 1985. It is not a comparison of two different survey results at two points in time. There is a possibility that management might have overstated their policy changes. However, the survey results can still be taken as an indication that the attitudes and general intended policy orientations after 1985 have shifted in a more positive direction.

Despite this, the situation as reported in the survey still awaits much improvement; 15.3 per cent of the companies still intended to continue their policy of restricting the utilisation of women to assistant type of jobs and another 15 per cent remained ambivalent with regard to their policies on women, which probably meant they had not taken any action in response to the law.

Extent of direct policy response to the EEO Law

Table 6.2 shows the extent to which companies have introduced changes in their personnel management practices in direct response to the requirements of the legislation, as reported in the Rodosho survey (MOL 1987b). It appears that companies are more willing to introduce changes both at point of entry (recruitment and conditions of employment) and exit (retirement) from the firm. These are areas which will cause least disruption to the core practices of the personnel management systems and tend to affect only those employees who are either joining or leaving the company. In the area of training, a high proportion of the firms replied 'no such training' which could either mean they did not conduct training in those areas, or the type of training they had was outside the scope of equal treatment requirements. This is because the present legislation only

Table 6.1 Policy orientations on women employees, before and
after 1985

	Before 1985 %	After 1985 %
Positive utilisation based on individual ability, disregarding sex	39.6	54.8
Utilisation of women mainly in specialist jobs (e.g. systems engineers, R&D jobs, etc.)	13.7	14.8
Utilisation of women limited to assistant type of jobs	33.9	15.3
Utilisation policies on women under examination	5.4	11.2
Do not intend to utilise women	6.5	3.3
Others	1.0	0.6
(Total no. of companies responding)	(2,005)	(2,005)

Source: NIVER (1987: 265)

prohibits discrimination in a narrow range of training, excluding
on-the-job training.

In the areas of assignment, job rotation (especially that involving
movement between establishments) and promotion, company responses to the equal treatment requirements stipulated in the guidelines have been relatively limited. A high proportion of the firms had
not complied: 35.1 per cent in assignment, 55.1 per cent in job
rotation involving geographical mobility and 41.5 per cent in
promotion (note that these figures are the sum total of those who
replied 'under examination', 'no action yet' or 'unclear' in the survey
results shown in table 6.2). These are the areas in which changes will
affect a large number of the existing employees. One would
therefore expect resistance to rapid changes from both the employers
and the male employees. Changes in these areas will probably
involve a long process of bargaining between the management and
different categories of employees within the enterprise. Judging from
the small proportion of firms which said they had introduced changes
in compliance with the equal treatment requirements, the legislation
does not appear to have had substantial impact in these areas.

Table 6.2 Extent of response to the EEO Law (in percentages)

	Already had equal opportunity change not necessary	Change introduced	Under examination	No action yet	Unclear
(Exhortation)					
Recruitment	68.0	19.8	6.3	5.8	–
Conditions of employment	78.7	18.9	1.9	0.4	0.1
Job assignment	56.1	8.8	13.6	–	21.5
Job rotation					
(a) Within same establishment	74.8	8.2	8.1	8.8	–
(b) Rotation involves geographical mobility	32.0	14.0	16.8	37.2	–
Promotion	53.8	4.8	11.5	29.8	0.2
(Prohibition)					
Basic training (for new recruits)	55.7	5.6	(No such training = 38.7)		–
Basic training (job-related)	42.3	4.7	(No such training = 48.0)		4.9
Management training	29.7	3.0	(No such training = 60.9)		6.4
Benefits (e.g. housing loan)	27.3	0.7	(No such benefits = 67.8)		4.3
Retirement age	82.1	15.0	–	–	2.9

Source: Compiled from Rodosho survey (MOL 1987b).

However, one can still argue that since a relatively high proportion of the companies replied that 'change was not necessary because they already had equal opportunity for women before the legislation was enacted', this need not mean that the hortatory provisions have had no effect. It could mean that some of the firms had introduced policy changes in anticipation of the new legislation. Therefore by the time the legislation came into force, there was no need to take any further action. It could also mean that more companies are now making false claims that they have equal opportunity policies because of increasing social pressures on companies to do so. Both interpretations could be true; it would be difficult to verify the precise contribution of each factor to the replies in the Rodosho survey.

There is some evidence to support the argument that many companies, especially the large ones, had taken steps to eliminate the most blatant forms of direct discrimination against women before the EEO Law formally came into force in April 1986. About one-third of the firms reported that they had completed reviewing their personnel management procedures (75 per cent in the case of firms with 3,000 or more employees) and half of them were taking some kind of action, according to a survey on 321 large major firms in March 1986 (Rosei Jiho 1986). Further, a comparison of the results of the Rodosho survey on companies' personnel management policies on women at three different points of time, namely 1977, 1981 and 1987, shows a dramatic decline in the number of firms reporting direct discrimination against women, with the decline especially sharp between 1981 and 1987 (see table 6.3). Between 1977 and 1981, there was some slight improvement but the extent of change was not as drastic as that occurring between 1981 and 1987. The change was most dramatic with regard to recruitment, conditions of employment and job assignment. The one area that appeared to be most resistant to change was promotion; 41.3 per cent of the firms reported not offering women management promotion chances or imposing different terms and conditions in 1987 as compared to 45.1 per cent in 1981 and 52.3 per cent in 1977. With regard to training, directly comparable data in the 1987 survey were not available due to the different way the question was asked.

Overall, the legislation has had an impact on the most blatant forms of direct discrimination against women, except in promotion. It has helped to eliminate the number of worst practice companies. The meagre improvement reported in the area of promotion is not difficult to explain. Equal opportunity for women (defined in the

Table 6.3 Proportion of companies admitting direct discrimination
against women (1977, 1981 and 1987) (in percentages)

	1977	*1981*	*1987**
Recruitment			
a) Male graduates only	78.3	73.0	19.6
b) Male high school leavers only	–	24.5	14.3
c) Mid-career entry limited to males only	–	19.0	14.1
Conditions of employment (Imposing different terms and conditions on men and women, e.g. different age limit, exclusion of married women, etc.)	38.1	32.6	8.7
Job assignment (Have jobs which excluded women completely)	91.5	83.4	35.1
Job rotation (Not offering women job rotation)	50.8	50.4	26.3
Training (No training for women or contents of training programme different for men and women)	70.3	60.0	–**
Promotion (No managerial promotion opportunities or imposing different conditions)	52.3	45.1	41.3
Retirement (Separate systems for men and women)	22.4	19.4	2.9

Source: Compiled from Rodosho surveys (MOL 1977, 1981a and 1987b).

Notes: * Questions in the 1987 survey were designed specifically to test the
extent to which companies had complied with the practical
requirements of the EEO Law. The way they were written differed
from that of the previous two surveys. The 1987 figures were adapted
by the author for comparison with the previous survey results.
** Comparable data on training were not available in the 1987 survey.

guidelines as 'not to exclude women' or 'not to treat women unfavourably') in recruitment or assignment can be fulfilled by allowing
some new recruits into areas which have previously excluded them,
even if it is only a few token women. This can be achieved within a
relatively short period of time. In contrast, equal treatment in
promotion is much more complex. It requires changing the policies
on existing employees: even promoting a few token women to
supervisory positions can be politically sensitive and seen as
disrupting the existing hierarchical order in the organisation. A

longer time span may be necessary before companies can claim they offer equal treatment to women in promotion.

TYPE OF POLICY CHANGES

The quick response of companies to the practical requirements of the EEO Law raises an important question: namely, the meaning of 'equal opportunity' as defined in the guidelines, and the standards of equal opportunities required. The present guidelines define equal opportunity as 'not to exclude women' or 'not to treat women unfavourably'; as long as companies adopt an equal treatment policy, the requirements of the law are fulfilled. Companies are merely required to adopt a 'non-discriminatory' approach in applying the personnel management rules and procedures but not necessarily change these established rules and practices. It could well be that companies have accepted the equal treatment requirement with little resistance partly because they have discovered that adopting it will not necessarily upset the *status quo*.

A more detailed examination of the type of policy changes introduced will illustrate more clearly the extent to which management have actually taken positive steps to initiate changes in their personnel management procedures and practices towards more egalitarian treatment of women, in respect of the spirit of the law.

Recruitment and conditions of employment for new entrants

Companies have responded most rapidly since the enactment of the EEO Law in the areas of recruitment and conditions of employment for new entrants. The effects are also more readily observable as changes in recruitment and selection policies would have an immediate impact on the large number of graduates and school leavers coming onto the job market in the spring of each year.

It is in job advertising that the most remarkable changes have taken place. The proportion of companies which excluded female job applicants (specifying that jobs were open to male graduates only) declined from 41 per cent in 1986 to 17 per cent in 1987; those which offered jobs to graduates without specifying the sex requirements rose from 36 per cent in 1986 to 77 per cent in 1987 (WVI 1986 and 1987). This has been reflected positively in the actual job placement ratio of female graduates, increasing from 75.4 per cent in 1985 to 82.4 per cent in 1989. The increase in the case of male graduates during the same period was a mere 2 percentage points, from 86.9 per cent to 88.9 per cent. Another notable positive change has been the increased entry of women to large firms. In 1985, 37 per cent of the female school leavers and graduates entering the job market joined large firms (those with 1,000 employees or more), with the proportion rising to 50 per cent in 1989 (Sato 1990: 102).

An increasing number of companies have also taken steps to remove the unfavourable terms and conditions applied specifically to female job applicants such as requiring women to have special qualifications or skills or restrictions that women should be commuting to work from their parents' homes, etc. A more remarkable change has been the move towards equalisation of starting wages for new recruits. Section 4 of the Labour Standards Law prohibits 'unequal wages for equal work' but many companies have been able to continue offering different starting wages to men and women by restricting women to certain low-paid job categories. The EEO Law has helped to reduce unequal treatment in this area, at least on the formal policy level. More companies have moved towards equal starting wages for men and women (see table 6.4).

The EEO Law has made companies find it difficult to specify the sex requirements in job advertisements and to impose obviously

Table 6.4 Changes in starting wages for new recruits, 1975–87

	High School			University		
Year	Equal wages %	Differ by sex/job %	No. of firms	Equal wages %	Differ by sex/job %	No. of firms
1975	46.7	53.3	420	31.7	68.3	205
1980	59.5	40.5	388	35.5	64.5	183
1985	62.0	38.0	332	49.0	51.0	259
1986	74.6	25.4	299	64.7	35.3	295
1987	82.1	17.9	184	78.9	21.1	190

Source: Rosei Jiho (1987:4).

Note: Enterprises with 500 or more employees, annual surveys by Romu Gyosei Kenkyu-sho.

unequal terms and conditions on women at the point of entry. However, the harsh realities confronting many female job applicants suggest that in some cases changes in recruitment policies are more in form rather than in substance. Staff at the universities' employment information office reported that even when they received job offers for both sexes, firms often revealed preference for men in the screening process (JIL 1987). There were also widespread complaints from female graduates that the changes in job advertising had only created false expectations and caused confusion in their job hunting activities as they only discovered that companies had no real intention of recruiting female graduates or offering them equal career opportunities when they approached the companies (*Asahi Shimbun*, 9 September 1987). In practice, 50 per cent of the firms still restricted recruitment for technical-related jobs to men, and over a quarter did not seek to recruit female graduates for administrative or sales jobs, according to the latest survey by the Ministry of Labour (MOL 1990: 4).

The EEO Law does not seem to have had much effect on eliminating many traditional Japanese recruitment practices which, although not in direct violation of the requirements stipulated in the guidelines, discriminate against women. Many companies still conduct their recruitment and screening activities for men and women separately. One common practice is to set aside different dates for accepting applications from men and women. Companies would normally finish the interviews for male job applicants first before they start interviewing female applicants. This could mean that companies only offer job opportunities to women after they have failed to recruit a sufficient number of men. In the case where recruitment activities for both men and women are conducted on the same day, it is still a common practice for companies to organise separate meetings for male and female job applicants. These practices do not constitute discrimination against women, as defined by the Ministry of Labour, because companies have not 'excluded women' in the recruitment procedures.

Sex is still one of the most important criteria on which many companies base their annual recruitment plans and make their manpower decisions. In 1986, three out of four companies still decided in advance the number of men and women they intended to recruit each year (Rosei Jiho 1986). Out of these more than half indicated that they did not plan to change this practice in the near future. The main reason for this, as pointed out by the companies, being that 'the type of jobs' for men and women were different. This raises a crucial question of how far the present legislation has helped to remove the traditional practice of recruiting men for core career jobs and women for assistant type of jobs. Equal opportunities for women will not come about unless companies are prepared to eliminate the practice of making a clear distinction between 'men's jobs' and 'women's jobs'.

Changes over the last few years seem to indicate that companies are moving towards more indirect, yet institutionalised, ways of segregating the majority of women into low status jobs.

A new selection system: 'career tracking'

Since the promulgation of the EEO Law, an increasing number of major firms have introduced a new recruitment system – the 'career tracking system' *(Kosubetsu koyo-seido)* – in which new recruits are offered a choice of different career tracks at the point of entry. Over 20 per cent of the firms which had no formal distinction for regular employees' career tracks adopted such a system after the EEO Law was introduced (WVI 1986). Among those firms which had introduced the system, half of them indicated that the main objective was to cope with the law. The number of companies adopting the system has been rising in recent years. It is most widely adopted by firms in the finance and insurance sector (MOL 1989). Figure 6.1 shows the extent to which companies have introduced this new form of selection system by firm size. Career tracking is primarily a 'big firm phenomenon': 42.3 per cent of firms with 5,000 or more employees have introduced the system as compared to 11.4 per cent for firms with 300–999 employees.

Although there are some variations in its implementation in different companies, the most common form of career tracking is to classify the regular employees into two streams: the managerial and the clerical. The managerial track (usually called *'sogoshoku'*) is usually defined with three characteristics: (a) jobs which require complex judgement, such as business negotiations, personnel management, designing or developing products, planning of company policies or strategies; (b) employees in this track are subject to comprehensive job rotation and transfers for career development and business necessities; and (c) there is no limit to promotion – employees can eventually become top-level managers or executives.

The characteristics of the clerical track (usually called *'ippanshoku'*)

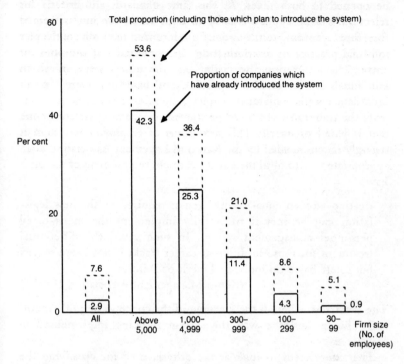

Figure 6.1 Extent of coverage of career tracking system, by firm size, 1989
Source: MOL (1990)

are in contrast with the above in the following ways: (a) jobs are considered less complicated and more manual; (b) job rotation and transfers are carried out within a limited scope (notably employees are not required to move to other localities); and (c) there is a formal limit to promotion (employees can attain only lower-level or local management positions). In some firms, an additional track is organised between these two tracks for 'specialist employees' (*senmonshoku*), who specialise in jobs requiring high-level skills or knowledge.

According to the Kanto Management Association (1986), the career tracking system is designed to clarify each individual's career choice at the early stage of their careers so as to facilitate career planning. It also points out that selection for entry to the different career tracks is solely based on 'merit' and that all career options will be opened to both sexes. As the same standards and criteria for selection will be applied equally to both sexes, the new system is therefore, according to the association, intended to eliminate the past informal practice of discrimination against women at the point of entry. The association also claims that the new system, in which individuals are recruited for specific 'jobs' based on 'merit' and in accordance with individual 'choice', signifies a fundamental shift from the traditional sex-based personnel management system to one that is based on merit. This new form of employment system is strongly recommended by the Kanto Management Association as an appropriate way to fulfil the equal treatment requirement of the EEO Law:

> treating women equally with men as required by the new legislation can be met if firms fully implement the merit-based personnel management system. In such cases, the differential treatment for those in different career tracks is not based on sex but solely based on individual merit or abilities.
>
> (Kanto Management Association 1986: 6)

The crucial issue here is the meaning of the concepts of 'job', 'merit' and 'choice' and the way the system is being implemented in practice.

First, one needs to look at the criteria used for classifying the different job categories or career streams. How far are they job related and how far are they behavioural requirements? In the majority of the cases, the job classification is no more than a broad distinction between the 'managerial' and the 'clerical' jobs. It is often not clear what precisely the job specifications are and what type of requirements and qualifications companies are looking for. The one common criterion used by all the firms adopting the new system is the mobility requirement for jobs in the managerial track. Some companies have instead simply used the commitment to mobility: calling the two tracks the 'mobile' and the 'non-mobile'.[3] Career progression for those in the 'non-mobile track' is normally limited to middle management.

Second, job specifications are often very broad and general. The job abilities and qualifications required for the different career streams are often no more than a set of behavioural expectations, such as a commitment to be geographically mobile. At those companies which have adopted the new system, there were complaints from women that they were doing the same kind of work as men but were classified into the inferior 'clerical career track' simply because they did not make a commitment to the mobility requirement (JERC 1987: 125–7). This is clearly a form of indirect discrimination against women. As the majority of women would find it difficult to commit themselves to the mobility requirement at the beginning of their career, companies could use this new system to exclude the majority of women from the mainstream career jobs. Recruitment by individual 'merit' is in effect a disguised form of sexual discrimination.

Third, implementation of the new system raises serious doubts about the fairness of the selection and screening procedures. Formally, the management career track is open to both men and women (in most cases restricted to graduates only), but in practice men are almost assigned to it automatically, whereas women are selected for it only exceptionally (JERC 1987: 121–4). In the process of selection interviews with management, women were often challenged with tough questions about mobility and potential sacrifices of family life. Men who intended to select the clerical (or non-mobile) career track were persuaded by the companies to change their mind (*Asahi Shimbun*, 1 September 1987).

Despite the formal offer of equal opportunities, in reality very few women managed to pass the selection procedures to enter the management career track. Table 6.5 gives some examples of firms which have pioneered the new employment system and recruited women for the managerial track in the spring of 1987. The number of female graduates who managed to enter the mainstream managerial track was extremely small.

A survey by the Women's Vocational Institute (WVI 1990) in September 1987 on forty firms in the finance, insurance and banking sector which had adopted the career tracking system found that only 1.3 per cent of the women employees were in the managerial track, as compared with 99.0 per cent of men (see table 6.6). In contrast with the managerial track, the clerical track has remained exclusively a female domain. Women constituted 98.9 per cent of those in the clerical track. Under the present EEO Law, it is considered acceptable for companies to restrict certain jobs to women only.

It is no exaggeration to say that the formal classification of employees into different career tracks is in effect institutionalisation of past informal practices which segregated women in the inferior dead-end jobs. The present system is more of a classification of employees by status rather than by job. It would seem that from

Table 6.5 Examples of companies which recruited female graduates for managerial career track (*sogoshoku*) in the spring of 1987

Name of company	Total no. of male graduates recruited (All 'managerial career track')	Total no. of female graduates recruited*	No. of females selected for 'managerial career track'
Orientorisu	56	152	2
Sumitomo Bank	420	60	20
Taisho Kaijo Kasai Insurance	120	43	3
Tokyo Gas	108	12	12
Daiwa Security	300	(approx.) 130	3
Nikko Security	396	(approx.) 160	3
Mitsubishi Bank	385	30	(approx.) 10
Mitsubishi Trading	138	125	3

Source: *Nikkei Shimbun* (Evening), 14 April 1987.

Note: * Figures inclusive of those selected for 'managerial career track'

Table 6.6 Distribution of male and female employees by career tracks, 1987

	Male		Female		Women's share of each category
	No.	%	No.	%	
Managerial (*Sogoshoku*)	81,249	99.0	706	1.3	0.9
Clerical (*Ippanshoku*)	615	0.8	53,519	96.2	98.9
'Mid-way' (*Chukanshoku*)*	19	0.0	1,356	2.4	98.6
Specialist (*Senmonshoku*)	166	0.2	34	0.1	17.0
Total	82,049	100.0	55,615	100.0	40.4

Source: WVI (1990: 26).

Note: *This is a kind of 'middle-of-the-road' career track recently introduced by some companies to enable some selected women to take up more responsible jobs, but unlike those in the managerial track, there is no requirement for geographical mobility.

management's viewpoint, the offer of a 'choice' to individuals at the point of entry not only fulfils the equal treatment requirement of the EEO Law, but also automatically justifies the differential wage systems, training and promotion opportunities accorded for the different 'class' of employees in different career tracks. Employers thus could justify paying a woman lower wages, offer her less training and little promotion opportunities by the fact that she has made a 'choice' to enter the clerical career track.

The above account does not imply that the new selection system will be without effect in improving women's career opportunities. The formal offer of equal treatment will lead to some changes, and some women will take advantage of it and seek to pursue the managerial career route. But the move towards equal opportunities for women will be gradual and extremely limited; only a minority of women who are capable of and willing to accept the challenge of adopting the male working pattern will be offered a chance.

Job assignment and promotion

Job assignment and promotion are the 'core areas' of the personnel management systems which Japanese companies resisted strongly against any kind of external intervention during the drafting stage of the EEO Law. As with recruitment and hiring, the present legislation urges companies to 'make efforts' to offer women equal opportunities in these areas. Policy changes in these areas have been few and extremely limited.

Only a relatively small proportion of the companies said they had introduced some kind of change in these areas since the legislation was introduced, according to the Rodosho survey (see table 6.2) (MOL 1987b). Over one-third of the companies surveyed either had not taken any action or were unclear about their future policies for women in job assignment and promotion. Even among those companies which reported they had initiated some kind of policy changes in response to the legislation, the type of changes introduced were extremely limited and restricted to women employees who could satisfy certain terms or conditions imposed by the companies (see table 6.7).

In job assignment, among those companies which reported having introduced some policy changes, 21 per cent had opened up all job categories to women, while 79 per cent said they had only opened up some of the traditionally 'male jobs' to women (MOL 1987b).

Table 6.7 Type of policy changes in job assignment, job rotation and promotion (percentage of companies reporting changes in policies following the introduction of the EEO Law)

Job Assignment	Open up all jobs to women	Open up some jobs to women	
	20.9	79.1	

Job rotation (within same establishment)	All women offered same opportunity as men	Only women who satisfy certain conditions	Women who choose rotation
	27.2	36.0	36.8
Job rotation (involves geographical mobility)	24.3	30.8	44.9

Promotion	Equal opportunity for all women	Only women in certain job categories	
	47.4	52.6	

Source: Compiled from Rodosho survey (MOL 1987b).

Note: ˙ The base (100 per cent) is the number of companies which reported they had introduced policy changes since the EEO Law was introduced (refer to table 6.2)

The Rodosho survey does not indicate what type of jobs have been opened up for women, but evidence from the JERC study and the NIVER survey shows that the dominant trend in recent years has been the expansion of more opportunities for women in areas such as sales, marketing and technical development (NIVER 1987: 270–1; JERC 1987: 84–5). Most of these are specialist jobs which require some kind of technical or specialist skills. Management's attempts to open up more job opportunities for women in these areas started well before the introduction of the new legislation. Increased market competition and skills shortages have been the major factors prompting companies to expand opportunities for women in these specialist areas. The legislation has probably helped to accelerate these 'market-pushed' tendencies at a much faster pace rather than brought about any path-breaking changes.

In the area of promotion, changes are very few and limited. The fundamental policy adaptations in this area have been towards more formalised and institutionalised screening and selection procedures for women employees who aspire to pursue a long-term career. An increasing number of companies have adopted the 'career conversion system' which allows selected female employees to apply for conversion to the managerial career track, opening up promotion possibilities up to top management level. Career conversion constitutes an important element of the career tracking system discussed earlier. It is not an entirely new policy innovation in response to the legislation. Early in the 1980s, several major banking and security companies adopted the conversion system as a means to open up promotion opportunities for women with long years of service (see chapter 4). Since the introduction of the EEO Law, this system has spread rapidly and companies have introduced more formalised and sophisticated procedures. It is most widely adopted and well-developed among the large firms in the female-intensive industries such as finance, banking and retailing.

Under this system, equal promotion opportunities would only be offered to those women who satisfy certain terms and conditions and manage to pass the screening tests and interviews for conversion to the managerial career track. In some cases, the terms and conditions would include age and length of service requirements plus performance criteria. For instance, in the case of Mitsubishi Trading Corporation, only women who are aged over 37 and with good continuous performance over the previous three years would be eligible to apply for conversion to the managerial career track which, automatically, would also require a commitment to be geographically mobile. Many companies, however, do not specify clearly the terms and conditions required apart from the requirement to make a commitment to be geographically mobile (Rosei Jiho 1988). Such a requirement almost automatically justifies the exclusion of the majority of women from promotion. The crux of the problem is that under the present conversion system, all the male employees are automatically converted to the managerial track while only a selected number of women are eligible to apply for conversion.

Furthermore, as pointed out in chapter 4, career conversion would hardly have any real impact on promoting women's position unless they were given the requisite training and job experience from the early stage of their careers. So far, there is little evidence that there has been much progress with regard to equal training opportunities for women.

Education and training

The effects of the legislation in this area have been largely limited to the elimination of unequal treatment in basic induction training for new recruits. Changes beyond this initial stage of training have been extremely limited (JERC 1987: 140). For instance, for job rotation which constitutes the most crucial part of education and training in Japanese companies and is closely related to promotion, equal opportunities for women are basically limited to those who can satisfy certain terms and conditions imposed by the company (see table 6.7). Job rotation involving geographical mobility is still one of the most controversial areas which the majority of companies hesitate to initiate any fundamental policy changes.

The present legislation prohibits 'discrimination against women in provision of training for basic skills necessary for performing their jobs and duties'. Prohibition of discrimination against women in management and specialist training only applies to those who have already been formally accepted for promotion to jobs which require these skills. The offer of equal treatment for women in more advanced types of training will be no more than a hollow promise unless they are offered equal job assignment and promotion opportunities.

POLICIES FOR HARMONISING WORK AND FAMILY: RE-ENTRY AND CHILDCARE LEAVE MEASURES

In the Rodosho survey (MOL 1987b), over 50 per cent of the employers pointed out that women's 'short years of service', and another 34 per cent indicated that 'women's responsibilities in the family' were the greatest problems they saw in utilising women. Despite this, only 11 per cent of the employers regarded the introduction of re-entry or childcare leave systems as one of the policy priorities they intended to consider in the future.

The Japanese government emphasises that the fundamental spirit of the EEO Law is to 'promote measures to enable women to harmonise working life with family life'. The present legislation urges employers to introduce re-entry and childcare leave systems for their female employees. Special financial incentives have been introduced by the Ministry of Labour to encourage companies to take actions in these areas.[4] So far, policy initiatives in these areas have been limited. In 1989, the proportion of companies with re-entry schemes, including those operating on an informal basis, was 16.6 per cent (MOL 1990). Although there have been some improvements in the provision of childcare leave in recent years as a result of collective bargaining by some unions (rising from 15 per cent in 1985 to 19 per cent in 1988), the number of women covered by childcare leave schemes was less than a quarter of the total female workforce (Sato 1990: 189). At present childcare leave as a statutory right is only granted to nurses and women teaching in state schools. The number of companies in the private sector providing childcare leave systems is very small.

The situation might improve with the recent enactment of the Childcare Leave Act (1991). In August 1987, the opposition parties submitted a childcare leave bill to the Diet. It was initially rejected by the Ministry of Labour on the grounds that it was 'too soon' for Japan to introduce such a bill. However, severe skills shortages and a continued decline in the birth rate have pushed the government to change its stance. A bill guaranteeing a maximum of one-year childcare leave for working parents eventually passed the Diet in May 1991, despite strong opposition from *Nikkeiren*. The law will take effect from April 1992, with enforcement in small firms (with 30 employees or less) delayed by three years.

SUMMARY AND CONCLUSIONS

This chapter has reviewed companies' response to the EEO Law. In terms of reducing the number of worst practice companies by removing the most obvious forms of direct discrimination against women, the present legislation has been quite effective. Companies in general have responded fairly rapidly (both before the implementation of the legislation or immediately afterwards) to the prohibitory provisions and the practical requirements stipulated in the guidelines with regard to the hortatory provisions. Changes at the point of entry to the company have been most significant, especially in terms of opening up job opportunities for female graduates. Many less obvious forms of discrimination in recruitment still persist. This is not because companies have failed to comply with the requirements stipulated in the guidelines, but more because of the way equal opportunity is being defined by the Ministry of Labour.

So far, there is little evidence that companies have taken more positive steps initiating changes in their personnel management procedures, especially with regard to job assignment and promotion, apart from adopting a passive policy of equal treatment. On the contrary, the requirement to offer women equal treatment has stimulated companies to formalise and institutionalise many of the past informal practices which operated to segregate men and women into entirely separate career tracks. Companies have now introduced more formal screening and selection procedures for those women who intend to pursue the mainstream career jobs. Career tracking preserves the core personnel management system even better and ensures that equal opportunities will be only offered to a limited number of women, in the majority of cases university graduates, who can satisfy the requirements and conditions imposed by the company. Discrimination is indirect and is justified by the 'logic' of the personnel management system.

Many of the changes observed were in fact a continuation and acceleration of the trends already going on before the introduction of the legislation. The EEO Law serves a symbolic function of formally ratifying these changes and perhaps has acted as a catalyst pushing forward these changes at a much faster pace.

The present equal opportunity debate, both within companies and at the societal level, appears to have been biased towards the 'career-oriented women' and to have neglected an increasing number of Japanese women who aspire to combine employment with having a family. According to attitude surveys by the Prime Minister's Office, the proportion of women believing they should re-enter the job market after child rearing rose from 39 per cent in 1979 to 55 per cent in 1983 and shot up further to 64 per cent in 1989 (PMO 1979, 1983 and 1989). The EEO Law urges companies to introduce re-entry and childcare leave systems. There has been little evidence that companies have taken active steps in these areas to ease women's career constraints.

Unless companies are prepared to go beyond the minimum equal opportunity standards as stipulated in the guidelines, the present legislation clearly can only have a limited direct effect in removing the structural sources of unequal opportunity between the sexes. The symbolic importance of the legislation, however, is that it does appear to have a general educative effect on the attitudes of employers. The NIVER survey shows that less employers now regard women merely as an auxiliary workforce. More employers are prepared to offer a few token women the opportunity to enter the male career stream, though these women should be prepared to follow the male working pattern. To an increasing number of companies, equal opportunities for women has become an important policy issue to be put on the management agenda for discussion. However, it still remains to be seen how far some good practice companies are prepared to take more active measures to set the pace for further change.

The analysis in this chapter has been mainly based on secondary surveys. Although they are reasonably reliable for assessing the extent to which companies in general have taken actions in response to the EEO Law, they are inadequate for the examination of more specific policy changes that might have taken place but not been revealed through the broad questionnaire surveys. The national surveys are useful for assessing how far the law has raised the 'average norm of equal opportunities', but they do not necessarily tell us whether good practice companies have been 'making efforts' to move beyond the requirements of the law.

So far, the government's administrative guidance has focused primarily on removing bad practice companies, and surveys conducted by the Ministry of Labour have intended to measure policy effectiveness in these terms. It is difficult to gauge from the large-scale questionnaire surveys whether companies have been 'making efforts' in respect of the spirit of the law. In-depth enterprise level information is necessary for a more complete evaluation of the situation.

There is also a methodological reason for using an alternative approach to assess the operation of the law. Up to the present, the majority of the large-scale surveys are either conducted or sponsored by the Ministry of Labour, which is not a disinterested party. From the ministry's point of view, conducting surveys and the dissemination of results are all part of the processes of administrative guidance. The ministry might want to use survey results to exert pressures on companies to conform to the 'emerging norm of equality'. Survey questions could be deliberately designed to show positive effects in general rather than to reveal persistence of discrimination. This is not to suggest that all government surveys are necessarily biased. However, there are inherent institutional and political incentives for the government to emphasise positive results. Thus, the Ministry of Labour surveys and reports should be used with some caution.

This further emphasises the need for an in-depth case study for evaluating the impact of the law on management practices and the implications of the changes for women. If the real significance of the law depends on the extent to which good practice employers are prepared to comply with its spirit, and not just follow the letter of it, then it is important to look at how a leading-edge company like Seibu might set the pace for further improvement.

Part III

A case study

Chapter 7

The Seibu case: an introduction

This part of the book presents a detailed case study conducted at Seibu Department Stores Ltd, one of the biggest department store groups in Japan. Although department stores employ a high proportion of women and are often regarded as a 'women friendly' industry, until recently women in Japanese department stores did not enjoy higher organisational positions than their counterparts in other industries. The majority of women were employed in low status selling jobs at the bottom of the organisational hierarchy. The mainstream career jobs in buying, product planning and management were predominantly male preserves. However, beginning in the mid-1970s, there were signs of change. A series of managerial reforms were introduced at Seibu aimed at promoting the position of women by bringing more highly qualified women into key business functions. Seibu was not the only company to initiate changes in employment policies on women; similar tendencies could be observed throughout the whole department store industry (Rosei Jiho 1978). However, among the major department stores, Seibu has been regarded as a pioneering model in introducing personnel policy reforms for women.

The main objectives of the study at Seibu were threefold. First, to analyse the major commercial and market factors prompting Seibu's management to shift its employment and personnel policies on women after the mid-1970s and the type of new policies and practices introduced. Second, to examine how a large Japanese company, one which is deemed as 'progressive' in personnel management reforms and is regarded as a leading edge company in promoting career opportunities for women, has responded and adapted its practices to comply with the spirit of the EEO Law. Third, to test the outcomes of the equal opportunity policies on the position and status of women and to explore how far the EEO Law and the equality debates have brought about a shift in women's work attitudes and career expectations. The study was conducted both before and after the introduction of the EEO Law. The initial study was conducted in 1983–4 and the follow-up in 1988. The present chapter introduces the background of the study.

WHY SEIBU?

Seibu was chosen for this study because it is a major company in a sector which has been relatively active in developing new personnel policies for the effective utilisation of women. Especially since the mid-1970s, the onset of slower growth and increased market competition have pushed many major department stores to look to their sales workforce, the majority of whom are women, for ways to improve productivity. Many of the big department stores started to recruit female graduates and introduce better career opportunities in order to raise their morale and productivity (Rosei Jiho 1978). For business reasons, department stores have been more sensitive to 'women's issues' and they have been acting as 'pace setters' with regard to their personnel policies on women.

Among the major department stores, the author's attention was directed to Seibu because it is a unique company. It has pioneered many new personnel policies on women and has a high profile reputation as a leading-edge company in promoting career opportunities for women.[1] This is partly because Seibu is a relatively young company in the department store industry. In order to compete with stores with a longer history and well-established tradition, Seibu management has been putting great effort into building up a new corporate image through innovations in retail concepts, management strategies and personnel policies. Seibu's innovative management policy is also partly a result of the special company culture fostered by the top management of the company – a culture which favours ongoing change and reform (Wada 1981).

A series of new personnel policies introduced for women employees since the early 1970s has won the company a 'pro-women' corporate image (NNKC 1981; MOL 1981c). Seibu began to recruit female graduates in 1970, much earlier than other large companies. In 1975, the company began to introduce specialist jobs for women and a specialist career route was formally introduced in 1978 to expand promotion opportunities for all the employees. The company also introduced a re-entry scheme for women employees in 1980. A more path-breaking step was the creation of a company creche in 1982 – the first attempt of its kind in the history of Japanese business. With respect to these policies Seibu was far ahead of many large Japanese companies in the early 1980s. It was among the top three companies most favoured by female university graduates; women believed they had a good chance of getting promotion at Seibu, according to a survey conducted by the Recruit Company (a Japanese company specialising in monitoring the employment situation in the country) in 1984 (*The Japan Times*, 22 September 1984).

Preliminary individual interviews with thirty-four Seibu women employees show that many women graduates came to Seibu not because they were particularly interested in a career in retailing as such, but because they believed that there were better career opportunities for women in the department stores industry and, most important of all, many of them mentioned the appeal of Seibu's 'good corporate image'. Many young women were attracted to Seibu because they believed that there was less discrimination against women than elsewhere. Such perceptions and expectations of women reflect the success of Seibu in portraying a modern 'pro-women' corporate image. Although the majority of women interviewed pointed out that the reality was far from satisfactory, they felt that Seibu's top management had been putting in great efforts to promote career opportunities for women. The majority of them appeared to be rather happy that 'Seibu is better than elsewhere'.

Seibu's 'pro-women' corporate image has caused much talk both inside and outside the company. Nevertheless, the company's concern about the 'women's issues' stems not so much from a sense of social justice for the promotion of equality between the sexes but more from pragmatic business needs. This will be discussed in greater detail in the sections that follow.

When the initial fieldwork was being carried out in 1984, the author did not have in mind that the case study would turn out to be a 'critical case' for examining the effects of the EEO Law. The Japanese government passed the EEO Law in May 1985. This put the author in the advantageous position of being able to examine the effects of the new legislation by comparing the situation at the case company before and after the passing of the legislation. This unexpected opportunity was immediately seized upon by the author. In the summer of 1988, the author returned to Seibu with the specific objective of seeing whether the EEO Law was having any impact on the company's personnel policies towards more egalitarian treatment of women and whether there was evidence that the position of women had improved.

The research at Seibu was adapted to take advantage of the opportunity given by the new development in the research environment. This was not simply because the timing of the legislation had made it possible to do so, although this historical factor had provided a unique opportunity. A more important reason for carrying out a follow-up study was because Seibu, being a leading-edge company in the development of equal opportunity policies, is one of the companies most likely to comply with the spirit as well as the letter of the EEO Law.

As discussed in chapter 5, the Japanese EEO Law is not only aimed at improving the equal opportunity standards of the worst practice companies by removing the most blatant forms of direct discrimination against women, but also at raising the standards of equal opportunities in Japan closer to the 'western' norm by means of moral pressures. The EEO Law has two objectives. The first is to remove the most blatant forms of direct discrimination through its prohibitory provisions and the practical requirements stipulated in the guidelines; this first objective is aimed at enforcing changes at the worst practice companies, not a leading-edge company like Seibu. The law's second objective is to use the hortatory provisions to exert further moral pressures on employers, those which have already moved beyond the first stage, to move closer to the ideal norm of equal opportunity by giving women equality in job assignment and promotion. Seibu falls into this second category. Although Seibu has been seen as a best practice company by the Japanese standard, the initial study in 1983–84 showed that Seibu nevertheless fell far short of full equal opportunities for its women employees. Market pressures had pushed the company to make minor adjustments by creating specialist work roles for a small number of women. However, the majority of women were still segregated in low status selling jobs, with the mainstream career jobs in buying, product planning and management being predominantly male preserves. The major structural and attitudinal changes which were needed to bring about egalitarian treatment of women in training, job assignment and promotion had not come about. The pre-EEO Law practices in Seibu required much improvement in order to comply with the spirit of the EEO Law.

The choice of Seibu for our case study has a special significance. It is a critical case. We are examining the possibility of bringing about positive changes towards greater equality for women in a company which already has strong economic incentives to employ and utilise women. Further it is a company which has capitalised on its 'pro-women' corporate image for more than a decade. If the law is going to exert moral pressures on employers to accommodate improvements in equal opportunities for women, such pressure is most likely to be effective on a 'goodwill' employer like Seibu than elsewhere. If positive changes have not occurred in such a company, one can assume that it is unlikely to have happened elsewhere.

THE COMPANY: BACKGROUND, MANAGEMENT PHILOSOPHY AND CORPORATE CULTURE

Seibu Department Stores Ltd is the core company of the Seibu Department Stores Group.[2] The group was established in 1940 making it a relatively young company, but among the six biggest department store groups in Japan (Okada 1982).[3] It currently consists of thirty-six companies primarily engaged in operations related to department stores. The group is organised into four divisions: department store operation, merchandising and commerce operations, new business operations, and purchasing and product development. Its sales totalled 1.12 trillion yen (8.75 billion US dollars) in the fiscal year 1987.

Seibu Department Stores Ltd, being the leading company of the group, develops and implements strategy for the group's stores nationwide. Apart from department stores operation, the company is also active in such areas as travel, automobile sales and leasing, and the operation of sports centres. It operates a total of forty-four branch and associated stores throughout Japan, with its three major stores in the centre of Tokyo: Ikebukuro, Shibuya and Yurakucho (Saison Group 1989).

In 1988, the company employed a total of approximately 20,000 people. Of these, about 12,000 were full-time regular employees of which women constituted about 43 per cent. The remaining 8,000 were non-regular employees, including mixed categories of contract and part-time workers, the majority of whom were women. In addition, Seibu also employs a large number of short-term *arubaito* workers for adjustment to seasonal fluctuations in sales. Women are much more 'visible' than men on the sales floor, as the great majority of them are assigned to first line sales or customer service jobs.

Since the early 1960s, the company had been carrying out a policy of expansionism through the opening of new branch stores. Between 1967 and 1973, the period when Japan was experiencing rapid economic growth, the company opened up seven new branch stores around the Tokyo and Tokai region. The annual rate of increase of sales started to decline in the mid-1970s, reflecting the general tendency of stagnation of the economy and the declining sales in the department store industry as a whole. However, even allowing for the generally poor performance of the industry, Seibu was able to maintain a relatively favourable annual growth rate. In 1982, the average annual rate of increase of department store sales in Japan bottomed at 2.3 per cent; in contrast Seibu was able to maintain a growth rate of 7.6 per cent (Shizuka 1983: 56–7). Seibu's relative success in a period of economic stagnation can be attributed to its innovative retail concepts and its ambitious venturing into non-traditional retail areas, such as the expansion of various types of personal services and cultural activities. In the 1980s, when most of the big department stores were turning to the renovation of their existing stores rather than opening up new stores, Seibu was planning its second stage of expansion through the opening of new 'high-tech' department stores using modern information technology.

The relative success of Seibu in a period of economic stagnation can be explained partly by its relative youthfulness as a company and partly by its innovative retail concepts and management strategy. Being a young company in the department store industry is both an advantage and a disadvantage in Japan. Japanese consumers are very conscious of good corporate image based on high quality, high social responsibility and the 'goodwill' of stores sustained over a long period of time. In this sense, Seibu was in a disadvantaged position compared to the more prestigious stores such as Mitsukoshi which had a long tradition of over a hundred years. In order to compensate for its short history and 'lack of tradition', Seibu has been putting great effort into building up a new corporate image through innovations in retail concepts, management strategies and personnel policies. In contrast to the more prestigious traditional type of department store, Seibu presents the new image of a fast-growing young company. It represents a young corporate culture and its target market has been mainly oriented to the 'new thirties' – the upwardly-mobile, affluent younger generation (Shizuka 1983: 115–16). This market orientation has led to tremendous business success because the 'new thirties' belong to a generation growing up in affluent Japan with a strong sense of consumerism. The women of this generation are either young affluent housewives or belong to an emerging new generation of career women with increasing spending power. One implication of more women entering the labour market and becoming economically independent is that they are becoming a larger and more independent market segment (Wada 1981: 101–2). Given that women are so vital to department store success, the changing values and orientations of women in modern Japan is certainly having an important impact on the retail strategies of department stores (ibid: 76–8).[4] Thus the corporate culture of Seibu is not only aiming at appealing to the younger generation of consumers, but more importantly to the 'new women' in Japan.

The most significant strategy adopted by Seibu during the high growth period was expansionism. From the mid-1970s onwards, the company shifted to a policy of specialisation and expansion on lines of commodities and services. In both 1975 and 1980, the flagship store was twice renovated to include new specialised areas of business such as food, sports and various cultural activities.

From the 1980s onwards, Seibu started to plan a new phase of expansion through large-scale investment in new business areas including the development of information industries and the introduction of modern technology to the stores. Seibu's top management believe that modern department stores are undergoing a revolutionary change from the selling of 'goods' to the selling of 'information' and 'services'. These are seen as new markets with good potential for further development. Since the mid-1970s, Seibu has projected the concept of 'the people's industry' (*Shimin-Sangyo*) as its new managerial philosophy. Department stores are no longer places where only material goods are being sold, they are rapidly transforming into an industry catering for all aspects of people's lives. Seibu's top management emphasise that the main task of department stores in the 1980s and 1990s is the 'selling of new lifestyles' to customers (*Seibu Nyusha-Annai* 1985). The management of Seibu also say that they believe that people who are working in the retail industry should also have broad experience in various aspects of life and have the ability and sensitivity to perceive changes in consumer needs and demands (Wada 1981: 217–20). The management, therefore, regard the role of women as crucial to the company's success in the new business areas because of the important role of women in services in Japanese society and the fact that women almost completely dominate the consumer markets in Japan (Ido 1985: 56).

THE CHANGING RETAIL ENVIRONMENT AND NEW BUSINESS STRATEGY: IMPACT ON THE ROLE OF WOMEN

Three major concepts can be used to describe Seibu's new business strategy in the 1980s, namely diversification, specialisation and market-orientation.

Diversification

Diversification into new areas of business and venturing into non-traditional retail areas were the major strategies adopted by Seibu in the 1980s. The most significant changes in the consumer market were seen by Seibu top management as first, declining expenditure on material goods while expenditure on leisure, sports and various kinds of cultural activities had been increasing. Second, the rising segmentation of the consumer market; unlike the period of mass consumption in the 1960s and early 1970s, consumers in the 1980s had more diverse preferences and sophisticated individual tastes. The strategy adopted by Seibu was to capture the growing new markets through the 'selling' of new lifestyles and the 'selling' of various kinds of services. The five major target growth markets to be captured included: the market of living styles, such as interior design; the food market; the leisure and culture market; the sports and health market; and the new fashion market (Wada 1981: 105–17). Seibu top management regarded these growing markets as 'new lifestyle markets' and believed that all these were 'women's markets', given that women in Japan are leaders in the consumer market and 'innovators' in new styles of living. The company's management pointed out that the future success of the department store industry would depend, to a great extent, on whether companies could establish a new personnel system to utilise women as 'specialists' in these growing areas (Wada 1981: 76).

Specialisation

The 'specialty store' approach was devised as a strategy to meet the challenge of other forms of retailing such as superstores and specialist shops, and to cope with the changing tastes of consumers in modern Japan. This approach was based on the idea that a department store should be a big store composed of many specialty shops. Each specialty shop was targeting a certain segment of the consumer market, to provide specialised merchandise to suit that particular market segment and to provide high quality and specialised services. Management believed that in order to capture modern consumers who were becoming more knowledgeable, more sophisticated and who had more individualistic tastes, department stores should be able to offer a wider range of merchandise than before. However, specialisation in each range of merchandise was necessary in order to attract such sophisticated customers and, most important of all, department stores should be able to offer high quality personal services. Thus one priority condition was to have high quality sales staff with specialised product knowledge who were able to provide consulting services in the selling of commodities; it was therefore necessary to change the 'sales clerk' to a 'professional salesperson'. This was an important factor motivating Seibu to recruit more highly-educated women after the mid-1970s. In order to attract more competent women into sales jobs, it was also important that these jobs should be seen as stepping stones to better career opportunities in the company.[5] The specialist career route was introduced in 1978 to provide a career route for women in first line sales jobs (see next chapter).

Market orientation

Seibu management believed that in order to maintain a favourable position in the rapidly changing retail environment it should focus on the market through changing the organisation (products, distribution and promotion) to fit the market place. This market-oriented approach required fundamental changes in the traditional organisational structure. Traditionally, the buying groups and people in the centralised management system were the major driving force of the department stores; first-line sales staff (women) played a secondary role in selling whatever was bought by the stores. However, the need for greater sensitivity to changes in consumer tastes meant that staff in day-to-day store operations, particularly the sales staff, needed to play a more central role in the running of the store. Seibu management saw an increasing need to bring the customers' perspective into the central decision-making process and to create a new structure to enable continuous sensitivity to the concerns of consumers. According to Seibu management, a more aggressive response to consumers' tastes implies that department stores are no longer simply selling whatever is bought from the manufacturers or wholesalers, but are acting as purchasing agents for the customers. The company describes this as a 'reverse type' of marketing, different from the traditional approach (*Seibu Nyusha-Annai* 1985).

Another important strategy adopted by most of the department stores since the mid-1970s has been the development of their own brand products. Seibu management stated that they regarded the product development function as the major driving force to revitalise the stores, and to enhance sales in the market and product development should be closely linked with the promotion of its corporate image (Wada 1981: 129). All these factors meant that there was a growing need to bring the 'women's perspective' into central decision-making and product development functions; first line sales staff who were in direct contact with customers acquired the most essential information for predicting changes in consumer tastes and needs. Seibu was faced with a situation in which there was a need to bring in more qualified women and to create a new organisational structure and personnel system which gave women a more central role in the operation of the stores, in product planning and in decision-making processes. The traditional sexual division of labour – 'women should sell and men manage', with men at the top and women at the bottom of the hierarchy was proving to be an obstacle to the efficient operation of the business. Early in the 1970s, complaints from the sales clerks about the inefficiency of the traditional arrangement were reported in the company's newsletter:

The majority of the shop-floor supervisors (*kakaricho*) are lacking in product knowledge. In the face of rapid opening of new stores, men with little experience were assigned to supervisory positions. In reality women with long years of experience in sales have more product knowledge and experience than the male supervisor.

(Seibu 1973)

In the light of all these changes, top management at Seibu called for a re-evaluation of the role of women in the company. There was a growing concern that the traditional organisational and career structures had to be changed in order to give women a greater say in the planning and decision-making mechanisms of the company. Early in 1972, Seiji Tsuzumi, chairman of Seibu, made a self-critical remark on the company's lack of utilisation of women:

> We have about 170 buyers in our product planning department. According to world standards, 80 of them ought to be women. In the United States, probably about 100 of them are women and in the Soviet Union the figure may be as high as 150. In our company, only 10 of them are women . . . . In the coming years, the competitiveness of department stores will depend on whether companies can effectively utilise woman power.
>
> (Seibu 1972)

Seibu started to introduce a series of personnel policy changes to enhance the utilisation of women after the mid-1970s. These will be examined in the next chapter.

A NOTE ON THE METHODS OF RESEARCH

Seibu is a complex organisation. To acquire information about such a huge organisation and to understand a complex, evolving situation, a mixture of methods was used throughout the various stages of the research. These included in-depth interviews with personnel management and some thirty women employees, a one-month period of participant observation during the beginning stage of the initial study in 1984 and questionnaire surveys on about 1,100 male and female regular employees in 1984 and replication of the questionnaire survey on 800 employees in 1988. The personnel data obtained from the head office cover the whole company (the head office and all the branch stores); the interviews with the women employees and the questionnaire surveys were carried out at the flagship store in Ikebukuro and another major city-centre store in Shibuya. These two major city-centre stores were chosen mainly because they were the key stores of the company in terms of their location (both are in Tokyo), size, and most important of all, they are the strategic centres of the company where top management put their greatest efforts in the development of new policies. They employed the largest number of people. In 1988, there were about 2,000 full-time regular employees working at the Ikebukuro store, and 900 at the Shibuya store. The number of full-time regular employees at these two major stores together constituted about one-quarter of the total full-time regular employees of the whole company.

Details of the field study methods, data sources and the survey samples are contained in appendix A.

Chapter 8

The Seibu case: changing company practice

This chapter first examines the pre-EEO Law situation at Seibu, looking at the company's policy orientation on women after the mid-1970s and gives an account and evaluation of the new policies and practices introduced. The chapter then moves on to examine whether and how the EEO Law has had an impact on Seibu's policy on women. The main objective is to see how much further Seibu has progressed in promoting equal opportunities since the law was introduced.

NEW PERSONNEL POLICIES ON WOMEN IN RESPONSE TO CHANGING MARKET ENVIRONMENT

The need for better quality professional sales staff and a growing awareness of the importance of bringing in the 'women's perspective' in product development and strategic business planning were the main factors prompting Seibu management to adopt more positive personnel policies on women. Beginning in the mid-1970s, new policies and practices were introduced to raise the quality of the female workforce, to improve the utilisation of women and to provide better career opportunities for the experienced staff in first-line sales jobs.

Increased intake of women graduates

Like many other major companies, Seibu has been employing an increasing number of women graduates since the mid-1970s. This represented an important departure from past policies which restricted the recruitment of graduates to that of males. The number of female university graduates joining Seibu increased by more than four times between 1976 and 1985 (see table 8.1). In 1976, women university graduates constituted 4.4 per cent of the total number of women recruited; the figure rose to 22 per cent in 1985. There has also been a steady increase of junior college graduates. These, together with the university graduates, constituted 50 per cent of the total number of women recruited in 1985.

Seibu's shift towards recruiting more highly-educated women was not merely a reflection of the rise in the overall educational level of the female working population but was also very much a result of the company management's deliberate effort to raise the quality of the core female workforce. For example, until the mid-1970s the proportion of women graduates recruited by Seibu was under-represented (for national figures, see chapter 4, table 4.2). However, by 1985, women university graduates constituted 12.7 per cent of the total female population entering the job market; the proportion recruited by Seibu in the same year was 22 per cent.

The long-term implication of the increased participation of highly-educated women in an industry which had traditionally seg-regated women to low status selling jobs was proving to be signifi-cant. The career orientations of the women graduates differed significantly from women with a lower level of education. The survey conducted in 1984 showed that only 4 per cent of women graduates would want to remain as ordinary sales clerks, as compared to 19 per cent and 36 per cent in the cases of junior college graduates and high school leavers. The majority of women graduates joining Seibu were seeking a career as specialists in sales (28 per cent), as buyers (21 per cent) and as administrative and planning staff (25 per cent). Particularly notable was the high proportion of women graduates seeking their careers in the buying function – a traditionally male-dominated field in Japanese department stores. Seibu management saw a need to develop new personnel policies to cope with the career aspirations of the increasing number of highly-educated women (Ido 1980a).

Improving the utilisation of women: the specialist career route

Early in 1975, when Seibu began to set up 'specialty shops' selling high quality merchandise within the stores, a new job title called 'shopmaster' was created. A shopmaster is a manager of a specialty shop who supervises a small number of staff, normally no more than

Table 8.1 Changes in the proportional distribution of women recruited annually, by educational levels, 1976–85

	1976	1977	1978	1979	1980	1981	1982	1983	1984	1985
University	4.4	10.3	16.0	16.4	19.0	16.0	18.6	22.3	24.0	22.0
Junior college	6.9	20.9	16.4	23.4	16.0	18.0	17.2	12.3	17.0	28.0
High school	88.7	68.8	67.6	60.2	65.0	66.0	64.2	65.4	59.0	50.0
Number recruited	(679)	(747)	(797)	(708)	(765)	(1,080)	(751)	(690)	(476)	(613)

Source: Data provided by personnel department, Seibu Department Stores Ltd.

ten people, and is entrusted with full autonomy in running the entire business of the shop from purchasing to selling. The job is defined as a 'specialist' job (*senmonshoku*) equivalent to the managerial role in terms of status, wages and working conditions.

When the shopmaster role was first introduced in 1975, twenty-one women were appointed, constituting one-third of the total number of shopmasters appointed in that year. Over the years, the number of women appointed increased faster than that of men. In 1984, out of the total number of 202, women constituted 116 of them. This specialist role had proved to be very popular among the women employees, giving them opportunities to perform a great variety of duties in addition to selling, including the supervision of a small number of staff. Many of the specialty shops were run entirely by women staff so it was often a situation of women supervising women, which as some female shopmasters pointed out 'made life easier for them'. Job satisfaction and morale appeared to be high among women appointed to the new role.

This encouraged Seibu management to go one step further. A specialist career route was introduced in 1978 (see figure 8.1). Major restructuring of the personnel system also took place.

A new job classification system was introduced. It classifies all the jobs into eight functional areas, namely, sales expert, sales consultant, shopmaster, outdoor sales, buyer, staff (planning/personnel), technician and management. The specialist career route refers to a career in the non-managerial job functions. In theory, Seibu emphasised that the management function was to be included as a specialist job in supervising and managing people. This represents a deliberate attempt made by the company to remove the status distinction between management and specialists (Rosei Jiho 1979: 44). In the early 1960s, some Japanese companies made attempts to introduce specialist functions in their companies but most of them failed because specialists often ended up being seen as positions created for people who could not make their way into management (Tsuda 1981: 173–4).[1] Seibu was well aware of the difficulties in introducing specialist functions in an organisation which had been geared to the formation of generalists. To ensure that the specialist career route would not be seen as inferior to that of management, Seibu made a pioneering attempt to include management into the specialist job classification system. However, in practice, the managerial career route is still seen as distinct from the specialist career route.

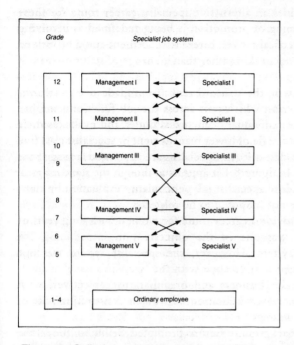

Figure 8.1 Seibu's specialist career system (*Senmonshoku-seido*).
Source: Seibu Department Stores Ltd.

The new personnel system also brought about two important changes in the promotion system. First, as a job system was introduced alongside the standard rank system, promotion had two different meanings. It could mean promotion in rank (*shokaku*), i.e. moving up the standard rank according to age and years of service; and it could also mean promotion in position according to job performance (*shoshin*). In the past, there was no clear distinction between the two and promotion was largely determined by age and length of service. In the new system, young people with high performance can be promoted to higher-level job positions without upsetting the standard rank which is still based on seniority. Second, in the past, promotion more or less meant becoming management which often required a breadth of experience acquired through regular job rotation. This implied that women who spent many years in sales jobs or specialised functions had little opportunity to move up the company hierarchy as their experience was often regarded as 'too narrow' and hence not qualify for managerial positions. The new system provides an alternative specialist career route for these people. The meaning of promotion is being redefined as involving lateral as well as vertical moves; career advancement could be viewed in terms of advances in skill rather than a change of status or span of authority.

In the new system, the standard rank (from grade one to twelve) is a common criterion which cuts across the job functions; the job system defines the individual's functional duties and evaluates their performance from a scale of lower management or specialist class five (V) to the highest class one (I). Specialists are appointed among those above grade five. In figure 8.1 it appears as though the standard rank (grade) corresponds to specialist job performance evaluation by class; in theory they are not supposed to be related.

The need to provide a career route for women with long years of sales experience was one of the objectives in introducing the specialist career system. However, the specialist system was not specifically designed only to cope with the 'women's issue' as such. It stems from wider business and organisational objectives, with policies on the increased utilisation of women constituting part of the new business strategy.

Three major background factors prompted Seibu to adopt the specialist career system. First, from the viewpoint of business objectives, there was an increasing need to train more specialists in different product areas to cope with the more sophisticated and specialised consumer markets. The specialist career route was introduced in line with the company's new business strategy to capture the highly diversified and individualised consumer market through the creation of many small specialty shops within the department stores.

Second, the specialist system was also intended to help solve the twin organisational problems of career blockage and escalating labour costs resulting from the growing proportion of middle-aged employees. In the late 1960s and early 1970s, when the company was expanding rapidly, a large number of male graduates were recruited. Most of them had reached middle-age by the early 1980s and were expecting promotion to managerial positions. However, since the late 1970s, expansion of the scale of business was becoming more and more difficult in the face of slower growth of the Japanese economy. When the company was not expanding as rapidly as before, it implied that an increasing number of employees would be facing the problem of career blockage due to the shortage of positions. The specialist career route was introduced as an alternative career route to expand promotion opportunities for the growing number of middle-aged employees. Further, faced with an increasing number of middle-aged and older employees, Seibu was finding it more difficult to maintain the *nenko* promotion and wage system because of escalating labour costs. The specialist personnel system was also intended to bring about changes in the reward system towards greater emphasis on merit.

Third, the specialist career route was also intended to provide promotion chances for some able women with many years of experience in specialised product areas. It represents a compromise strategy to bring more women into responsible positions without causing major disruption to the existing male career hierarchy. Seibu top management did not think that women were suitable for managerial jobs but believed that to place them in specialist jobs was a viable approach to promote their positions in the company. The following remarks made a managing director of Seibu, clearly expressed the company's view on this matter:

> If we want to utilise fully women's ability, we would need to change the management-oriented personnel system to one that is more oriented to specialists. Such a change in orientation will also fulfil the new demands of our business environment . . . . A management-oriented personnel system often operates to women's disadvantage because the majority of women do not want to become management. Thus, women's performance is often not properly evaluated. For women to become management, they often have to follow the male working standards and become like men. This means that they cannot utilise fully their special feminine qualities. *We do not wish our female employees to deny their roles as mothers and wives in the family by adopting the male working pattern.* Therefore, the proper approach is to develop the special qualities of women and to utilise them as specialists.
>
> (Ido 1980a: 46–7; emphasis added)

An evaluation

By the middle of the 1980s, women constituted about 15 per cent of the specialist jobs and 6 per cent of the managerial positions. Although 90 per cent of the women in these positions were in the lowest class five which was equivalent to the first supervisory level (*kakaricho*), the specialist career route had at least provided a chance for some women who had had many years of work experience in first-line sales jobs to gain promotion chances which otherwise would have been more difficult had there been only a single managerial career route.

Compared with the *ad hoc* and informal policy adopted by many other companies, Seibu had gone one step further in its policy for promoting women's careers. The specialist career route was introduced on a company-wide formal basis, and it was integrated into the whole personnel system. In addition, Seibu had sought to upgrade the status and image of specialists by emphasising that the managerial function is also a specialist job, which is a very unique approach among the Japanese companies. How far Seibu has been successful in equalising the status of the two career routes is a separate issue.

The policy adopted by Seibu represents a pragmatic strategy to try to 'make way' for women in a traditionally male-dominated organisation; bringing more highly qualified women into the organisation through the specialist career route rather than through the conventional managerial career path is certainly less threatening to men. This reduces the risk of a male backlash as women in specialist roles are not seen as competing directly with men for the limited number of managerial posts.

Further, the new personnel system at Seibu had full backing from the top management and the 'utilisation of women as specialists' approach was seen as an integral part of the company's new business strategy rather than a 'women specific' policy as such. Theoretically, the successful operation of the specialist career system in the long run should benefit women's careers in two important ways. First, it seeks to expand promotion opportunities for all the employees, not through expanding the number of vertical opportunities but the number of lateral prospects through greater emphasis on upgrading skills and competence in specialist jobs. This should give women a better chance. Second, evaluation of performance is based more on merit rather than *nenko*. Seibu had increased the proportion of job-related pay from 10 per cent of the basic monthly earnings to 15 per cent in 1978 when the specialist career route was first introduced and up further to 30 per cent in 1985. This means that women, with shorter years of service, should be less disadvantaged as job competence is seen as equally important as *nenko*. The increased emphasis on 'merit' should be beneficial to women in the long run.

However, the potential weaknesses of this 'women as specialists' approach are twofold. First, to typecast women as specialists reinforces the rather poor image of specialists in Japanese companies – that the specialist career route is a secondary choice for people who cannot make their way into the mainstream managerial career route. Second, there is the danger of perpetuating the traditional belief that 'women are different' which often serves to reinforce the existing pattern of sexual division of labour by segregating women into certain 'women's jobs'.

The argument put forward by Seibu management that women were more suitable for specialist jobs was based on two traditional stereotypical assumptions about the role of women: women are not suitable for managerial jobs because these are male domains and, second, women themselves do not want to become managers.

This may not be because women are uninterested in managerial jobs but because they tend to perceive themselves as lacking managerial ability or because they perceive a lack of opportunity for promotion to management. The following quotations from the author's interviews in 1983 indicate that many women felt that they had no choice because it was the company's policy to put women in specialist roles:

'It is easier to pursue a career in the specialist role because this is the way our company wants us to be'

'I don't think I have a choice because the company has decided that women are to be specialists, not management.'

'It seems to me that the specialist career route has greater appeal because it is easier for women to utilise their abilities as specialists. That is why our company introduced the specialist career route; it is much easier if I follow this route'

'I do want to pursue a career in management but women often ended up lacking the breadth of experience for managerial positions'

The 'women as specialist' approach can only be effective in promoting the status of women in the company provided that the specialist career route is not seen as a low-status secondary career route and that there is a balanced distribution of men and women in different specialist jobs. Data from the 1984 survey suggested that the situation was far from meeting these two criteria.

Despite Seibu's effort to remove the status distinction between the specialist and managerial career routes, employees still perceived the two career routes as quite different. The questionnaire survey in 1984 showed that a higher proportion of male employees wanted to pursue a career in management (see table 8.2). Men who were in specialist jobs appeared to be less satisfied with their positions in the company as compared with those in management; although the difference was not obvious in the case of women (see table 8.3).

If there is still a general perception that specialists are inferior in status to management, then to stress that 'women are to be utilised in specialist roles' will have a doubly negative effect − specialist jobs will tend to be seen as 'women's enclaves' and this will reinforce the image that women are secondary workers. This situation can only be avoided provided that men and women are evenly distributed in different kinds of specialist jobs. Evidence indicates that this is not the case.

If we look at the distribution of male and female specialists by their job functions (see tables 8.4 and 8.5), there is a clear-cut job segregation between men and women. Women were heavily concentrated in two first-line sales jobs: 'sales expert' and 'shopmaster'. Among all the female specialists, 60 per cent of them were in first-line sales jobs (sales expert, shopmaster and sales consultant), while the equivalent figure for men was 14.7 per cent. Women had made very few inroads into the traditionally male-dominated jobs such as buyer, outdoor sales and management. The most important business functions at a department store − buying, product planning and managing − were still dominated by men. The specialist system had not changed the traditional pattern that 'women should sell and men manage'. The new personnel system had opened up a career route for a small number of women with long years of selling experience to be promoted to a higher grade, but the existing pattern of job segregation remained undisturbed. If one of the main objectives of the new personnel system was to bring the 'women's perspective' into central buying and product planning functions, the specialist system had not made much progress in this respect. From the viewpoint of business needs, there ought to be more women in the buying function as the company stressed the need to bring in the 'women's perspective' in product planning and development. In both the United States and Britain, women have made considerable progress in gaining managerial positions in the buying functions in department stores

(Williams and Faltot 1983; Gable *et al*. 1984). In Japan, the buying function was still very much a male preserve. This was not because Seibu women did not like the buyer's job. On the contrary, over 20 per cent of women graduates wanted to become buyers when they joined the company. In reality, opportunities for women to become buyers were extremely scarce; in 1984, out of a total of 190 buyers, only twelve of them were women. The figure in 1972 was ten – the situation had remained virtually the same since the chairman of the company first made a formal policy statement in the company's newsletter about the need to train more women as buyers.

Something was hindering women from pursuing the buyer's role. The company's job requirements indicate that one of the prerequisites for becoming a buyer is to have managerial experience on the sales floor and to move to the local stores at some stage in the career. These requirements are clearly obstacles to women as very few of them have the opportunity to become managers and many women have felt they could not meet the mobility requirement.

Despite the changes in the business environment which made Seibu management aware of the need to change its traditional policy orientations on women, by the mid-1980s there were still very few women in high level jobs. The small number of women appointed as specialists were concentrated in the first-line sales jobs. Women virtually disappeared beyond grade 5 – the minimum grade required to become first-level supervisor (*kakaricho*) or qualified to be appointed as specialists. The department stores were still very

Table 8.2 'Which career route do you intend to pursue at this company?' (1984 survey)

	Male %	Female %
Management	33.8	5.8
Specialist	20.9	20.4
Either	43.1	57.6
Haven't thought about it	1.8	15.1
Others	0.3	1.1
Total	100.0	100.0
Number in survey	(325)	(550)

Table 8.3 'How satisfied are you with your present position?'
(1984 survey)

| | Male | | Female | |
| | Specialist | Management | Specialist | Management |
	%	%	%	%
Satisfied	57	78	78	80
Dissatisfied	43	22	22	20
Total	100.0	100.0	100.0	100.0
Number in survey	(81)	(93)	(54)	(20)

much operating on a two-tier structure with the majority of women
in bottom level selling jobs and men in central planning, decision-
making and management functions. From the viewpoint of achieving
Seibu's initial business objectives, the 'utilisation of women as
specialists' approach has only been half successful. However, for the
promotion of equal opportunities for women, Seibu management has
only touched the surface of the real issues. Seibu cannot be said to be
a true equal opportunity employer unless it can satisfy two
conditions. First, there is a more balanced distribution of men and
women in different job functions – there must be a major shift in the
traditional pattern of job segregation that it is 'women's job to sell

Table 8.4 Distribution of male and female employees by job
position (as of December 1983)

| | Male | | Female | | Women's share of each category |
	No.	%	No.	%	
Specialist	1,915	33.7	345	5.9	15.3
Management	1,694	29.8	113	1.9	6.2
Ordinary employee	2,072	36.5	5,395	92.2	72.3
Total	5,681	100.0	5,853	100.0	50.7

Source: Data provided by personnel department, Seibu Department Stores Ltd.

Table 8.5 Distribution of male and female specialists by job functions
(as of December 1983)

Job function	Male		Female		Women's share of each category
	No.	%	No.	%	
Sales expert	69	3.6	67	19.4	49.3
Shopmaster	86	4.5	116	33.6	57.4
Sales consultant	128	6.7	24	7.0	15.8
Outdoor sales	479	25.0	6	1.7	1.2
Buyer	190	9.9	12	3.5	5.9
Staff	787	41.1	115	33.3	12.7
Technician	176	9.2	5	1.4	2.8
Total	1,915	100.0	345	100.0	15.3

Source: Data provided by personnel department, Seibu Department Stores Ltd.

and men's job to manage'. Second, there must be more women in central management functions otherwise women can only be seen as 'second-class' members of the work organisation. To achieve these conditions, there needs to be a more fundamental review and change in the rules and practices governing training, career planning, job rotation and promotion which perpetuate the existing structure of male dominance. Seibu has superimposed a specialist career system on top of the existing personnel system without taking positive steps to introduce more fundamental changes.

OBSTACLES TO EQUAL OPPORTUNITY

Our analysis of Seibu's personnel management system in the mid-1980s showed that career planning and promotion were still based on the assumption of a continuous lifetime career. Training and job rotation policies were designed to be geared to the needs and expectations of such a career. In spite of the growing attention paid to a person's ability and job performance, in practice advancement in the career hierarchy was still commonly regulated by minimum age levels for each rank. The career patterns laid down by this type of planning made assumptions about the need for movement into certain types of jobs, by a certain age and for geographical mobility. All this had negative implications for women.

Career planning and promotion

An important part of the new personnel system introduced by Seibu in the late 1970s was the establishment of a systematic job rotation policy which was built into the employees' long-term career planning in accordance with age and length of service. Figure 8.2 shows the career path and job rotation requirements for different job categories. For a long time, Seibu has emphasised the importance of promotion based on job performance and individual ability rather than age and length of service. The specialist career route was intended to bring about a more merit-based personnel system. In spite of all these policy changes, the company still stressed the importance of the age and length of service factors in career planning. Career development and promotion was still built upon the assumption of the necessity to move into certain jobs by a certain age. The most crucial period for career formation, as can be seen from figure 8.2, is around the employees' late twenties to early thirties. This is the time when an employee is required to decide which career route to pursue and marks the beginning of systematic training through job rotation. As the majority of women at Seibu would prefer to interrupt their career when they have a family (see chapter 9, table 9.13), the rigidity of the career structure puts the majority of women in a disadvantaged position.

Job rotation and mobility requirements

Frequent job rotation constitutes an essential part of career development at Seibu. Except for jobs in first-line sales, most of the jobs require some kind of job rotation at some stage in a career. It involves not only movement between different jobs but also moving between the head office and the branch stores and between the different branch stores. The requirement to be geographically mobile is one of the greatest barriers to women's advancement into the mainstream career jobs. All the jobs in management, staff and buying functions – the areas where women are most under-represented – require some kind of mobility between different branch stores.

Women as a group are often assumed to be less mobile and are often not considered for promotion to jobs which require geographical mobility.

Training

Despite the introduction of more formal training opportunities in recent years, on-the-job training (OJT) still constitutes the most essential part of training at Seibu. The majority of the women interviewed pointed out that in terms of formal training offered by the company, men and women were treated equally if they were assigned to the same jobs. They pointed out that the major differences were in day-to-day OJT. Our survey in 1984 showed that over 50 per cent of the respondents (both males and females) did not think that men and women were receiving the same kind of OJT. As regards the concrete differences, 79 per cent of the respondents pointed out that the 'type of tasks assigned were different'.

Most of the women interviewed were aware of the sex role distinction in their day-to-day work. When asked whether women were given the same training opportunities as men, a 34-year-old woman who had been with the company for fourteen years and was a member of staff in the personnel department said:

> Of course, men and women were treated differently. As men were expected to become management eventually, they were taught how to run the entire business of the shop including managing the accounts of the shop. Women were to stand in the shop and sell. Standing in the shop was our training. Even if we were interested in learning how to manage the account of the shop, we were not given any chance to learn. As a result, it becomes very difficult for us to take up managerial positions because we know so little about managing and financial matters.

Another 24-year-old woman graduate who had been with Seibu for two years said:

> Well, we are offered the same formal opportunities by our company. But in our day-to-day work, men and women are treated differently. Men are trained towards becoming management. Women, even the graduates, are not given the same opportunity. When I first joined the company, I felt that my female colleagues were more capable than men. However, after a

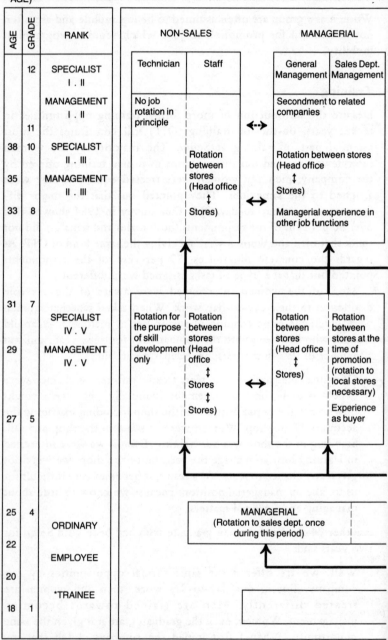

Figure 8.2 Seibu's job rotation chart.
Source: Seibu Department Stores Ltd.

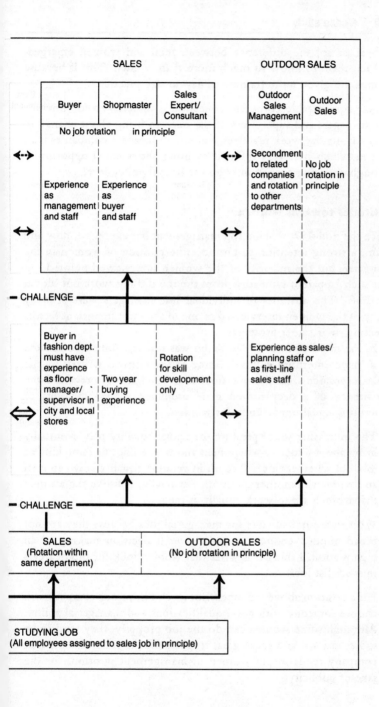

year or so, the difference between men and women emerged. Men seem to know so much more than women. This is because men are given more training in day-to-day practice.

Unless considerable corporate education is undertaken to convince line managers and supervisors of the need to bring about change in their day-to-day work practices, training in Japanese companies is an area in which it is very difficult to bring about equal opportunity through changing programmes on the formal policy level.

Attitudes towards women

Since the mid-1970s, Seibu top management has expressed, now and again, a strong intention to promote the position of women in the company, but the majority of the women interviewed pointed out that such 'apparent sympathy' from the top did not work out 'down the line'. The attitudes of individual line managers were seen by many of the women interviewed as one of the most important factors affecting their career prospects.

In the middle of the 1980s, Seibu was still very much dominated by a 'male enterprise culture'. Some of the remarks written by the male respondents on the questionnaire (1984 survey) revealed the persistence of a deep-rooted male prejudice against the idea of promoting equal opportunity for women:

> The increasing social pressure for sexual equality may eventually bring about a society where men and women do the same kind of job, but whether this will result in genuine equality between men and women is another question. Personally, I dislike the attitude that women are to work equally as men.

> Women are not suitable for managerial jobs because they are not broad-minded enough to make overall decision making in an organisation. I think it is wiser that women look for their careers in specialist jobs.

> For a position above the supervisor level, I hope our company will choose someone with good qualifications and managerial ability. Although some women can do the job properly, they tend to be too emotional and cause great troubles for the subordinates. Our company tends to put women in management positions for the sake of publicity.

The increasing participation of women may change the world and even change human history. But these are not necessarily changes in a desirable direction . . . . I resent over-evaluation of women's ability.

Work and family: the unresolved dilemma

Women's responsibilities in the family constituted one of the greatest barriers to their advancement to senior positions. It was very rare for Seibu to promote married women to senior positions. Over 90 per cent of the women in management or specialist jobs were single and over 30 years of age – most of them had passed the 'marriageable age' in Japanese society. In the mid-1980s, over 60 per cent of the female workforce in Japan were married; among the female regular workforce at Seibu, only 13 per cent were married. Middle-aged women working at Seibu were largely employed on a part-time or temporary basis. Married women were seen as secondary workers.

Most of the women interviewed pointed out that working conditions at the department stores made it extremely difficult for them to combine work with family. Late-opening hours, the need to work overtime and change their work schedules during peak seasons and the fact that rest days do not necessarily fall on the weekends (Japanese department stores are opened on Sundays) cause adjustment problems for those with a family.

Seibu's management was aware of the dilemma faced by its women employees. Management also realised that many women had low morale because of a lack of a long-term perspective in their relationship with the company. In April 1980, a re-entry scheme called the 'licence system' was introduced to enable women to return to work for the company after a career break. In order to be qualified for applying for a re-entry licence, a woman employee has to work for a minimum of six years with the company (or four years in the case of a university graduate) and her job performance should be 'above average' as evaluated by the personnel department. The 're-entry licence' enables the woman to return to work for the company within ten years of leaving and provided that she is under 40 years of age. However, it is neither a formal agreement nor a contract. It merely states that when the employee returns to work 'she will be given first priority and guaranteed better conditions when compared to other ordinary job applicants'. There is no guarantee of employment nor any guarantee of returning to her former position. The ultimate decision for re-employment rests on the company and the forms of employment, that is whether she will be re-employed on a full-time or part-time basis, will be 'determined by the company taking into consideration her request' (Kurihara 1980: 60).

The re-entry scheme has gained the company much publicity as a 'progressive' employer. However, the majority of the women interviewed were critical of the scheme. Most of them said they would apply for the licence if they decided to have a family as a kind of 'safety valve' for the future, but they really had no intention of coming back once they decided to leave the company. Most of the women described the scheme as 'not practical' because there was no guarantee of re-entry and no guarantee of returning to their former positions.

At the end of 1988, eight years since the scheme was introduced, there were altogether 950 women who had received the re-entry licence and only fifty-four of them (5.6 per cent) had returned to work, among them thirty-two were re-employed as regular full-time employees and the rest as non-regular contract employees.

Given the rigidity of the career structure and the ambiguity of the scheme, it is unlikely that the re-entry scheme will help women at Seibu to resolve the dilemma of choosing either work or family. For the majority of women, interrupting their career to have a family means losing their position in the company. The majority of them knew that when they returned to work, the options available would be extremely limited and the chance for them to gain entry to the career jobs was very slim. The choice open to the majority of the women was either to continue their career without interruption like men or to leave when they had a family.

The limits of managerial reform

Although the majority of the women interviewed tended to believe that they were 'better off' than women in other companies, very few of them were optimistic about the future prospects for women to gain higher positions in the company.

The analysis in 1984 indicated that the major structural and attitudinal changes which were needed to bring about a more egalitarian treatment of women had not come about. This is not because Seibu was a backward organisation; Seibu was anything but backward, and it was acutely aware that women constituted a reserve of unused and undeveloped talents which, if given the opportunities to be tapped and developed, would be a powerful factor in determining the success of the industry. The problems encountered by Seibu in bringing more women into the core of the organisation illustrate some common dilemmas faced by most Japanese companies when they are confronted with the challenge to offer women equal opportunities.

The core group of employees were still governed by a set of rules and practices which stressed lifelong commitment, long-term career advancement regulated by age and length of service, a requirement for total devotion to the company by working long hours and a willingness to be geographically mobile at the request of the company. Such a career structure was not flexible enough to permit women to leave the company for a number of years without losing their positions.

Seibu's ideal image of female employees, as openly stated by the personnel director, was 'those who would not deny the fact they are women and would not refuse to carry out their roles as mother and wife in the family' (Ido 1980b: 11). Sexual equality in employment will not come about unless Seibu also recognises the importance of 'men's roles as father and husband in the family' and is willing to make career jobs more compatible with family life.

One year after the initial case study was conducted, the Japanese government passed the Equal Employment Opportunity Law. The rest of this chapter examines how many further policy changes have occurred at Seibu since then.

'POST-EEO LAW' POLICIES ON WOMEN

In the three summers between 1987 and 1989, the author visited Seibu to find out whether the company had taken any new policy initiatives to promote women's career opportunities and how much further the company went than the pre-EEO Law policies. Information and data presented in this section are mainly based on interviews and discussions with personnel staff at the flagship store and the head office, internal documents provided by the personnel department and individual interviews with twenty-five women employees, twenty-one of whom were first interviewed in 1983 (see appendix A for more details of the follow-up study).

Broadly speaking, two types of policy responses to the EEO Law can be distinguished: first, direct policy responses, i.e. changes in personnel policies and practices in order to comply with the practical requirements of the law and, second, new policy initiatives undertaken by management to promote equal opportunities for women which are not directly required by the law, but appear to result from a growing consciousness of Seibu's management to 'move ahead' and to comply with the spirit of the law.

In terms of direct policy responses, the personnel manager at the head office pointed out that it was not necessary for the company to review or introduce any changes in their personnel policies and practices, because Seibu's policy on women had always been more 'advanced' than that required by the new legislation. The personnel departments in all the stores, however, did run special seminars to explain the major changes resulting from the legislation to those in supervisory and specialist positions. According to those women who attended the meetings, there was no explanation of the contents or implications of the EEO Law as a whole. The main focus of the meetings was on the amendments of the Labour Standards Law relating to the relaxation of overtime work and holiday work restrictions. At the meetings there was no mention of those parts of the law dealing with the elimination of discrimination. The seminars were mainly intended to explain the practical details of the changes in overtime work arrangements rather than explaining the implications of the law on equal opportunity.

However, an examination of the new developments in the company's utilisation policies on women since 1986 shows that several important changes have occurred. First, in October 1986, a two-track career system was introduced which functions as a formal screening system to select some 'able' women for special training and career development. Second, the general policy orientation on women has shifted from the previous emphasis on utilising women as 'specialists' to an emphasis on the appointment of more women to management positions. There are indications that the company is gradually moving towards an emphasis on the importance of adopting 'positive action' for achieving 'equality in outcomes'. Finally, several new policy measures were introduced to improve the general support environment to help women compromising between work and family.

The two-track career system: selecting and training a core group of 'elite women'

Seibu introduced the two-track career system in October 1986. The new system classifies all employees into two types: the 'global employee' and the 'local employee'. Employees who choose the 'global career route' are required to accept the rule that they could be transferred to any office or subsidiary located in any part of the country or even foreign countries, i.e. they are required to make a commitment to be nationally mobile. For those who choose the 'local career route' transfer will be within commutable distance.

On the surface, no formal career advantages are offered to those who choose the 'global' career track apart from a small mobility allowance added to their monthly payments. Unlike many other companies which set a formal limit to the level of promotion possible to middle-management level to those in 'local' career tracks, Seibu management emphasises that there is no discrimination between employees in the two career tracks with regard to promotion. However, in practice, one would expect 'global employees' to end up having a greater breadth of job experience and training opportunities, which will make them more 'qualified' and eligible to be promoted to key senior positions in the company.

The new system does not apply to all employees equally. At the time when the new system was introduced, all the female employees were asked to declare their choices of career routes. All the male employees, except those who were over 55 years old, were automatically assigned to the global career route. As a general principle, all women employees newly joining the company since the system was introduced have been asked to declare their choices when they reach the age of 27 although the company does allow the possibility for individual application for choice of career track at other stages if special circumstances arise.

Women who choose the global career route have to undergo a two-stage screening process including paper screening and interviews with top management. At the initial stage of implementation of the new system, about 5 per cent of the female employees (276 out of a total of 5,620 female employees) passed the screening. It is not at all clear what criteria the company used to judge the 'suitability' of women to be placed in the global career route. There are no such specifications in the official document issued by the company. Information on the personal background and characteristics of the

276 women recognised as global employees was not available at the time when the author visited the company. However, based on the interview data, it is not too difficult to have a glimpse of the characteristics of the 'global type women'. Out of the twenty-five women interviewed, six women had chosen the global career route and four of them eventually passed the screening procedures (see table 8.6).

Cases E and F dropped out after the interviews with management. Case E was the only child in the family and during the interview she was asked whether it was all right for her to leave her parents behind if she was asked to transfer to a distant place. She dropped out after some consideration, feeling that the management had helped her to make a right decision. Case F said she changed her mind after the interview because she was thinking of getting married in the near future. The question of her likely marriage was raised during the interview and she was asked to reconsider her choice by the management.

It is not clear how many women dropped out from the 'global career route' choice after interviews with the management. The above two cases, nevertheless, do illustrate that appraisal interviews, which are very important in personnel development in Japan, could be used as informal channels to exert pressure on women to ensure their full commitment to the career requirements imposed by the management if they desire to be treated equally as men.

Although the interview sample is small, the above data indicate that those women who chose to pursue the global career route and eventually passed the screening procedures shared some common characteristics: they were highly educated, in their mid- or late-30s,

Table 8.6 Characteristics of the 'global women'

	Education	Age	Job	Grade	Family
A	University	34	Specialist (sales)	6	Single
B	University	34	Specialist (planning)	6	Single
C	Junior college	39	Specialist (sales)	7	Single
D	Junior college	38	Specialist (sales)	6	Single
E	University	37	Specialist (sales)	7	Single
F	University	28	Specialist (buyer)	6	Single

Source: Individual interviews carried out in 1987

single and were in specialist jobs. They were a select group of 'career-minded women' without family obligations, who would be prepared to be transferred to any distant places. It is also clear that these women have all passed their marriageable age in Japan. The risk of these women leaving the company for family reasons is thus minimised. The only young woman (case F) in our sample who applied to be placed on the global career route eventually changed her mind after being questioned about her likely forthcoming marriage during the interview. The individual interviews with management appear to be an important screening procedure used by management to exert pressure on women who might not go ahead with their careers, to reconsider their choice.

The two-track career system is intended to function as a formal procedure to screen out and distinguish a small number of 'elite' women who are willing and able to comply with the requirements to be 'mobile employees' and manage them accordingly. In a formal company document describing the system, the company states the following:

> In considering the fact that women are normally more closely attached to their local areas due to societal expectations, the system formally recognises the restriction of the location of their job assignment. However, the system is also intended to make a clear distinction in the management of different types of (women) employees. This enables the company to plan their job rotation and utilise them positively in line with their choices.

Following the selection of 276 'global' women at the end of 1986, a special training programme was designed for these women. The first step to be implemented was to put these women in small groups, each under the direct supervision and instruction of top management for a period of six months.

Seibu management point out that the main reason for selecting a core group of 'elite' women stems from the commercial need to train and assign more women to key positions in the company. The career tracking system enables the company to spot the 'able' women at an early stage and facilitates training and manpower planning in the long term. Seibu has every commercial reason to train more able women and in fact it had begun to do so after the mid-1970s, although not on a formal and systematic basis. Why did Seibu adopt the career tracking system in October 1986? The timing of the system clearly suggests that the EEO Law has added extra reason for the company to formalise the practice and perhaps to implement it more systematically and on a much wider scale in the future. Sections 7 and 8 of the EEO Law 'exhorts' employers to provide equal opportunity to women in job assignment and promotion. The rationale underlying Seibu's career tracking system is probably not so different from that of many other major companies which have introduced the system recently. The system serves the purpose of screening the 'right' kind of women to whom the company will be prepared to offer equal job assignment and promotion chances. However, in several respects, Seibu appears to have gone much further. First, Seibu is not merely using the career tracking system to make a formal claim that it has offered women equal opportunity by having a few token women selected; 5 per cent of its women employees had passed the screening at the time when the system was first introduced. Although this is a small number in relation to the total female workforce, it is not a token few. Second, unlike many other companies which make a clear-cut distinction in the level of promotion for the two different career tracks, the only formal distinction in the case of Seibu is the scope of job rotation. Third, women who are selected into the 'global career track' are given special training. It is not so clear whether such special attention is offered to men as they are all automatically put on the 'global career track'. In this respect, Seibu's career tracking system is designed specifically to distinguish a small number of 'elite' women from the rest of the female workforce rather than aimed at separating the 'male career track' from that of the 'female career track'.

Seibu is implementing the career tracking system with goodwill, intending to select more 'bright women' to be put on the elite career course. However, like many other major companies, Seibu is only prepared to offer such special favour to women provided they are prepared to make a full commitment to work like their male colleagues. The number of women who will be able to do so is bound to be small despite the goodwill efforts on the side of the management.

A shift in policy orientation: developing more women managers

In early 1987, Seibu stated its intention to design new career development programmes to improve the utilisation of women further. In the summer of 1987, three special project teams were set up to examine specific issues related to women's careers in the company.

The special project teams included a management development team to design training programmes to develop women's managerial potential; a career development team to examine the role of women in the company and to design job rotation policies for women; and a women's working environment team to devise new policy measures to improve the working conditions for women.

Formal policy proposals were put forward in an internal document in January 1989 which represented the most thoroughgoing new policy programmes on women documented by Seibu in recent years. In the policy document, it was pointed out that there were two approaches to the development and utilisation of women: first, to utilise women's 'special qualities' by appointing them to specialist jobs in first-line sales and services and second, to select and utilise women in the same way as men by appointing them to managerial and staff positions in key product areas and departments. The company emphasised the importance of continuation of the first approach but at the same time pointed out that new efforts should be made to develop more women managers. The following statement made in the new policy document indicates the shift in policy emphasis:

> The first important step in the long-term development policy for women in regular full-time jobs is to implement policies for the development of more young women as managers. At the present stage, no matter how difficult it is, the company should press forward to increase the number of women in managerial positions and help women managers to form a sense of consciousness. At the same time, it is necessary to set concrete targets and make them known to all the employees.

In terms of concrete steps to be taken to increase the number of women managers, the project teams suggested the creation of 'women only' departments in one of the stores as a trial attempt. The rationale for this was to avoid job differentiation between men and women so as to allow women to have proper practical management training opportunities at an early stage and to ensure the absolute increase in the number of women managers in management positions. For the first time, Seibu has actually set concrete targets for increasing the share of women in the next ten years. The proposed target was to increase the share of women in lower management (*kakaricho*) from the current 14.7 per cent to 50 per cent by the year 1998 and that of middle management positions from 3.6 per cent to

20 per cent. This, in effect, is a kind of positive action aimed at 'equality in outcome', which to the author's knowledge, is the first of its kind that has ever been proposed in a Japanese company. At the time of writing, there was no information on whether Seibu had actually gone ahead with these policy proposals. None the less, the EEO Law appears to have stimulated Seibu's management to undertake new policy initiatives in promoting women's careers. How far these will have a positive impact on women's position in the long-run is a separate question.

Enabling women to compromise between work and family

In this area, some minor policy improvements were introduced. First, the re-entry scheme was extended to women in non-regular jobs who had worked continuously for the company for a minimum of six years. Second, staff from the personnel department together with union officials were to set up a special counselling service to provide help and advice to women employees who needed childcare facilities. Third, a modified form of the re-entry system was introduced which enables women in full-time regular jobs to change their employment status to part-time while child-rearing, and re-enter the company as full-time regular employees when their children reach school age. The shift in employment status requires a termination of the previous contract and the renegotiation of a new contract at each stage.

All these show that Seibu is a 'pro-women' employer aimed at improving the welfare and working conditions for their women employees in respect of the spirit of the EEO Law, which also encourages employers to introduce measures to help women who are compromising between work and family. However, in terms of developing more concrete policies for enhancing women's career continuity as full-time regular employees, Seibu cannot be said to have gone very far. The re-entry scheme does not provide such a guarantee. At present (1991), Seibu does not have a formal childcare leave system, and there was little indication (at the time when the author visited the company in the summer of 1989), that the company was intending to do so in the near future. Seibu set up a company creche providing some thirty nursery places for its 5,000 plus full-time regular employees in 1982, which was regarded as an exceptionally progressive policy. However, in its recent policy proposals on promoting equal opportunities for women, Seibu has ruled out the possibility of extending such facilities. The cost factor was pointed out as the major impediment. It seems that policies which will encourage a larger number of women to maintain their full-time career continuity are not high on the company's policy agenda for women.

CONCLUSIONS

There is no doubt that Seibu management has adopted more positive policies aimed at selecting more women for responsible jobs since the introduction of the EEO Law, although causality cannot be inferred from the timing of two events. The commercial reasons for Seibu to introduce positive utilisation policies on women remained equally strong in the late 1980s as they had been in the early 1980s. Staff in the personnel department pointed out that it was inevitable that Seibu needed to promote more able women to managerial positions and other key business functions previously dominated by men, because of the gradual decline in the proportion of full-time regular employees as a result of the increased employment of a large number of part-time and contract employees on a mass scale in recent years (see next chapter). The absolute shortage of full-time regular staff has forced the company to utilise the abilities of both men and women to the full, in return for offering them the benefits of permanent employment.

However, the timing of the new policy measures and the major shift in the policy orientations suggest that the EEO Law has added reasons for Seibu to push forward its 'pro-women' policies at a much faster pace than they might otherwise have done. Also being a leader in managerial reforms means that Seibu is very concerned about its well established corporate image as a 'pro-women' employer and this means making every effort to maintain it.

Seibu has taken some new steps in observing the spirit of the EEO Law. On the policy level, it has moved much further in promoting women's careers than many other major companies. Nevertheless, one should not be over-optimistic about the overall 'equal opportunity effects' of the policies pursued by Seibu. There are several reasons for this. First, Seibu's equal opportunity policy has focused on a small number of highly-educated 'elite' women, mostly university graduates, among the regular full-time employees. Among those women interviewed in 1983, there were complaints from those with lower educational qualifications that they were being left out.

Such complaints came out more vividly and frequently during the interviews in 1987. Second, the policies are only applicable to a declining number and proportion of women in regular full-time jobs. An increasing number of women are outside the framework of Seibu's 'pro-women' policies (see chapter 9, table 9.1). Lastly, and most importantly, equal opportunities means that women have to formally accept and commit themselves to work 'like men'. The career planning, promotion and job rotation systems which we discussed previously, as the major structural factors hindering the majority of women from pursuing equal opportunities, remain basically the same. Seibu has done very little to review and change those rules and practices. The career tracking system serves the purpose of justifying and formalising the core personnel system which operates to exclude the majority of Seibu's women employees. Despite the 'goodwill' efforts made by Seibu management, the operation of the two-track career system is in effect both directly and indirectly discriminatory against women. It is directly discriminatory because it does not apply equally to both men and women, and indirectly discriminatory because it has a disproportionate impact on women – only a small minority can comply with the mobility requirements and pass the screening procedures.

Although some women have benefited from the policies adopted by Seibu, it is an extremely small number. The EEO Law has stimulated some new policy efforts at Seibu but it is unlikely that there will be path-breaking changes in terms of the position and status of the majority of women. The next chapter looks at the evidence of this argument.

Chapter 9

Changing roles and attitudes of Seibu women: towards equal opportunity?

Having examined the personnel policy changes introduced by Seibu management in the previous chapter, the spotlight now turns to the women employees – the intended beneficiaries of the policy changes. The objectives of this chapter are twofold: to examine first, changes in the employment pattern and status of women employees, and second, changes in their work attitudes.

The primary intention of the first part is to see how far the policies pursued by Seibu are helping women's careers. Whether career opportunities for women employees at Seibu have improved or not over the years of personnel policy changes and in the period during which the EEO Law was introduced has wider implications beyond this one case. Seibu represents a critical test of the possibility of introducing equal opportunities for women in a large Japanese company. The company operates in an industry which has the greatest need to open up career opportunities for women. All the more important, it is regarded as a leading-edge company in personnel management reforms. An important underlying objective of the EEO Law is to use the legislation as a moral force to stimulate further policy changes in good practice companies and use them as leading models to establish new equal opportunity norms and standards in the future. Since the introduction of the EEO Law, Seibu management has taken some new steps in giving women greater access to the core career jobs. It is therefore important to examine the effectiveness of the model of equal opportunity policy pursued by Seibu. If improvements in women's position have not occurred in a 'progressive' company like Seibu, it is unlikely that they would have taken place elsewhere.

The chapter also examines how the work attitudes of the women at Seibu have changed as a result of the sexual equality debate in recent years, and especially after the introduction of the EEO Law. Women's work attitudes are important factors in affecting their desire for upward mobility and consequently in determining the effectiveness of equal opportunity programmes (Martin *et al.* 1987). The future direction of equal employment for Japanese women will depend not only on changes in employer policies and attitudes, but also on how far women themselves start to perceive the possibilities of change and begin to make more demands on their employers. Further, the extent to which Japanese women's labour supply pattern might shift in the future will be an important determinant of employers' labour force strategies. How have Seibu women reacted to the 'new environment' and the possibility of better career opportunities brought about by the EEO Law? Is there evidence that the EEO Law has raised the women's career expectations and made them more 'career-oriented' and less 'home-bound'? Answers to these questions have important policy implications.

The questionnaire surveys conducted at Seibu in 1984 and 1988 enable a comparison of the shift in women employees' attitudes over time. Interpretation of the survey results is supplemented by data obtained from in-depth individual interviews with twenty-one women at both points in time.

SHIFTS IN THE POSITION AND STATUS OF WOMEN

An examination of the shifts in the position and status of Seibu's women employees between 1983 and 1988 indicates two important changes. First, the absolute number and proportion of those employed on a non-regular contractual basis to take up bottom-level sales or clerical jobs has expanded tremendously. Second, for those women employed on a full-time regular basis, there has been some increase in their share of specialist and managerial jobs. The general trend appears to be towards an increased polarisation of career opportunities for women according to their employment status.

Changes in employment patterns

Between 1983 and 1988, the total number of Seibu employees increased by 48 per cent and in absolute number from 12,947 to 19,110 (see table 9.1). The increase, however, did not constitute a balanced distribution among different categories of employees. For men, the number employed on a regular full-time basis increased by

24 per cent over the period, while that of women declined by 10 per cent. The most dramatic increase was in those employed as non-regular contract employees. For women, between 1983 and 1988, the number employed on a non-regular basis had increased over three times from 1,413 to 5,230. Although the company also started to employ a small number of men on a non-regular basis, the proportion was rather small when compared with that of women.

The big growth in female numbers employed at Seibu has been accompanied by a dramatic shift in their employment status. In 1983, 81 per cent of women working at Seibu were employed on a permanent regular basis, whereas by 1988 the proportion had declined to only 50 per cent. By 1988, the number of women employed on a contractual non-regular basis had surpassed those in full-time regular status.

Over the last few years, Seibu has reduced the recruitment of women as permanent regular employees. Figure 9.1 shows the changes in the number of men and women recruited as regular employees over a period of ten years between 1977 and 1987. The general tendency since the early 1980s has been towards the reduction of employment of regular employees. The decline in the employment of women has been more drastic than that of men in recent years. If we look at the number of women recruited annually by educational qualifications (Figure 9.2), it shows that the reduced

Table 9.1 Composition of male and female employees by employment status (1983 and 1988)

	1983		1988		% change between 1983–88
	No.	%	No.	%	
Male (regular)	5,681	(43.8)	7,055	(36.9)	+24
Female (regular)	5,853	(45.2)	5,284	(27.7)	−10
Male (non-regular)	–*	–	1,473	(7.7)	–
Female (non-regular)	1,413	(11.0)	5,298	(27.7)	+275
Total	12,947	(100.0)	19,110	(100.0)	+48

Source: Data provided by personnel department, Seibu Department Stores Ltd.
Note: *The number of male non-regular employees was almost negligible and no formal record was available.

recruitment of women has mainly affected the high school leavers.

The cut in new recruits was not due to contraction of business. Seibu has embarked on a second phase of expansion since the early 1980s. The company opened up three new branch stores between 1983 and 1987, and the total sales floor area had expanded from 233,231 square metres to 273,399 square metres. The company adjusted to the increased volume of business by recruiting a large number of non-regular contract employees. Clearly, there has been a gradual substitution of full-time regular employees by non-regular contract employees, the majority of whom are women.

The 'contract employee system'

Traditionally, department stores have always been one of the largest employers of part-time and temporary female workers. Seibu was no exception. What makes the recent phenomenon worthy of special attention is that Seibu introduced a new 'contract employee system' in 1984 which formalised and institutionalised the employment of non-regular contract employees on a long-term and large-scale basis.

The new category of contract employees includes the traditional type of part-time and temporary workers and a new category of contract workers whose contract of employment is for one year and subject to renewal on an annual basis. Under the 'contract employee system', the company defines three sub-categories of non-regular employees (as distinct from the permanent regular employees). These non-regular employees can work either on a full-time or part-time basis.

First, there are temporary casual workers employed for miscellaneous sales, maintenance and clerical support jobs. The term of contract is in principle up to one year but a shorter contract is also possible. Payment is entirely on an hourly basis. The company's job advertisement states that these are jobs intended for students, housewives and the aged.

Second, are contract sales clerks employed specifically for first-line sales or customer service jobs. The term of employment is for one year which is subject to renewal on an annual basis. Payment can be by straight hourly rates or a combination of basic pay and commission. The company states in its job advertisement that these are 'women's jobs' intended to utilise the life experience of women on the sales floor. The flexibility of working hours was meant to suit the needs of women for combining work with family responsibilities.

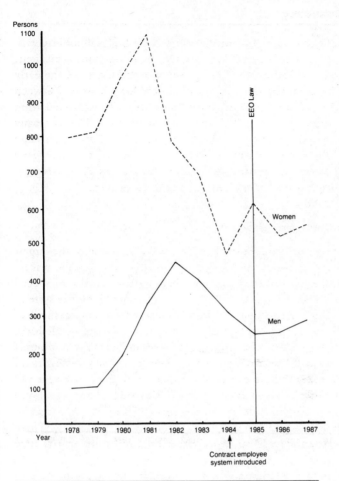

Year	Men No.	Women No.
1978	101	797
1979	105	709
1980	195	765
1981	339	1,080
1982	447	783
1983	393	692
1984	310	476
1985	252	613
1986	253	521
1987	287	549

Figure 9.1 Number of men and women recruited annually (as regular full-time employees), 1978–87.

Source: Data provided by the personnel department, Seibu Department Stores Ltd.

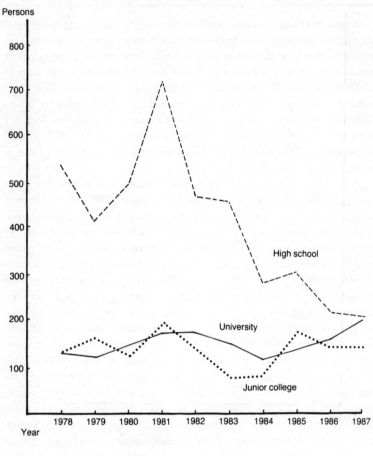

Year	University No.	Junior college No.	High school No.
1978	127	131	539
1979	119	163	427
1980	145	123	497
1981	175	191	714
1982	171	142	470
1983	148	82	462
1984	114	82	280
1985	137	172	304
1986	162	140	219
1987	199	143	207

Figure 9.2 Number of women recruited annually (as regular full-time employees), by educational levels, 1978–87

Source: Data provided by the personnel department, Seibu Department Stores Ltd.

Third, there are contract specialists employed for high-level consulting, or technical jobs such as consultants in music, specialists in product development or engineers. The system of payment and working hours are all subject to individual negotiation on an annual basis. Each contract period lasts for one year. In the job advertisement for this specialist category, the company emphasises its 'non-discriminatory' employment policy and states that 'any individual with specialist skills and abilities will be welcomed'. This category of specialist employee is clearly not intended for women only, but is aiming at both sexes.

Among the above three categories of non-regular employees, the company clearly encourages women to apply for the first two categories of sales and clerical support jobs which are traditionally regarded as 'women's jobs'. Table 9.2 shows the composition of the three different categories of contract employees by sex. The former two categories are predominantly female domains while men constitute about two-thirds of the specialist third category. The second category is the largest of the three and is composed mostly of women.

The contract employees are entirely distinct from the regular permanent employees in terms of pay structure, working conditions and grading system. For instance, the grading structure for the full-time regular employees ranges from grade one to twelve, while the contract employees are on a separate grading system which ranges from grade one to five. In terms of pay, full-time contract employees of grade three earn 83 per cent of the annual basic income and 59 per cent of the annual bonus of full-time regular employees of an

Table 9.2 Composition of contract employees (as of October 1987)

	Male No.	Female No.	Women's share %
Temporary/casual	261	752	74.2
Contract sales	899	4,329	82.8
Contract specialists	313	217	40.9
Total	1,473	5,298	78.2

Source: Data provided by personnel department, Seibu Department Stores Ltd.

equivalent grade. There is no formal system for the contract employees to convert their status to that of a regular permanent one. Contract employees could be doing the same kind of job in the same workplace as regular employees but are paid less and their terms and conditions of employment are less favourable.

What were Seibu's motives for introducing the contract employee system? Seibu management pointed out that a major motive was to reduce labour costs and to increase flexibility in future manpower planning. However, even before the introduction of the contract employee system, Seibu had been employing temporary contract employees, though not on such a large scale. The contract employee system was introduced one year before the Japanese government passed the EEO Law. Under the present legislation, it is entirely acceptable for employers to specify that certain jobs are intended for 'women only'.

One cannot verify a direct casual relationship between the dramatic increase of women in non-regular contract jobs and the introduction of the EEO Law. Neither is it possible to use the timing of the new employment system as an indication that Seibu management has deliberately introduced a policy to restrict the number of women in full-time regular jobs as a strategy to 'dilute' the impact of the anticipated legislation. However, the crux of the problem is that the present EEO Law has created a loophole which allows companies to continue their policies of segregating men and women into different employment statuses.

The company's management stated that one of the new personnel policy initiatives from the mid-1980s onwards was to differentiate the jobs of the permanent employees from those of the contract employees. The ultimate target appears to be to 'hive off' the first-line sales jobs and the peripheral support jobs to the contract employees while the regular permanent employees are to be assigned to core supervisory and managerial jobs. Given that 80 per cent of the contract sales clerks are women, the tendency is towards the increased segregation of women in bottom-level sales jobs.

The increased employment of a large number of women as non-regular contract employees implies that in effect a larger proportion of women working at Seibu in 1988, as compared with 1984, were segregated into secondary employment status with little chance for career advancement. As a result, the overall position of women employees was worse in 1988 because about half of them were virtually shut out from the core career jobs at the point of entry. This movement towards contract employment might, in the long-term, swamp any attempts made by Seibu management to promote the status of women in the company.

Shifts in job status of male and female regular employees

If the overall position of Seibu's women employees as a whole was worse in 1988 because a larger proportion of them were segregated into inferior employment status, how has the position of those women with regular full-time employment status changed over time?

Up to the present, the main aim of Seibu's equal opportunity policies (and also that of the EEO Law) has been oriented towards regular full-time women. Thus, any evaluation of the 'effectiveness' of the equal opportunity policies introduced by Seibu ought to be judged by the extent to which it has helped to promote the job status and career opportunities of its intended beneficiaries, i.e. women employed in regular full-time jobs. The following analysis focuses on the shifts in the job status of women in regular full-time jobs as compared with their male counterparts.

Women's share in management and specialist jobs

Over the five-year period between 1983 and 1988, despite an increase of nearly 80 per cent in the *number* of women in managerial and specialist jobs, their *share* increased only slightly from 6.6 per cent to 8.5 per cent and from 14.5 per cent to 17.3 per cent respectively (see table 9.3). This small positive change, however, did little to correct the imbalance between men and women in specialist and management jobs. Thus, the unequal job distribution was equally striking in 1988 as it was in 1983. Management was still predominantly a male preserve in 1988. Although Seibu management had been putting strong emphasis on utilising more women as specialists since the late 1970s, the increased share of women in specialist jobs was not particularly impressive.

Changes in distribution by job functions

Table 9.4 shows the number of women and men in different specialist job functions and the changes in the share of women in each category between 1983 and 1988. Although women were still highly concentrated in direct sales-related specialist jobs such as sales

LIVERPOOL JOHN MOORES UNIVERSITY
LEARNING SERVICES

Table 9.3 Job position of male and female regular employees (as of June 1983 and September 1988)

| | Male | | | | Female | | | | Women's share of each category | |
| | 1983 | | 1988 | | 1983 | | 1988 | | 1983 | 1988 |
	No.	%	No.	%	No.	%	No.	%	No.	%
Management	1,592	28.0	2,210	31.3	113	1.9	204	3.9	6.6	8.5
Specialist	1,863	32.8	2,681	38.0	316	5.4	562	10.6	14.5	17.3
Ordinary employee	2,226	39.2	2,164	30.7	5,424	92.7	4,518	85.5	70.9	67.6
Total	5,681	100.0	7,055	100.0	5,853	100.0	5,284	100.0	50.7	42.8

Source: Data provided by personnel department, Seibu Department Stores Ltd.

expert and shopmaster, there had been some small but potentially important changes – an increasing number of women were entering the traditionally male-dominated jobs such as buyers and outdoor sales. Between 1983 and 1988, the increase in almost all the specialist job categories (except for sales expert) had been faster for women than for men. Especially in those areas where women were extremely under-represented such as outdoor sales, buyer and technical specialists, the rate of increase was relatively fast as compared with other job categories.

The gradual entry of women into the traditionally male-dominated specialist jobs might not necessarily be a result of deliberate attempts to reduce job segregation between the sexes, but could simply reflect a shortage of experienced male staff because the proportion of regular full-time employees in relation to the total number employed at Seibu had shrunk dramatically over the past five years. The dramatic expansion in the number of non-regular contract employees in bottom level sales and support jobs implies the use of

Table 9.4 Number and share of women in specialist and managerial jobs (as of June 1983 and September 1988)

	1983			1988			
	Male No.	Female No.	% of women (A)	Male No.	Female No.	% of women (B)	(B–A)
Sales expert	57	57	50.0	125	82	39.6	–10.4
Outdoor sales	457	5	1.1	526	24	4.4	+3.3
Sales consultant	103	20	16.3	144	34	19.1	+2.8
Shopmaster	90	111	55.2	64	149	69.9	+14.7
Buyer	209	12	5.4	172	24	12.2	+6.8
Staff (planning/ personnel)	767	106	12.1	1,318	237	15.2	+3.1
Technician	180	5	2.7	191	12	5.9	+3.2
Marketing	–	–	–	141	–	–	–
Management	1,592	113	6.6	2,210	204	8.5	+1.9
Total	3,455	429	11.0	4,891	766	13.5	+2.5

Source: Data provided by personnel department, Seibu Department Stores Ltd.

existing experienced regular employees, whether male or female, in core specialist and managerial jobs.

The above evidence suggests that the job position of the regular female employees at Seibu has improved over the period observed. The major shift in Seibu's employment policy towards the expansion of the non-regular workforce has benefited a small number of women in regular full-time jobs. This improvement for a small group of 'elite' women employees, however, does not necessarily mean there has been an overall reduction of discrimination against women in job assignment or promotion. There are many compositional variables such as age, length of service and education which might have caused the shift in women's job position over the period studied.

The next section examines the importance of the 'sex factor' in explaining the variations of employee status and the extent to which its relative importance has shifted over time.

MORE EGALITARIAN TREATMENT OF WOMEN IN PROMOTION?

To see how far sex has remained a significant factor contributing to variations of employee job status and whether its relative importance has changed over time, the ANOVA procedure was used.

The 'job status' variable is measured by the employees' grade (for explanation of the grading system, see chapter 8). Table 9.5 shows the changes in the distribution of male and female regular employees by grade between 1984 and 1988. (Note: The employees' grades are rank ordered into 5 grade groups). For both sexes there has been a substantial reduction of those of grade 3 or below (ordinary employee grade). This reduction reflects the reduction of the number of new recruits, especially women, in recent years. In the case of men, the proportion of those in senior grade 8–9 (section manager level) increased by 11.7 percentage points; while in the case of women, the greatest increase was in junior grade 4–5 (team leader level). The variations by grade between men and women at both points in time were statistically significant, though more so in 1984 than in 1988.

The effects of the following four factors on an employee's grade were examined in the ANOVA procedure: length of service, age, educational level and sex. The result shows that in both 1984 and 1988, all the four factors are significant in explaining the variations in grade (see table 9.6). The multiple R squared, as shown in table

Table 9.5 Distribution of male and female regular employees by grade
(1984 and 1988), in percentages

Grade groups	1984		1988	
	Male	Female	Male	Female
Below grade 3	24.3	61.5	7.9	35.2
Grade 4–5	28.9	29.7	30.7	48.4
Grade 6–7	39.1	7.8	41.4	13.9
Grade 8–9	7.4	0.9	19.1	2.6
Grade 10 or above*	0.3	0.0	0.9	0.0
Total	100.0	100.0	100.0	100.0
Number	(325)	(548)	(215)	(465)

*Differences (x^2) between male and female for 1984 and 1988 are both
significant at 0.001 level.*

Source: Surveys conducted in 1984 and 1988.

Note: * The survey did not include employees in top management positions
(*bucho* or above), hence the small proportion of those in grade 10 or
above. Actual company data (as of September 1988) showed that
among the 7,055 male regular employees, 541 (7.7 per cent) of them
were in grade 10 or above; whereas in the case of women, only 6 out of
5,284 (0.1 per cent) of them were in equivalent grades.

9.7, gives the variance of the dependent variable that is explained by
the independent variables. In 1984, age, length of service, sex and
education all together explain 81 per cent of the variations in grade;
while in 1988, these variables explain 75 per cent of the variation.
The change over time, however, is not significant.

The relative importance of the four significant factors affecting
grade (as shown by the adjusted beta weights in table 9.7) has
remained unchanged. The most critical finding is that sex explains
more of the variation in grade in 1988. If we look at the adjusted beta
weight in table 9.7, which indicates how much change in the
dependent variable is produced by a standardised change in one of
the independent variables when the others are controlled, in 1988,
the 'pure sex factor' explains 22 per cent of the variation in grade as
against 18 per cent in 1984. Further, at both points in time, being
male is a more positive factor in determining the average mean
grade. In 1984, being male, after controlling for other variables (the
'pure male effect') adds 0.21 of a grade group to the average grade

Table 9.6 Analysis of variance (1984 and 1988 data)

Dependent variable: Job status (grade group) (1984 data)

Source of variation	Sum of square	DF	Mean square	F	Significance of F
Main effects	529.84	17	31.17	213.75	p < 0.001
Age[1]	57.03	7	8.15	55.87	p < 0.001
Length of service[2]	36.21	7	5.17	35.48	p < 0.001
Education[3]	2.46	2	1.23	8.45	p < 0.001
Sex	14.27	1	14.27	97.89	p < 0.001
Explained	529.84	17	31.17	213.75	p < 0.001
Residual	122.19	838	0.15		
Total	652.03	855	0.76		

Dependent variable: Job status (grade group) (1988 data)

Source of variation	Sum of square	DF	Mean square	F	Significance of F
Main effects	410.58	17	24.15	117.22	p < 0.001
Age[1]	48.06	7	6.87	33.32	p < 0.001
Length of service[2]	12.57	7	1.79	8.71	p < 0.001
Education[3]	2.48	2	1.24	6.02	p < 0.005
Sex	18.06	1	18.06	87.65	p < 0.001
Explained	410.58	17	24.15	117.22	p < 0.001
Residual	134.87	655	0.21		
Total	545.44	672	0.81		

Notes: [1] Age is measured in terms of eight categories at an interval of five years in each category: 24 or under, 25–29, 30–34, 35–39, 40–44, 45–49, 50–54 and 55 or above.

[2] The annual number of working years is classifed into eight categories: 0–1, 2–3, 4–5, 6–7, 8–9, 10–15, 16–20 and 21 or above.

[3] The level of education is ranked ordered in terms of high school, junior college and university.

group; and in 1988 it adds 0.29 of a grade group. In contrast, 'being a female' has a negative effect at both points in time, −0.12 in 1984 and −0.13 in 1988. These results certainly imply that in terms of grade promotion there was no less discrimination against women in 1988 as compared to 1984. How could this be explained?

Have women been losing out in the race for promotion because competition for promotion was more intense in 1988 as the proportion of middle-aged employees, especially men, had increased rapidly over the previous few years? As senior positions have gradually become saturated, the speed of promotion has slowed down and this might have hit women harder than men. Table 9.5 clearly shows that men were progressing more rapidly to senior grades over the period observed, while the bulk of women were still in junior grades. Women virtually disappeared beyond grade 6–7; there was very little improvement over time.

Table 9.7 The 'pure sex effect' on job status (grade group*) (1984 and 1988 data)

	1984	*1988*
Beta for age variable	0.47	0.54
Beta for length of service variable	0.43	0.29
Beta for education variable	0.08	0.08
Beta for sex variable	0.18	0.22
Multiple R squared of all independent variables	0.81	0.75
Grand mean of dependent variable (grade group)	1.77	2.11
'Male effect' on grade group	+0.21	+0.29
'Female effect' on grade group	−0.12	−0.13

Source: This table is derived from the multiple classification analysis in the ANOVA procedure. For the original multiple classification analysis tables and further explanations, see appendix B.

Note: * See table 9.5.

CHANGES IN WOMEN'S WORK ATTITUDES: GROWING CAREER CONSCIOUSNESS?

Although only a very small number of women have gained entry to senior jobs and there is little evidence of a decline in discrimination against women in promotion, our survey results show that more women in 1988 believed that men and women were treated equally in their workplace than those that did in 1984. In 1984, 24.6 per cent of the women said they felt men and women were treated equally; the figure rose to 36.9 per cent in 1988. This change in perception is especially prominent among younger women (see table 9.8).

There are two possible explanations for this positive shift in the perception of Seibu women. First, it may reflect actual improvement in the general working environment at Seibu towards greater equality, such as more egalitarian task assignment for younger women and more equal treatment of men and women in day-to-day, on-the-job training. There is some evidence suggesting that such general improvements might have occurred. In 1984, 26.7 per cent of the women in the survey said they received the same kind of on-the-job training as their male counterparts; the figure increased

Table 9.8 Women's perception of equality: 1984 and 1988 compared ('Do you think men and women are treated equally in your workplace?') (by age cohorts)

| | Aged under 24 | | Aged 25–29 | |
	1984 %	1988 %	1984 %	1988 %
Yes	28.2	44.9	21.2	36.8
No	36.6	26.4	63.6	40.2
Don't know	35.3	28.7	15.2	23.0
Total	100.0	100.0	100.0	100.0
Number	(238)	(149)	(151)	(143)

Differences (x^2) between 1984 and 1988 for aged under 24 are significant at 0.005 level, and for aged 25–29 are significant at 0.001 level.

Note: There were some positive changes among the older age groups but because they were smaller and the sample was also smaller, they failed to show statistical significance.

to 32.2 per cent in 1988. A second possible explanation is that the company's formal selection of a small number of 'elite women' through career tracking and the special attention these women are getting has given women an impression that career chances are opening up. This might have made them feel that men and women are treated more equally than before. The author's interviews with twenty-one women in the summer of 1987 provides some relevant information for supporting this second explanation. The majority of the women interviewed, although appearing somewhat hesitant to give a straightforward reply when asked if they thought women's promotion chances had improved over the previous three years, did indicate that they believed there were some positive changes. Most of them referred to some concrete examples of women moving into lower or middle-level management positions:

> There are now more young women becoming shopmasters . . . and there is also one female senior manager (*bucho*) . . . I think the company is making some efforts . . .

> Promotion for woman is still very slow. But I think there is now relatively more chances for women to move into first-level supervisory positions. There has been an increase in the number of women becoming assistant managers.

> I don't think there has been much change. There are not so many women in management positions . . . but I think there will be some improvement from now on . . .

The women's perception of improvement in equal opportunities, whether or not it reflects the actual reality, might have important implications in the long-run. The 'hope hypothesis', an important component of relative deprivation theory, posits that when economic conditions improve, the disadvantaged should have higher aspirations for upward mobility (Crosby 1976 and 1982). Thus, if women believe that the company is moving towards a more egalitarian treatment of women, this should lead to an increase in their aspirations and expectations for upward mobility. Further, the introduction of the EEO Law itself, as an additional 'external factor', might have raised their career consciousness. The reactions of women to equal opportunity policies and the shifts in their attitudes and expectations are important factors in determining the effectiveness of equal opportunity programmes and can create their own dynamics for further change.

In the following sections, three major aspects of Seibu women's attitudes will be examined. First, their job preferences; second, their aspirations and expectations for upward mobility and third their intention to pursue a continuous career. The analysis will focus especially on the shifts in the attitudes among the younger women and the graduates. If the recent equal opportunity debates are having a positive impact on women's work attitudes and career aspirations, one would expect it to be more prominent among the younger generation, especially those who joined the company in recent years. Further, as already discussed in the previous chapter, women graduates have been the major focus of Seibu's equal opportunity policies. In the Japanese labour market as a whole, they have been the main beneficiaries of recent changes in companies' recruitment policies. If equal opportunity policies are having an impact on raising the aspirations and expectations of the potential beneficiaries, one would expect such an effect to be greatest on the graduates.

Job preferences: do Seibu women desire entry into 'male jobs'?

One prerequisite for equal opportunity is to eliminate the traditionally clear patterns of job segregation by sex. This is a formidable task, especially in department stores where the traditional pattern of the sexual division of labour – 'women should sell and men manage' – is so deeply rooted in the psychology of men and women and the culture of the organisation. Breaking down the sexual barrier between jobs involves not only positive action on the side of the company but also changing the sex-typed conception of the jobs.

Although over the past few years, there has been some slight improvement in women's share of specialist and management jobs, women are still under-represented in the major specialist and management jobs. In particular, the two most high-status core work roles, buyer and management, have remained fundamentally male-dominated areas (see table 9.4). Seibu has appointed more women as buyers (women's share increased by seven percentage points between 1983 and 1988) in recent years but the increased share of women in managerial jobs was almost negligible (a mere two percentage points increase over the five-year period observed).

The inital job preferences of men and women reflect the existing patterns of sexual division of labour (see table 9.9). Buyer and management were the jobs most preferred by men. The majority of women either 'had no particular preference' or intended to work as ordinary sales clerks or as specialists in direct sales. Management was at the bottom of women's job preference.

However, there have been some shifts in young women's job preferences over time. Less of them would want to remain as ordinary sales clerks; more indicated they wanted to become staff (i.e. non-managerial specialists in organisational planning or personnel) or buyers. Despite these signs of positive change, management remained an area in which young women did not appear to show much interest in either 1984 or 1988.

Table 9.9 Job preferences of men and women (1988); young women only, 1984 and 1988 compared ('Which job did you wish to pursue when you joined the company?')

Type of job	Male 1988 %	Female 1988 %	Young women only* 1984 %	Young women only* 1988 %
Ordinary sales clerk	6.5	19.4	36.3	29.3
Sales expert	4.7	4.2	0.8	3.5
Sales consultant	4.2	3.8	3.4	2.3
Shopmaster	3.3	10.0	9.7	3.9
Outdoor sales	1.4	1.2	0.0	1.5
Buyer	21.4	11.4	5.5	8.8
Staff (planning/personnel)	12.1	12.2	12.7	16.0
Technician	7.0	4.0	5.9	5.5
Management	21.9	3.6	1.3	0.6
No preference	14.4	25.4	21.9	20.6
Others	3.3	4.7	2.5	8.1
Total	100.0	100.0	100.0	100.0
Number	(215)	(461)	(237)	(147)

Differences (x^2) between male and female in 1988 are significant at 0.001 level; differences between 1984 and 1988 for young women only are significant at 0.025 level.

Note: * Women aged 24 or under.

Women's job preferences appear to be partly influenced by the existing sex ratios of the job. The increased entry of women into the buyer's role in recent years has provided role models to follow and has stimulated younger women's career interests in this traditionally male-dominated job. The unattractiveness of managerial jobs to women appears to be a self-reinforcing cycle in which the lack of representation of women in turn attracts very few women. This would seem to be the result partly of the nature and customary demands of the managerial work role. Male resistance to women's entry into managerial roles is much stronger, as it means disruption of the traditional hierarchical relationships between the sexes. The demand for those in supervisory positions to work long overtime hours presents another major obstacle to women. Several female supervisors indicated in the interviews that they would prefer switching to specialist work roles once they had a family as the pressure for overtime work is less. Unless more deliberate efforts are made to change the 'male work practices' and positive action taken to change the sex-type conception of the management job itself, it seems that even when given the opportunity women would still 'voluntarily' refuse the chances offered and 'self-select' themselves into the traditionally 'female jobs'.

Aspirations and expectations for promotion

In the questionnaire survey, the respondents were asked two questions relating to their aspirations and expectations for promotion: 'Do you desire promotion to a higher position?' and 'If you continue to work in this company, up to which level do you think you will be promoted?' The first question aims at probing a general response indicating aspirations, that is, whether women want promotion, and the second question asks the respondents to predict the specific level which they think they can achieve. The same questions were asked in the 1984 and the 1988 surveys.

If the EEO Law and Seibu's new personnel policies are having a positive influence on women's career attitudes, one can hypothesise the following: first, that women's aspirations and expectations for promotion should have increased over time; second, that such a shift in attitude should be more prominent among younger women as they are most likely to be affected by the EEO Law and benefit from the policy changes; and third, that the aspirations and expectations of women graduates should have gone up more than that of other groups of women as this group of women has been the major beneficiaries of the EEO Law.

Contrary to our expectation, there is no evidence that women's aspirations for promotion have increased (see table 9.10). The proportion of younger women who 'desire promotion to a higher position' has increased very slightly (from 30.0 per cent to 32.0 per cent for those aged under 24 and from 43.0 per cent to 46.0 per cent for those aged 25–29). The changes were, however, too small to be statistically significant. Our prediction that the aspirations of women with a higher education background should have increased more than those with less education is also refuted by the results. On the contrary, a higher proportion of women graduates said they 'would prefer to remain in the same position' (increased by six percentage points) and the figures for those who 'desire promotion to a higher position' has declined by a two percentage points. To summarise, there is no evidence that the women employees' aspirations for promotion have risen over time.

Table 9.11 shows the responses of female and male employees to the question, 'If you continue to work in this company, up to which level do you expect to be promoted?'. For analytical purposes, the responses were classified into four groups: low expectation, medium expectation, high expectation and 'don't know'.

The majority of women either had a low expectation or they gave a 'don't know' response, while the majority of men exhibited a high

Table 9.10 Women's promotion aspirations: 1984 and 1988 compared ('Do you desire promotion to a higher position?')

| | All women | | Women graduates only | |
	1984 %	1988 %	1984 %	1988 %
Higher position	36.8	37.7	56.3	53.5
Same position	19.7	19.7	5.8	13.4
Don't know	41.9	40.6	35.0	30.7
Others	1.7	2.0	2.9	2.4
Total	100.0	100.0	100.0	100.0
Number	(544)	(463)	(103)	(95)

Differences (x^2) between 1984 and 1988 are not significant for both categories.

expectation in both 1984 and 1988. In the case of women, those with a low expectation decreased by over eight percentage points and yet there was only an increase of two percentage points of those with a high expectation. More women in 1988 replied 'don't know'; an increase of six percentage points.

The shift in attitude over time is especially significant among women aged under 24 (see table 9.12). Those with a low promotion expectation dropped rather sharply from 50.8 per cent in 1984 down to 32 per cent in 1988. Those with a moderate or high expectation remained a small minority at both points in time. The most striking feature is the increase in the proportion of those with an 'uncertain' attitude (those who replied 'don't know') – the figure rose from 42.9 per cent in 1984 to 61.6 per cent in 1988. In comparison, the change in the attitudes among older women, especially those aged 30 or above, is not significant.

Another crucial observation is that, contrary to our expectation, the proportion of female graduates with a high expectation has declined slightly over time, from 11.7 per cent in 1984 to 9.5 per cent in 1988, and those with an 'uncertain' attitude increased by ten percentage points, from 28.2 per cent in 1984 to 38.5 per cent in 1988. In comparison, male graduates with a high expectation increased rather significantly over the same period observed – from 50 per cent in 1984 to 56.6 per cent in 1988.

On the whole, the findings support our prediction that equal opportunity policies should have a greater impact on the career expectations of younger women. However, this observation needs some qualification. What could be said is that young women, especially those aged under 24, appeared to be less pessimistic about their chances for promotion in 1988. Less of them expected to remain in a low position, yet there is no clear-cut evidence that their expectations for promotion to higher positions have increased over time. Instead, a great majority of them expressed an 'uncertain attitude'. The 'uncertain group' increased from 42.9 per cent in 1984 to 61.6 in 1988. The proportion of the 'uncertain group' among the graduates also increased by ten percentage points from 28.2 per cent in 1984 to 38.5 per cent in 1988. The significant observation is that women who are most likely to benefit from the company's equal opportunity policies appear to display a greater degree of uncertainty about their career future than before. How do we explain this?

There are two possible explanations: the first relates to women's practical reaction to the 'new situation' and the second concerns the conflicts in values experienced by the Seibu women.

First, women's increased ambivalence about their future career could be a reaction to the fact that core career jobs have become much more demanding, especially in terms of working hours. Our survey results show that both men and women worked many more overtime hours then they did in 1984. The increase was particularly remarkable among women graduates; in 1984 only 2 per cent worked more than twenty hours overtime per month, the proportion increased to 22 per cent in 1988. This was also confirmed by the author's interviews with a group of 'elite women' in 1987. Among the twenty-one women interviewed (they were initially interviewed in 1983), two-thirds of them worked more overtime hours than they

Table 9.11 Promotion expectations of men and women: 1984 and 1988 compared ('If you continue to work in this company, up to which level do you expect to be promoted?')

	Male		*Female*	
	1984 *%*	*1988* *%*	*1984* *%*	*1988* *%*
Low expectation[1]	9.5	7.9	48.7	40.1
Moderate expectation[2]	23.6	21.8	7.8	8.5
High expectation[3]	38.3	44.4	2.9	5.1
Don't know[4]	28.5	26.0	40.6	46.2
Total	100.0	100.0	100.0	100.0
Number	(326)	(216)	(549)	(461)

Differences (x^2) between 1984 and 1988 are not significant for males but are significant for females at 0.05 level.

Notes: [1] Low expectation group: those who replied that they expected to remain as ordinary employees or up to team leader level (*kakaricho* level).

[2] Medium expectation group: those who expected promotion up to middle management level (*kacho* level).

[3] High expectation group: those who expected promotion up to top management or senior executive level (*bucho* level or above).

[4] 'Don't know' group: those who replied that they had not thought about the issue. This could either indicate a lack of interest in promotion or uncertainty about future career.

Table 9.12 Women's promotion expectations: 1984 and 1988 compared (by age cohorts)

| | Aged under 24 | | Aged 25–29 | | Aged 30–39 | | Aged 40 or above | |
	1984 %	1988 %	1984 %	1988 %	1984 %	1988 %	1984 %	1988 %
Low expectation	50.8	32.0	52.3	46.5	48.6	49.5	22.7	30.2
Moderate expectation	4.2	3.9	5.2	6.4	12.6	12.4	25.0	17.4
High expectation	2.1	2.6	2.6	6.0	3.6	4.3	6.8	9.9
Don't know	42.9	61.6	39.9	41.2	35.1	33.7	45.4	42.5
Total	100.0	100.0	100.0	100.0	100.0	100.0	100.0	100.0
Number	(240)	(149)	(153)	(143)	(111)	(99)	(44)	(69)
	(x^2 significant at 0.005 level)		(x^2 not significant)		(x^2 not significant)		(x^2 not significant)	

did in 1983. Some younger women, especially those regarded by the company as 'high flyers', worked up to an average of 50 hours overtime per month. The majority of the women interviewed had more doubts about the possibility of combining work with having a family.

In addition to the *actual* increases in career demands, the company's new policies of career tracking and adoption of more formal selection procedures also appear to have made women, especially the 'potential beneficiaries' of the new policies, *more aware of* the 'negative aspects' of upward mobility such as long working hours, showing loyalty to the company and a commitment to the mobility requirement. Seibu introduced the career tracking system in 1986. Younger women who joined the company after 1986 were likely to be informed of the demands the company would make on them if they intended to select the 'mobile career track' (see chapter 8). The selection and screening processes themselves might have had an impact on women's attitudes. Both our survey results and interviews show that in comparison with the pre-EEO Law situation, women in 1988 perceived greater 'availability' of equal opportunities. At the same time, they were also more clearly informed of the terms and conditions required for equality. The increased degree of uncertainty among the young women and the graduates could reflect their reaction to the new situation. It is as if these women were saying 'Now that I can have it, I am not so sure I want it'. Could this reaction also explain why the career aspirations of the graduates – the 'target population' of Seibu's equal opportunity policies – have declined over time? Fewer graduate women said they wanted promotion to a higher position and more of them wanted to remain in the same position in 1988 (see table 9.10). The possibility of giving women access to better career opportunities also means that women are asked to make more clear-cut choices at the early stages of their careers in order to facilitate the company's training and manpower planning policies. The 'pressure of equality' was becoming more obvious to women in 1988 than in 1984.

There is another reason why women would appear to have become more ambivalent about their future career. This could be a manifestation of a greater degree of value conflict experienced by the women at Seibu in the post-EEO Law era. Such conflict is likely to be greater among women who are more career conscious. The EEO Law is a symbolic representation of the value of sex equality and the importance of women's role in employment. The introduction of the law might have in fact raised the career consciousness of women. The fact that the attitudes of the young women – the post-EEO Law generation (those aged under 24) – have shifted most is a suggestive piece of evidence. It is possible that the law does not seem to have raised women's aspirations for promotion because of women's reaction to the 'real situation' at Seibu. The 'law effect' and the 'Seibu effect' might have generated opposing influences on women's attitudes. This may help to explain why the group of women who are most likely to be affected by both factors exhibit a high degree of 'uncertainty' about their future career. Another point worthy of note: both the EEO Law and Seibu's policies have stressed giving women access to equal opportunities without introducing positive measures to ease women's career constraints. Women at Seibu might have felt it easier to leave employment before when they were confronted with the conflicting demands. However, the value of sex equality as a desirable goal has put more women in the dilemma of choosing between 'either work or family'. Hence, more of them displayed a greater degree of 'uncertainty' in 1988.

Attitudes to career continuity

The author's follow-up interviews of the twenty-one 'elite women' in 1987 showed that more than half of them appeared to have changed their minds about their intention to combine work with family and had become rather pessimistic about the possibility of pursuing a continuous career:

> It would be very difficult to continue working here if I get married. Working hours are too long and it is just physically not possible to combine both. (43-year-old, senior manager (*bucho*), single)

> It is becoming very difficult . . . . I wish I had more time with my family. The amount of work is too much. I simply do not have time for myself . . . . (33-year-old, in staff function, who was married and had one child)

> I have no confidence in combining both work and family. If I consider getting married one day, it will be very difficult for me to decide what to do. (33-year-old, in first-level supervisory position, single)

A comparison of the survey results in 1988 with that of 1984 shows that the proportion of women wishing to pursue a continuous career has declined over time, from 16 per cent in 1984 to 12 per cent in 1988 (see table 9.13). An increasing number of women would prefer to seek a compromise by adopting a two-phase work profile, that is, retire from their job to raise children and re-enter the job market at a later stage in their life.

The decline in the proportion wishing a continuous career was greatest among women in their thirties – a drop from 26.6 per cent in 1984 to 13.6 per cent in 1988. This is correlated with the fact that many of the women in their 30s were already married and were probably more aware of the practical difficulties of combining employment with family responsibilities.

Seibu management might have allowed more women to compete with their male colleagues on an equal basis, but the intensive demands of the core career jobs, the practice of long working hours as a sign of commitment and the lack of policy measures to ease women's career constraints mean that such opportunities are seen as irrelevant by the majority of the women. There is some evidence suggesting that women are actually refusing the offer of senior jobs. It was mentioned to the author by a senior personnel manager at the head office that the company had made several attempts to assign women to senior positions in the personnel department, but they

Table 9.13 Women's attitudes to career continuity: 1984 and 1988 compared ('Do you intend to continue working after childbirth?')

	1984 %	1988 %
Continue working	15.7	12.3
Quit and re-enter*	27.1	35.1
Retire permanently	24.6	17.5
Haven't considered	25.9	28.5
Others	6.7	6.7
Total	100.0	100.0
Number	(536)	(393)

Differences (x^2) between 1984 and 1988 are significant at 0.05 level.

Note: * This means retiring from work at childbirth and re-entering the labour market after the children have grown up.

encountered great difficulties in persuading women to take up the posts offered. This issue was also discussed during the interviews with the women employees. One woman confirmed that she was offered the post of personnel manager (*jinji-kacho*) but eventually decided to turn it down because 'it was not the kind of job she had wanted'. Another woman pointed out that the company appeared to be more willing to appoint women to senior management positions than it was three or four years ago but such efforts often turned out to be futile because women appointed to management positions tended to resign afterwards. There is a lack of company-wide data to verify the extent of this phenomenon. If the incidents mentioned were representative, then it further confirms our argument that the 'equal opportunity efforts' made by Seibu management might not have much effect on women's position.

SUMMARY AND CONCLUSIONS

This chapter has presented a case study of organisational change in a situation where one could have expected the greatest changes towards greater sex equality as a result of many social and economic reasons and especially after the introduction of the EEO Law. Nevertheless, the study shows that change towards equal opportunities for women has been very limited.

Over the period observed, there has been a small increase in the number of women appointed to specialist or managerial jobs, but numerically much more important has been the increase in the number of women in contract employment, being segregated into inferior employment status and treated as a distinct sub-group of 'second class' employees with virtually no prospect for career advancement. It can be argued that the overall position of women was worse in 1988 as compared to that of 1984. Seibu's increased utilisation of women as non-regular contract employees in bottom-level sales and clerical support jobs appears to have swamped the company's policies to promote the status of women in the company.

There is little evidence that overall discrimination against women in grade promotion has been reduced. Despite a small increase in the numbers of women in senior grades, their relative share was as negligible in 1988 as it was in 1984. Management has remained predominantly a male bastion.

The study also examined whether the equality debates and the

EEO Law have raised women's career consciousness at Seibu, especially among the younger women and the graduates, who are most likely to be affected by the law and benefit from the company's policy changes. The results indicate a rather complex situation. The overall results show little evidence of positive change in terms of more women wanting promotion to senior positions. Contrary to our expectation, the aspirations of the graduates have declined over time. In terms of women's expectations for promotion, there have been some significant shifts, especially among the younger women. This suggests that the law might have had an impact on their expectations. There was a significant decline in the proportion of women aged under 24 who expected to remain in a low position. Above all, the most striking finding is that a much greater proportion of the young women and the graduates displayed an 'uncertain' attitude regarding their future career. The tendency towards greater 'uncertainty' can be observed across the whole female sample, but most strikingly among the groups of women who are most likely to have been affected by the law and Seibu's new policies.

The results show that it is necessary to distinguish the general 'consciousness raising effect' of the law from the specific 'Seibu policy effect' on the attitudes of women. It appears that any positive consciousness raising effect that the law might have had on women was being mediated by their actual experience at Seibu. The equal opportunity policies adopted by Seibu, although appearing to offer women greater access to core career jobs, have made women more aware of the 'price of equality' and put them under greater pressure to make their career choices through formal screening at the early stages of their careers. The new situation has put those women who might have wanted equal opportunities in a greater dilemma than before. The conflict between the new value of equal opportunity as symbolised by the EEO Law and the traditional familial ideology has become more apparent. This explains why women who are most likely to have been affected by the law and benefit from Seibu's policies have become more ambivalent and uncertain about their future career.

In the long run, it is more likely that women at Seibu are going to make a pragmatic choice. Fewer women in 1988 intended to pursue a continuous career without interruption and more of them, especially the married women, would prefer to retire from work when they have children. The intensive demands on employees in career jobs to work extra long hours – much more so than in 1984 –

and the requirement to make a commitment to relocation for those who intend to pursue the mainstream career route has driven a growing number of women employees to become more 'home-oriented' in 1988. The majority of the women interviewed by the author in the summer of 1987 pointed out that if equal opportunity meant that they had to forgo having a family and work like their male colleagues, they would rather seek a compromise by adopting a 'two-phase work profile'. For the majority of women at Seibu, this is probably a pragmatic choice in a system which does not allow career jobs to be compatible with family life and in a society which expects women to take up sole responsibilities for raising children.

Any attempt to improve the position of women in an organisation raises a wide variety of issues, many of which extend far beyond the organisation. Equal opportunities for women necessitate structural and attitudinal changes at the organisational and societal level which may take many decades to achieve. This case study, however, seems to indicate that if the present trends continue, it is unlikely that there will be a major shift towards a brighter prospect of equal opportunities for women at Seibu, and indeed, for women employed elsewhere.

One final question that might be raised: Why Seibu management, which has for a long time stressed the crucial role of women for the successful operation of the business and has capitalised on the company's 'pro-women' corporate image, has failed to make more use of the talents of their female workforce? Equal opportunities for women are not marginal issues at the company. Seibu management has made 'further efforts' since the introduction of the EEO Law in an attempt to select and promote more able women to senior positions. The management was well aware of the difficulties the company might encounter in retaining some of their talented women in the long run. When the author visited the company in the summer of 1989, a senior personnel manager at the head office pointed out that the company had reached a 'deadlock' in their equal opportunities policies. He remarked that the present career system was fundamentally 'male-oriented' and that the current situation presented a great dilemma for the company's personnel management policies.

The nature of the dilemma is that in order to attract and retain more able women in responsible jobs, the company would need to change the promotion rules and the work practices governing the core career jobs; for example, allowing for greater flexibility in career planning, enabling women to retain their seniority after a career break, reducing the intensity of work and allowing for the mobility rules to be applied in more flexible ways. However, altering these rules too radically would have two 'undesirable' organisational consequences for management. First, offering women true equal opportunities would imply a redistribution of the promotion chances between men and women. This would disrupt the job security and long-service promotion expectations of the male employees which are part of the long-standing implicit understanding between Seibu management and the male employees. This long-standing customary expectation has been the major force generating high commitment, high output effort and a willingness to co-operate in furthering the aims of the company. The benefits the company derives from these long-standing practices are considerable and it is not at all clear that Seibu management is willing to give them up. As long as 'good employers' in the Japanese enterprise community are still expected to be able to offer long-term job security and stable career progression for their (male) regular employees, giving up the benefits of the traditional system too rapidly might jeopardise the status of Seibu in the enterprise community and their ability to attract good quality male graduates. Moreover, as pointed out by Doeringer and Piore (1971: 161), seniority and promotion arrangements are customary in nature, and their complete elimination may require changes in custom itself. Seibu management's desire to protect the stability of the core career jobs imposes a severe constraint on the company's willingness to alter the promotion rules and work practices too drastically.

Second, introducing fundamental changes in the career rules to allow more women to retain their seniority and career continuity would not only imply an absolute increase in labour costs, but would also lead to an expansion of the number of employees under the guarantee of lifetime employment with its associated career expectations. The guarantee of lifetime employment under the *nenko* wage and career progression system is extremely costly and rigid. The 'core' system can only be maintained if there are a large number of low cost 'peripheral' workers to provide the necessary flexibility. Seibu is faced with a fundamental dilemma of how to get some 'good' women ('*noryoku to iyoku aru josei*', meaning women with the 'right ability and motivation') into top jobs without raising the career expectations of all women, and more importantly, how to ensure that the dualistic character of the employment structure continues to be accepted by the majority of women, amid the growing pressures for equal opportunities. Seibu management has adopted two strategies to cope with the dilemma. The first strategy is through career tracking, using the mobility requirement as a main criterion. The differential treatment accorded to the selected 'elite women' is therefore justified by the fact that they can conform to the 'male career rules'. A second long-term strategy adopted by Seibu is through segmentation by employment status. The contract employee system serves the objectives of cost reduction, enhancing manpower flexibility and at the same time helping to 'dilute' the potential destabilising effects of equal opportunity pressures. In the 1980s and 1990s, the increased pressures for greater equality for women has pushed Seibu to adopt more cautious policies in maintaining a delicate balance between the need to give some selected women equal opportunities and, at the same time, ensuring that the long-standing employment practices governing the internal career jobs will not be disrupted.

The present manpower strategies might not help Seibu management to resolve their dilemma in the long run. The fact that some women are turning down promotion and that more of them appear to have become more 'home-oriented' is an indication that Seibu might be failing to attract and retain enough 'good' women. The new strategy of segregating a large number of women into 'dead end' contract sales jobs is potentially unstable. Management has begun to show concern about the low morale of the contract sales workforce and the decline in the quality of service – an important factor in maintaining the competitiveness of the department stores. A potentially more explosive element is that the contract sales employees are mixed together with the regular full-time workforce. The differences in their treatment are immediately obvious. Several women supervisors interviewed by the author pointed out the increasing difficulties in managing the 'emotional conflicts' between the regular and the contract female employees. In the long run, Seibu management might find it difficult to justify to the majority of women why some women are treated better than others. In the past, segmentation of the workforce at Seibu was justified by the sex role distinction that 'men should manage and women should sell'. Such clear-cut sexual division of labour has become blurred in recent years. The new policy at Seibu is that 'men and some talented women should manage and the majority of women should sell'. This new segmentation strategy is potentially unstable. The disruption to the clear-cut sexual divisions of labour might begin to generate its own dynamics of instability.

Whether Seibu management will be pushed to institute more fundamental changes in the sexually discriminatory employment practices in order to attract and retain more 'good' women and to avoid the demoralisation of the female sales workforce is a question which cannot be predicted purely on the basis of 'efficiency needs'. One crucial insight to be gained from Doeringer and Piore's internal labour market analysis is that internal labour market rules and customs tend to persevere in the face of contrary economic pressure: that institutional survival is not dependent upon the logic of economic efficiency alone and that custom has an influence upon management decisions as well as being a constraint (Doeringer and Piore 1971: 24).

The Seibu case nevertheless illustrates that the continued stability and persistence of the internal labour market rules in their present forms cannot be taken for granted. The nature and dynamism of internal labour market rules need to be interpreted in the wider context of social and power relationships between the 'privileged' and the 'exploited'. The special type of internal labour market in Japan has traditionally operated on the basis of hierarchical sexual divisions and cultural repression of women. The social conditions of women have provided 'resources' for Japanese management in their development of labour market segmentation strategies. If these social conditions shift, management might be forced to adopt a different strategy of workforce segmentation. The continued persistence of the special type of internal labour markets in Japan is therefore partly dependent upon the social condition that the majority of Japanese women continue to accept a male-dominated system.

Part IV

Conclusions

Chapter 10

Equal employment for women in the Japanese employment system: limitations and obstacles

The empirical evidence presented and discussed in the previous chapters indicates that neither market pressures nor the EEO Law have caused Japanese companies to introduce fundamental reforms in their employment and personnel management systems. Although there have been some changes in companies' policies on women, especially after the introduction of the EEO Law, none of the policy adaptations have sought to change the nature of the rules governing job assignment, promotion and career structure in the core employment system. The model of change adopted by the companies is based on the premise that only those women with the 'right ability and motivation' (*noryoku to iyoku aru josei*) – meaning those who can conform to the existing organisational rules and practices like their male counterparts – will be granted equal opportunities. The 'two-track employment system', beginning to be widely adopted by an increasing number of major companies in recent years, typifies the superficiality of the companies' responses to the demands for equal opportunities. The policy responses have had very little effect in reducing the structural sources of inequality between the sexes.

Parallel with this is the increased pursuit of labour flexibility and the systematic utilisation of women as part-time and contract workers on a mass scale. This diminishes the career chances for an increasing number of women faster than the present EEO Law could ever help to improve them.

Why has there been so little improvement in the provisions of equal opportunities for women? This chapter examines the conservative forces within the employment system and the broader state policy context which constitutes a powerful mechanism to maintain the status quo.

MANAGEMENT'S CONTINUED ATTACHMENT TO THE 'JAPANESE EMPLOYMENT SYSTEM'

Preserving 'lifetime' employment

The extent to which major firms are willing to open up core career jobs to women and offer them equal promotion chances depends greatly on the importance they attach to the traditional practices of lifetime commitment and the *nenko* wage and promotion system. These two distinctive employment features, which constitute the cornerstone of Japanese personnel management, not only create tremendous practical barriers to women's entry into the core career jobs but are often used by management to justify unequal treatment of women from the viewpoint of economic efficiency. How far and how fast are these traditional practices losing their central importance in the employment system?

Despite much speculation about the inevitable dissolution of these long-standing practices, recent statistical evidence shows the opposite (MOL 1987a). A recent study by Dore *et al.* (1989) suggests that, far from disappearing, the lifetime commitment practice retains its centrality and there are signs that it is diffusing down the firm-size hierarchy. There are two major pieces of evidence.

First, the strengthening of the lifetime employment practice is indicated by the increase in the proportion of 'standard' workers over time (referring to those who were hired immediately after graduating and have worked continuously for the same enterprise). The proportion of standard male workers in the age group 30–34 has increased from 73.6 per cent in 1970 to 75.7 per cent in 1975 and to 77.9 per cent in 1984; for female workers in the same age group the corresponding figures are: 44.7 per cent, 51.2 per cent and 58.5 per cent (MOL 1987a: 16).

Second, the above observation is supported by concomitant figures showing a clear decline in the proportion of 'non-standard', mid-career recruits. Workers between the age of 30–34 who have less than five years of service may be deemed as 'deviants' from the standard lifetime recruitment from school or university – likewise for 35–39 year-olds with less than ten years of service and so on. For example, the proportion of 'non-standard' mid-career recruits in the age group 30–34 in firms with 1,000 plus employees has declined from 14 per cent in 1961 to 11 per cent in 1975 and further down to 8 per cent in 1984. Likewise, those in firms with 10–99 employees have also declined from 52 per cent to 41 per cent and further down to 38 per cent in the same respective years. Similar trends can be observed for other age groups (Dore *et al*. 1989: 57).

There is less clear-cut evidence, however, as to whether the *nenko* system is crumbling under the labour cost pressure exerted by demographic changes. The general indication is that it is being modified, i.e. the relative importance of *nenko* as a criterion for determining wage increase and promotion has declined, especially for white-collar workers but it still retains considerable influence (Hazama 1989: 206–8).

In the area of promotion, management has stressed the need to move towards a system which is based on individual merit and competition. There is, however, little evidence showing that this is happening in practice. More emphasis on competition and merit appointments should lead to a gradually increased dispersion in the ages of those occupying managerial positions. The trend is quite the reverse. In 1976, 32 per cent of sub-section chiefs (*kakaricho*) were in the modal age group 35–39, and 32 per cent were younger. In 1984 approximately the same 33 per cent were in the older modal age group, but only 20 per cent were younger. At the top end, the 1976 figures for department chiefs (*bucho*) were 34 per cent aged 45–49 and 25 per cent younger; eight years later, 37 per cent were in the former age group and only 15 per cent were younger (Dore *et al*. 1989: 64).

Some subtle changes in personnel practices may not be easily captured by statistical indicators. If there have been moves to de-emphasise the importance of lifetime commitment among the core employees, these are only moving at a very slow pace. The dominant opinion among the enterprise community is that companies should make their best efforts to create sources of flexibility out of the seemingly rigid lifetime employment system, such as expanding the sphere of employee loyalty and identity to the whole enterprise group so that excess manpower in one enterprise can be transferred or dispatched to another when necessary, buying in more specialist services in areas where technology is changing fast and increasing the utilisation of contract and part-time workers to extend the margin of greater employment flexibility. The fundamental orientation is that long-term employment should be maintained for the core employees because this is believed to be the source of vitality of the Japanese economy. Recent surveys on companies' personnel policies show that the desire and incentive to maintain their core employees' lifetime commitment is still strong. Over 80 per cent of the firms indicated an intention to maintain a guarantee of lifetime employment for their regular employees in the future. Although the framework of lifetime employment guarantee is to be modified, it might not necessarily mean lifetime employment within the same enterprise: over 90 per cent of the firms would want to guarantee lifetime employment at least within the same enterprise group (Hazama 1989: 205). As regards the main preoccupations of personnel policies, 87 per cent of the firms replied that the emphasis would be on training and manpower development (Inagami 1989: 8). This growing emphasis on training investment by the companies will serve to increase their incentive to maintain the long-term commitment of their employees.

In a period of rapid economic and social change, Japanese employers have been careful not to cause too great a disruption to the traditional personnel practices which are seen as the source of high commitment and high productivity. A recent report published by the Japan Productivity Centre stresses the importance of revitalising the lifetime employment practice:

> There are widespread opinions that the practice of lifetime employment needs to be modified in response to structural changes in the economy. Measures such as increasing mid-career recruitment, transferring or dispatching excess manpower are carried out in certain sectors of the economy or some departments of companies. These employment adjustment measures are necessary in order to maintain managerial efficiency. However, it is extremely important that the fundamental nature of lifetime employment is to be maintained. Career formation through long-term training and development under the guarantee of lifetime employment is a system which has many merits for the society, the economy, industrial relations and the management system. The merits of this system will continue to outweigh by far its demerits in the future. The framework and the form of lifetime employment may need to be modified but it is desirable that the nature of the lifetime employment relationship should be preserved.
>
> (JPC 1987: 9)

Strategies adopted by major companies to preserve the benefits of lifetime employment for their core employees include restricting the number of those who are under such guarantee, increasing the utilisation of temporary, part-time and contract workers, and ensuring that the top elite posts are reserved for those who are seen as 'committed' workers (presumably mainly men) through various forms of career tracking at an early stage. Unless women are prepared to commit themselves to work continuously without interruption, their chances of gaining core career jobs are going to be extremely limited. To force women to work like men under the lifetime employment system, according to a JPC report, will only cause many social dysfunctions:

> The practice of lifetime employment was originally formed in the large enterprises applying to the core male employees. It will create serious trouble if the practice is applied to women. In general, women are not geared to the practice of lifetime employment. To force women to comply to the requirements of long-term continuous employment and frequent mobility involving geographical movement will cause many practical difficulties for women and is socially dysfunctional.
>
> (JPC 1985: 77)

The fear that equal employment for women will upset the flexibility of the employment system and cause disruption to the social infrastructure which supports the system is deeply entrenched in Japanese management's thinking.

The increased utilisation of women as non-regular workers

While the majority of women continue to be excluded from the framework of lifetime employment, their role as non-regular workers, including those employed as part-time, *arubaito* and contract workers, is becoming increasingly important. The proportion of women employees classified as part-time, *arubaito* and contract workers increased from 26 per cent in 1981 to 36 per cent in 1990. In comparison, male part-time, *arubaito* and contract workers showed only a slight increase from 6 per cent to 8 per cent over the same period (Somucho 1981 and 1990).

The restriction of core career jobs largely to men and the utilisation of large numbers of women as a flexible non-regular workforce have served the Japanese economy well. Management will continue to restrict the employment of a disproportionate number of women to non-regular status and are not prepared to adopt active policies which will enhance women's career continuity. Even a 'leading-edge' company like Seibu does not have a childcare leave system at present (1991). The so-called re-entry scheme which was introduced in 1978 did not commit the company to re-employ the returnees in full-time regular jobs. Many companies use the re-employment scheme as a measure to maintain a large number of women, who retire from work for family reasons, as a pool of potential returnees and re-employ them as non-regular workers when the need arises. A re-employment scheme which guarantees an offer of re-employment at the same grade or employment status is almost non-existent in Japan.

Another reason why companies are not prepared to employ too many women as regular employees is the fear that, with an ageing workforce, it might intensify competition for the increasingly scarce managerial or specialist positions in the internal career hierarchy. A report submitted to the Ministry of Labour by an expert committee looking at personnel management policies in the ageing society made the following remark:

> The introduction of the EEO Law might have raised the career aspirations of women, but under the present *nenko*-based personnel system, increasing the number of posts for women means cutting the posts for men. The majority of the companies have very little intention in improving their treatment of women workers.
>
> (MOL 1988: 9)

Utilisation and cooptation of 'elite women'

To say that Japanese companies have not adopted active policies to ease women's career constraints is not to deny that there are economic benefits to be gained by offering some women better job opportunities. A company like Seibu genuinely needs to have more women in 'top jobs' because of the nature of its business. Given impending skills shortages, Japanese companies cannot afford to waste the talents and potential of a growing number of highly-educated women. The growing purchasing power of Japanese women and their dominance in the consumer market is another reason why companies cannot completely ignore the interests and demands of women both as employees and as customers. Many companies in the service sector such as retailing, banking and insurance and even manufacturers of consumer electronics recognise that 'the customer matters' and are aware of the need to use more women staff who could create the understanding and the link with their customers. Moreover, in an age of intense market competition, even using the theme of 'equal opportunity' as a public relations exercise might prove to be beneficial in promoting corporate image. Labour market changes and commercial needs have exerted powerful pressures on Japanese companies to provide better job prospects and employment conditions for some women. The EEO Law has added extra impetus for change.

Nevertheless, it cannot be taken for granted that the way companies choose to respond to these pressures will be good for the promotion of true equal opportunities for women in the long run. Our analysis of the responses of the major companies to these pressures cautions against having too high expectations.

Companies which are concerned about the 'women's issue' due either to the nature of their business or a desire to present a 'progressive' corporate image prefer to talk about policies for better 'utilisation' of women rather than using the term 'equal opportunity'. The former has a much broader and more flexible policy connotation, but does not necessarily involve comparing women with men. Popular 'women utilisation programmes' adopted by major firms include creation of women-only project teams in areas of consumer product design or marketing; and the creation of specialist work roles for women in areas which are deemed best for utilising their feminine qualities such as sales and customer services (see chapter 4). Moreover, most of these 'women utilisation programmes' are restricted to graduates rather than applying as general policies for all the female employees. This type of policy clearly has several advantages from the viewpoint of management's interests. It enables the company to utilise the best female talents to enhance product or market competitiveness in areas where female consumers dominate. By restricting the utilisation of women to 'women-specific' areas as defined in the traditional way, it ensures that the basic pattern of sexual division of labour is undisturbed, and by creating specialist work roles for women it produces ways for some ambitious women to take up more responsible jobs yet minimises the challenge to the established male career hierarchy. Also by targeting their new policies on the graduates, it helps to absorb the pressures for equal opportunity which is most likely to come from this group of women.

Market pressures and commercial considerations are triggering many changes in Japanese companies' utilisation policies on women, but these have not affected directly the nature of employment relationships, nor have they challenged the pattern of job segregation which underlies women's disadvantaged position in the labour market. A small number of 'elite' women might have benefited from the changes, but on the whole the great expansion of women's employment has been in low paid, non-regular jobs. The Seibu case clearly indicates the limits of management-initiated change programmes, and the persisting tensions between the need for flexible labour in order to maintain the viability of the core employment system and the full utilisation of women's labour potential on an egalitarian basis. The growing pursuit of greater flexibility in manpower planning and reduction of labour costs at Seibu since the mid-1980s has led to a systematic policy of utilising women as a form of cheap contract, first-line sales on a mass scale. By the late 1980s, over half of the women working at Seibu were non-regular contract workers with no prospect for career advancement. This has in effect almost completely reversed the company's previous attempt to improve the status of women in sales jobs. Japanese management's continued attachment to the 'traditional' employment practices and the increased pursuit of manpower flexibility cautions against too high expectations of management-initiated change programmes in bringing about equal employment for women.

Has the EEO Law made any difference to the above situation? The present legislation can be said to be quite 'effective' with regard to achieving its objectives. It has made bad practice companies reduce the most blatant forms of direct discrimination against women and has induced good practice employers like Seibu to take more positive steps in giving women formal choice and the possibility of access to core career jobs. However, the effects of these policies on women's position and status appear to be minimal. The model of equal opportunity as enshrined in the law accepts the persistence of the structural and institutional factors which contribute to women's unequal position. The review of the overall responses of companies and the Seibu case study reveals the inadequacies of the 'equal treatment approach' and the major loopholes in the legislation. The way 'equal opportunity' is being defined has permitted companies to create more part-time and contract jobs for women and segregate them into an inferior employment status which automatically justifies unequal treatment.

The present legislation has not undermined the mechanisms which perpetuate sexual job segregation in the employment system. On the contrary, it has helped to preserve the core employment system and to ensure that core career jobs will only be offered to those who can satisfy the requirements imposed by the companies.

THE STATE POLICY CONTEXT

It appears that any beneficial effects the present legislation might have on a small minority of elite women will in the long-run be swamped by other opposing forces which are working against equal opportunities for women. The broader context of state policies on women workers has not been pushing towards the direction of sexual equality.

The continuing marginalised position of the majority of women in the Japanese labour market is more than just the natural outcome of market forces. The overall political and economic perspectives underlying the form of policy adopted by the Japanese government towards women workers have helped to reinforce their marginal role in employment. The main orientation of government policies on women workers since the mid-1960s has been the emphasis on the importance of their role as part-time or temporary workers. This policy has been consistently developed and evolved in line with the needs of the economy since the mid-1960s up until the present day.

It was during the labour shortages beginning in the mid-1960s that women, along with the aged, were mentioned as a secondary labour force available to fill any gaps (EPA 1971). Part-time employment for women was encouraged and recognised by the government as a form of employment which suits the specificity of women's conditions (MOL 1964). The Working Women's Welfare Law was enacted in 1972 as part of the government's attempts to encourage more married women to enter the labour market as additional labour to cope with severe labour shortages.

In the 1980s, the government reactivated and reasserted its policy of reinforcing and consolidating the role of part-time and temporary workers in the Japanese economy. This time it was a response not so much to labour shortages, but more to the need to enhance the flexibility of the labour market to adjust to structural shifts in the economy and to technological change.

The Employee Dispatching Business Law, which recognises the

legitimacy of temporary workers' dispatching agencies previously prohibited under the provisions of the Employment Security Law, was introduced in June 1985.[1] Together with the recent policy proposals on part-time workers, attempting to consolidate what the employers called an 'intermediate' labour market, this represents the latest policy measures introduced by the government to provide a legal and administrative infrastructure to support the employers' increased pursuit of manpower flexibility (MOL 1987c).[2]

Despite the deterioration of the working conditions of part-time and temporary workers in recent years, neither the Employee Dispatching Business Law, nor the new proposals on part-time workers, include active measures for the protection of their working conditions. The issue of 'harmonisation' of the working conditions between the regular and the non-regular employees is not on the government's policy agenda (Ouwaki 1989; Nakajima 1989).

The Employee Dispatching Business Law and the proposals on part-time workers complement the EEO Law. The EEO Law does not apply so obviously to non-regular workers. It has allowed a loophole for employers to earmark jobs for women only. By consolidating the position of part-time and temporary workers, the present new policies will serve to reinforce the employers' segregation and segmentation policy. The proportion of women workers who are outside the scope of the EEO Law has expanded rapidly in recent years and will continue to expand.

The underlying ideology of government policies on women workers has always emphasised 'harmonisation of work and family', rather than questioning the prevailing assumption that a woman's primary role is that of housewife and mother. Under the government's recent 'administrative reform', the childcare budget was severely cut (JFWA 1987: 161–4; Hiroki 1988).[3] The number of public childcare facilities has declined since the mid-1980s. In the face of an impending ageing society, the government has put forward a 'Japanese-style welfare policy' which encourages 'self-help' and emphasises the importance of the traditional family foundation in supporting the aged (Takenaka 1983: 240–2; Hayashi 1986: 22–3). The traditional family ideology and the importance of the role of women as housewife and carer was recently reasserted in a government document entitled 'Perfecting the Foundation of the Family'. It put forward a priority policy to establish a new national holiday called 'Family Day' to acknowledge the housework and childcare performed by housewives. Further, recent reforms in taxation policy introduce extra tax benefits for women who are full-time housewives and those working part-time.[4] All these policies serve to endorse the traditional family ideology and constitute one of the greatest constraints inhibiting women's full integration in the labour market.

Sexual division of labour in the domestic sphere has a profound impact on women's work attitudes and their labour supply pattern. This would seem in part to explain why the EEO Law does not appear to have raised women's 'career consciousness'. In 1979, 20 per cent of Japanese women desired to pursue a continuous career even after marriage or childbirth. The figure dropped to 16 per cent in 1987 and down further to 14.4 per cent in 1989 (PMO 1979, 1987 and 1989). The author's interviews and survey results at Seibu also reflect this trend. This does not necessarily mean that Japanese women have become more 'conservative', as often lately pointed out by the Japanese mass media, but rather that the equality debate and the EEO Law have made women more aware of the practical constraints they are likely to encounter if they want to pursue a continuous career pattern similar to men. More women have chosen to adopt a pragmatic strategy, making a compromise between family and work. The proportion of women who prefer to adopt a two-phase work profile – retire from work when they have families and re-enter the labour market when their children have grown up – has increased from 39 per cent in 1979, 52 per cent in 1987 and 64.2 per cent in 1989 (ibid). This implies that the 'M-shaped curve' of Japanese women's labour force participation pattern will persist.

Employers will continue to design their labour force strategy by taking into account women's labour supply pattern, utilising them as a cheap workforce when they are young and employing them as part-time or temporary workers when they are middle-aged.

Social conservatism and 'market rationality' are the dominant forces shaping government policies on women. The national aggressive pursuit of economic growth since the mid-1950s, and the supposed virtues of the traditional familial ideology which defines the primary role of women as housewives and mothers have shaped the form and direction of state policies on women workers. By adopting a labour policy which helps to consolidate the formation of a secondary labour market on the one hand, and by reasserting the familial ideology in its recent family and welfare policies, on the other, the government is significantly responsible for the meagre improvement in the situation of women workers.

WOMEN'S CONSCIOUSNESS: AN OBSTACLE TO CHANGE?

Our study at Seibu shows little evidence that women have become more career conscious and prepared to demand better career opportunities. Does this indicate that equal opportunities are not desired by the majority of Japanese women? Or is it that there is a lack of awareness of the need for change? Opponents of equal opportunities for women in Japan often use the following observations to argue against the introduction of more drastic policy changes. First, improved career opportunities do not always seem attractive to women and second, Japanese women themselves endorse the sex role ideology and their psychological identity with the traditional feminine role renders external action ineffective. These observations are not entirely inaccurate but they should not necessarily be used as a guide for policy.

What deserves more consideration is why the majority of Japanese women are not prepared to accept the type of 'equal opportunities' offered by their employers. Under the present employment system, women who desire equal opportunities are asked to accept and conform to the male working norm which requires them to accept the mobility requirements in a very rigid way, to work excessive overtime as a sign of commitment to the company and to ensure that the occupational sphere remains aloof from the domestic sphere. All these practical constraints have made any expectation for career advancement unrealistic for the majority of women. Government surveys on Japanese women's attitudes often seem to confirm the view that women themselves appear to continue to endorse their familial roles (PMO 1984 and 1987).[5] However, many women may conform to the traditional role expectations not because they believe this to be right, but rather because there seems no worthwhile alternative.

Nevertheless, it is true that compared to their counterparts in western countries, Japanese women have been slow in developing their equality consciousness for equal rights. Experience in the United States and the United Kingdom suggests that active intervention by the government in the provision of equal opportunities policies for women was largely a result of political campaigning and lobbying by women's pressure groups (Meehan 1985). In Japan, women's pressure groups have not consolidated as a major social force to exert pressures on the government to intervene more actively in equal opportunity issues. The women's voice was almost unheard in the process of drafting the EEO Law. Two factors might have contributed to this. First, from the historical point of view, Japanese women's liberation from the bondage of the feudal society came only after World War II, as a result of the democratisation policies introduced by the Occupation. The original impetus for change did not come from grassroots social forces inside Japan. Second, the extreme degree of 'sex role specialisation' in Japanese society and the structural embeddedness of sex roles means that Japanese women are more rigidly bound by the social norms and structures than their counterparts in the more individualistic western societies (Lebra 1984: 301).

Until very recently, Japanese women have rarely expressed their discontent in the form of public protest. This apparent 'lack of demand' for change should not be taken as an indication that Japanese women are content with their lot and that changes are not desired by them. Our study at Seibu shows that the recent equality debates and the EEO Law have had an impact on the attitudes of the younger generation. The growing uncertainty and the greater ambivalence of the younger women towards their career future is a sign of change. The perceived tension between the value of sex equality, as symbolised by the EEO Law, and the familial ideology which continues to demand that women conform to the traditional 'housewife role', may in the long run generate greater discontent among the younger generation which believes that the new legislation is gradually opening up more career opportunities for them. In the past, women who were discontent with their treatment in the occupational sphere tended to 'retreat' into the family where the 'housewife role' could guarantee some compensatory fulfilment. However, the social picture has been changing fast and there are signs that even fulfilment from the 'housewife role' for Japanese women is crumbling rapidly as a result of the externalisation of many traditional family functions (Meguro 1980; Lebra 1984). More Japanese women are seeking fulfilment outside the domestic sphere and the continual exclusion of them from the occupational sphere may lead to growing discontent, especially among the highly-educated younger generation.

THEORETICAL AND POLICY IMPLICATIONS

This book has presented a detailed study of how major Japanese companies have adapted their employment policies and practices in response to the growing pressures for a more egalitarian treatment of women. The analysis indicates that the policy changes have had very limited positive effects on women's job positions. Although the EEO Law has helped to eliminate many of the formal written rules which discriminate against women directly, many substitute rules are written with sexual differentiation in mind and continue to discriminate indirectly against women. The study shows that unequal treatment of women, once built into the structural differences in the workplace, tends to perpetuate and reproduce itself through the operation of the seemingly 'sex blind' labour market rules and company practices. Institutional discrimination has maintained and perpetuated the structure of sexual inequality in the Japanese employment system. Major Japanese companies have been able to preserve and maintain the stability of the core employment practices governing the male-dominated internal labour markets in the face of growing pressure for change. A number of strategies have been adopted to absorb and dilute the 'destabilising effects' of equal opportunities. The career tracking systems have been designed to co-opt a small number of highly-educated women with strong career aspirations and, at the same time, to prevent the EEO Law from inflating the expectations of all women. Another important strategy has been the introduction of more clear-cut formal segregation at the point of entry. Many jobs which were previously carried out by women in the lower tier of the internal labour market have been externalised and become contract or temporary jobs. The 'contract employee system' adopted by Seibu is a good example of this new strategy of segmentation.

Japanese management's continued attachment to the 'traditional' employment practices, especially the pattern of 'lifetime commitment', imposes a powerful constraint on their willingness to introduce more liberal equal opportunities policies for women. Even a leading-edge company like Seibu, which has a reputation for its innovative equal opportunities policies, has not been able to introduce more path-breaking policy changes. The nature of the constraint is not only that women do not seem to possess the requisite behavioural traits such as employment stability or a strong commitment to intense work, but more importantly, that the smooth operation of the system requires a large number of women to be available as low cost peripheral workers. Full equal employment opportunities for women will not only destabilise the male career hierarchy and the established work practices, but will also upset the flexibility of the employment system.

One question remains unresolved: Why is it that Japanese management is able to preserve the male-dominated employment system despite the economic and legal pressures for change? In other words, why has the special form of internal labour markets continued to prosper in the way it has in Japan? This question is closely related to the recurrent debate about the origin and the nature of the Japanese employment system. It is a question which has preoccupied many Japanese and foreign scholars since Abegglen's pioneering study in 1958 first identified the Japanese employment system, characterised by the peculiar features of lifetime commitment and *nenko*-based wage and promotion, as distinctively different from the systems prevailing in western countries. Since then, a remarkable number of books and articles have been published on the subject. Broadly speaking, the various interpretations can be classified into two different approaches, namely the culturalist and the economic functionalist. Those adopting the culturalist approach (Abegglen 1958; Hazama 1971 and 1982) argue that the distinctive features of the Japanese employment system are a consistent and logical outgrowth of Japan's pre-industrial social organisation and have evolved from cultural values basic to the Japanese people. Abegglen (1958: 135) argues that 'the hard core of Japan's system of social relationships remained intact' in the face of rapid industrialisation. Hazama stresses the importance of social values such as 'groupism' as the driving force behind the peculiar features of Japanese management. In other words, these authors emphasise the role of social and cultural continuity carried over from Japan's pre-industrial past into contemporary industrial organisations.

Economic functionalists offer a different interpretation. Taira (1970) argues that Japanese labour market institutions and practices are basically the consequence of optimal economic choices of employers and workers given the labour market conditions prevailing during industrialisation. He presented historical evidence that the practices of lifetime commitment and the *nenko* wage system emerged as late as World War I as a reaction of employers in major firms in their attempts to cope with chronic shortage of skilled workers and their high labour turnover rates. Using neo-classical economic analysis, Taira purported to show that the peculiar character of the Japanese employment system is less a carry-over from feudal society than the result of an economic choice by employers.

How would the two different perspectives explain the origin and the perpetuation of labour market discrimination against women? Culturalists would say that it is a persistence of social discrimination against women. As the Japanese employment practices were modelled on the basis of the principles that regulated family life (the *ie* system) in feudal Japan, it was accepted as normal that only the male members were rewarded with permanent tenure and the benefits of the system. The exclusion of women reflected the inferior social conditions of women in feudal Japan and this has persisted into contemporary Japan. Many economists would argue that sociological forces such as 'culture' or 'tradition' have little role to play in a competitive market economy. Discrimination against women is no more than a by-product of the labour market rules and employment practices which represent the optimal economic choices made by employers. Discrimination has persisted because it is economically functional.

Our analysis of the changes in the 1980s illustrates that both of these general interpretations are too simplistic. The survival of the special type of internal labour markets in Japan and the persistence of discrimination against women cannot be fully understood from the viewpoint of efficiency-based economic theories. Nor is it adequate to interpret the contemporary situation as 'cultural continuity' in Abegglen's sense which sees 'culture' as a static historical phenomenon. One needs to develop a better understanding of how new employment practices and labour market rules become institutionalised and how 'culture' or 'tradition' are utilised as 'resources' and at times perceived as 'constraints' by the dominant parties – in the case of Japan, management – in the process of responding to the emerging economic and labour utilisation problems. Cole (1979: 22–3) has argued that 'no matter how innovative new institutions may appear, they do not develop in a cultural and structural vacuum . . . . It is the availability of these resources and the possible combinations among them which determines the mix in the emerging process of institutionalisation.'

Economic and sociological forces are not independent of each other. An important insight to be gained from the internal labour market concept developed by Doeringer and Piore (1971) is that sociological forces can influence labour market institutions and behaviour. Doeringer and Piore emphasise the important role of workplace custom in sustaining internal labour market rules and perpetuating discriminatory practices. Doeringer and Piore define 'custom' as the outgrowth of employment stability in the internal labour market. Implicit in their model is the assumption that discrimination is an incidental consequence of internal labour market rules designed for efficiency purposes. The Japanese experience suggests that it is necessary to develop this line of argument further in order to explain fully the survival of the Japanese type of internal labour markets and the nature of continued discrimination against women. Three major points are worthy of special note.

First, discrimination against women cannot be interpreted merely as an incidental by-product of 'neutral' internal labour market rules designed for efficiency purposes. Our analysis of Japanese management's adaptive strategies in the 1980s illustrates that gendered assumptions have been important factors in shaping and determining many of the employment practices introduced by management. Many of the company practices are designed with the traditional sex role model in mind. Japanese companies can continue to operate many of the discriminatory practices because (they assume that) the majority of women continue to accept their conditions. Moreover, the dominant role of management in Japanese society implies that they have a 'free hand' in shaping the new labour market rules and practices. Management has continued to exploit the cultural repression of women as a 'resource' in the institutionalisation of new employment practices. The persistence of discrimination against women needs to be interpreted in the socio-political context that Japanese management has a dominant political role in the society and that Japan is still fundamentally a male-dominated society. Power and status issues are relevant in understanding the formation of many of the company practices which operate on the basis of dis-crimination against women. The mass utilisation of the rural-based unmarried women as transient low cost labour in the textile industry before World War I is an example of the employers' strategic policies in exploiting the most subordinated members of the society. At that time women constituted the majority of the industrial workforce partly because industrial jobs had the lowest status in the society. In developing and consolidating the internal labour markets in the core sector of the Japanese economy after World War II, employers have consciously transformed sexual differentiation into structural differences in the workplace. Once such sex-based stratification is institutionalised in the employment practices, the perpetuation of discrimination against women becomes reinforced by the nature of the workplace relationship. In the 1980s and 1990s, the institutionalisation of many new employment practices continues to discriminate against the majority of women. In this study, we have seen that Japanese employers have, in designing their strategies to cope with the emerging economic and technological demands, consciously exploited women's social conditions and used them as a source of cheap labour. Discrimination cannot be interpreted as an incidental by-product of 'sex blind' labour market rules.

Second, Doeringer and Piore explain the survival and stability of internal labour markets and the issue of discrimination entirely in terms of the internal logic of the core workforce. The Japanese case has demonstrated that one cannot explain the dynamism of internal labour markets and discrimination entirely in terms of factors internal to the core workforce. The relationship between the 'core' and the 'periphery' is crucial. Changes affecting the peripheral groups can be critical to the survival of the internal labour markets for the core groups. The Seibu case illustrates that the continued stability of the rules governing the internal core workforce is dependent on the continued acceptance by the 'periphery' of their conditions. This explains why Seibu management has been anxious not to disturb the delicate balance of the relationship between the 'core' and the 'periphery'. This has imposed a severe constraint on Seibu's equal opportunities policies for women.

Third, Doeringer and Piore's model is inherently static and so does not provide a satisfactory explanation of how internal labour market rules might change over time. At the heart of Doeringer and Piore's argument is the observation that internal labour market rules persist because they are economically functional. Although their model emphasises the important role of workplace custom in sustaining inefficient rules and practices, they argue that the ultimate sanction against custom is economic failure. Thus they assume, as a matter of faith, that internal labour markets survive because they are economically functional. Their model implicitly assumes that 'mature' internal labour markets tend to persist and so does the structure of discrimination. However, the Japanese experience suggests that internal labour market rules do change and that the persistence of specific forms cannot be taken for granted. The Japanese type of internal labour markets has persisted because management has actively sought to protect its stability and because those who are excluded from the privileged jobs appear to continue to accept their exclusion. Nevertheless, in the face of economic changes and the growing pressures for equal opportunities, Japanese companies have had to introduce some changes in some of their rules and practices in order to protect the stability of the internal labour market: for example, by allowing a small minority of women to enter the core career jobs and by redefining the boundary of the core system through changes to the entry rules. As already pointed out in the previous chapter, the new practices introduced by Seibu have caused some instability in the company's personnel system. How far the present system at Seibu will continue depends not only on the intensity of market competition, but also on whether Japanese women will continue to accept the male-dominated system and how far the legal environment will continue to allow management a 'free hand' in structuring their workforce on the basis of gender differentiation. The present EEO Law has introduced some elements of potential instability in the employment system, but it does not have enough power to obstruct employers' sex-based workforce segmentation strategies.

In sum, this study shows the depth of resistance to change in the core employment practices governing the Japanese internal labour market. It also cautions against having too high expectations of management-initiated change programmes in bringing about true equal opportunities for women. If the present labour market trends are to continue, it is unlikely that there will be a major shift towards equal employment for Japanese women. If further improvement of Japanese women's labour market position is to be made possible and the norms and standards of equal opportunities in Japanese companies to be raised up to the commonly accepted 'western' standard, major legal reforms and stronger policy interventions are necessary. The problem of indirect discrimination must be dealt with. Career tracking rules and promotion procedures which obviously result in the exclusion of women must be scrutinised and less exclusionary alternative practices negotiated. The problem of women's increased segregation in part-time and contract jobs must be tackled if women's overall job status is to be improved. A long-term strategy for change will, of course, require the development of comprehensive policy measures in a wide variety of arenas, both inside and outside the sphere of employment, to bring about a gradual shift in social attitudes and a redefinition of sex roles in Japanese society.

The EEO Law represents the beginning of a willingness on the part of the government to step in and steer the course of change in women's employment conditions. However, the law will only be relevant if its spirit is effectively implemented through compulsion and voluntary action in parallel. In Japan, the existence of a skilled and dedicated governing bureaucracy which has a long history of active intervention in social and economic matters can be both a strength and a weakness, depending on how far the government is prepared to steer changes in a direction which is favourable to the majority of women.

One major lesson that Japanese women can learn from their counterparts in the West is that grassroots lobbying and political campaigns from women themselves are important means for propelling equal opportunity issues to the top of the political agenda (Meehan 1985). Unless there are stronger political pressures from Japanese women themselves to campaign for more active state intervention in both the economic and social spheres, the future of equal employment for Japanese women is unlikely to progress beyond its present limit. If Japanese women are to achieve full and real equality, it cannot be on men's terms. The male work norm will have to be changed and the Japanese management system will need to be challenged.

Appendix A

Field study methods and the survey samples

GETTING TO KNOW THE ORGANISATION

The first stage of the study was to acquire information about the company – its history, organisational structure, management philosophy and personnel system. These data were acquired from company documents such as annual reports, company newsletters, personnel records and the company union newsletters. During the first three months, numerous interviews and discussions, both formal and informal, were carried out with several senior members of the personnel department, including the personnel director (*jinji bucho*) at the head office and the personnel manager (*jinji kacho*) of the flagship store who were the key contact persons for the study. Often, by merely reading company documents, it was not clear why at a particular time certain new policies were introduced. The interviews and discussions with management gave a better insight into the underlying causes and processes of organisational change.

The fact that I was put into contact with the personnel director at the head office through a senior board member proved to be a very important asset throughout the various stages of the research. This not only enhanced my credibility, but also ensured smooth collaboration from staff at all levels. I was able to obtain internal company data which would not otherwise have been available to an 'outsider'. Apart from the 'credibility factor', establishing good personal relationships with the staff is also an important factor for carrying out research in Japanese companies. Throughout the various stages of the research, I built up a good network of contacts at the company from senior management to shop assistants. This greatly facilitated the research process and most important of all, informal discussions with these staff helped to improve the quality of the data obtained and made it possible to acquire an 'insider's view' of the company's situation.

GETTING TO KNOW SEIBU WOMEN

In the winter of 1983, in-depth individual interviews were carried out with thirty-four women employees at the Ikebukuro and Shibuya stores. The interviews were conducted partly as a pilot study for the questionnaire survey and partly as a means of acquiring in-depth qualitative information on the attitudes and working life of women at Seibu. The interviews were based on a semi-structured questionnaire with fifty open questions. The questions touched upon almost all aspects of the women's working life including their motives for working, reasons for joining Seibu, their attitudes to career development and to the company's policies on women, their consciousness of sex equality issues and their views on the relationship between work and family. Each interview lasted for an average of about sixty to seventy-five minutes.

The women interviewed were chosen by the staff in the personnel department, some were introduced by the women already interviewed. The majority of them were regarded as capable and having a promising career. A high proportion of them were graduates. This was because the company believed that equal opportunity had more to do with highly-educated women, and it expected these women to be more equality conscious and hence be prepared to discuss the issues in the interviews. Thus, the thirty-four women can be said to be a specially selected group of 'elite women'. Nevertheless, the sample included an appropriate mix of women with different educational levels and of different ages (see table A.1).

PARTICIPATION OBSERVATION

As a preliminary step to the questionnaire survey, a one-month period of participant observation was carried out. During that period I worked as a shop assistant in four different sales sections at the flagship store. The objective was to get to know the day-to-day work activities of the women employees and to become familiar with the culture of the company. The informal interviews and discussions with women on the sales floor contributed greatly to the construction of a meaningful and relevant questionnaire. Moreover, I was able to establish a network of contacts with the women who

Table A.1 The interview sample

Characteristics		Numbers interviewed	
		1983	1987
Age	Under 29	14	4
	30 – 39	16	11.5)
	40+	4	6
	(Average age)	(31.5)	(35.2)
Education	University	17	9.5)
	Junior college	8	7.5)
	High school	9	5.5)
Position in company	Ordinary employee	19	3.5)
	Specialis	11	16.5)
	Management	4	2.5)
Marriage	Single	28	16.5)
	Married	5	4.5)
	Separated	1	1.5)
Total number interviewed		34	21.5)

assisted the subsequent stages of the research. The contacts proved to be of great value when I returned to the company four years later – it was through these contacts that I was able to track down some of the women for the follow-up interviews.

QUESTIONNAIRE SURVEY

The company's new personnel policies on women cannot be meaningfully interpreted and their implications cannot be evaluated without looking at the attitudes and the career experience of the female employees, in particular their work attitudes and career experience as compared with their male counterparts. A questionnaire survey on approximately 1,100 employees (400 males and 700 females) was conducted in March 1984. The proportion of male and female full-time regular employees at Seibu at that time was about equal. However, we deliberately increased the proportion of women in our sample in order to have a reasonably large sub-sample of female graduates to allow comparison with their male counterparts (in 1984, female university graduates constituted 14.5 per cent of the total company female workforce, while 59.2 per cent of the male workforce were graduates).

The questionnaire survey obtained information on the respondents' personal characteristics, job position and status, career development experience including training and job rotation, their work attitudes, career aspirations and perception of sexual equality in the workplace.

The questionnaires were administered at the Ikebukuro flagship store and the Shibuya store. The sample was randomly selected from the male and female full-time regular employees. The questionnaires were distributed and collected through the personnel department of the stores. A total of 1,071 questionnaires were distributed and 879 were completed and returned, resulting in a response rate of 82 per cent (see later for more details about the samples).

THE FOLLOW-UP STUDY IN 1987–88

The follow-up study was carried out with the specific objective of finding out whether the EEO Law had made any difference to the company's policies and how it had affected the position and attitudes of the women employees. In the summer of 1987, follow-up interviews with the women first interviewed in 1983 were carried out. Out of the thirty-four women first interviewed in 1983, nine had left the company and four were not available at the time, resulting in a total of twenty-one women taking part in the follow-up interviews. In addition, four women who had joined the company after the EEO Law was introduced were also interviewed. Numerous informal discussions were carried out with the personnel staff at the head office and the flagship store.

The follow-up interviews proved to be very useful. They made it possible to examine the changes in the women's careers and the shifts in their perceptions and attitudes. Most important of all, face-to-face discussion with these women employees provided crucial information for assessing the validity of the claimed policy changes made by the management.

In the summer of 1988, a follow-up questionnaire survey on 800 male and female regular employees was administered at the same stores where the initial survey was conducted. A total of 800 questionnaires were distributed, of which 685 were completed and returned, resulting in a response rate of 85.6 per cent

The 1988 survey replicated the questionnaire used in 1984, with some minor modifications. It was not a follow-up study of the same individuals who took part in the 1984 survey as such. Some individuals might have taken part in both surveys but this could not be identified due to the anonymity of the respondents.

SAMPLE SELECTION METHODS AND SAMPLE SIZE

In both the 1984 and 1988 surveys, the male and female samples were drawn from the full-time regular employees, excluding senior executives, at the Ikebukuro and Shibuya stores. The employees at the two stores were treated as one single sampling population. The sampling population was divided into the male and female sampling frames and the samples were drawn randomly from the employee code numbers provided by the personnel department.

In the 1984 survey, the male sample size was 25 per cent of the male population and the corresponding figure for the female sample was 35 per cent. In the 1988 survey, the male sample size constituted 20 per cent of the male population. For women, a disproportionate stratified random sampling method was used. The female population was stratified into three groups according to their educational levels, namely, university graduates, junior college graduates and high school leavers, with the sample fractions for the three groups of women at 50 per cent, 40 per cent and 30 per cent respectively. The reason for varying the sample fractions in reverse proportion to the actual distribution of the female employees by educational levels was to ensure that the survey sample would provide a sufficient number of female university graduates as a sub-sample for statistical analysis. In 1988, female graduates constituted about 20 per cent of the female regular employees at Seibu as compared with 63 per cent in the case of men. All the statistical analysis of the female responses as an overall sample was weighted by the sample fraction.

Table A.2 shows the size of the sample population, the samples selected and the number of responses for the 1984 and 1988 surveys. The sample population figures for 1984 as shown in the table differ slightly from the actual numbers of the sampling frames as the figures shown in the table were obtained from the company's personnel records at the end of 1983 and the samples were drawn in March 1984.

Table A.2 Sample population, sample size and response rates

(a) 1984

	Sample population (persons)	Sample fraction %	Sample size (persons)	No. of responses (persons)	Response rate %
Male	1,526	25	386	327	84.7
Female	1,879	35	688	552	80.2
Total	3,405		1,074	879	81.8

(b) 1988

	Sample population (persons)	Sample fraction %	Sample size (persons)	No. of responses (persons)	Response rate %
Male	1,323	20	265	218	82.3
Female					
University	280	50	140	127	90.7
Junior college	497	40	199	165	82.9
High school	654	30	196	175	89.3
Others	–	–	–	3	
Sub-total	1,431		535	470	87.8
Total	2,754		800	688	86.0

CHARACTERISTICS OF THE SAMPLES

Table A.3 shows the composition of the 1984 and 1988 samples by age, length of service, educational levels, marital status and entry to the company. The characteristics of the samples have not changed a great deal between 1984 and 1988. Nevertheless, the 1988 sample was slightly older, had been with Seibu longer and was more highly educated.

Table A.3 Characteristics of the samples (regular full-time employees)

| | 1984 | | | | 1988 | | | |
| | Male | | Female | | Male | | Female | |
	No.	%	No.	%	No.	%	No.	%
Age								
Under 24	35	(10.7)	240	(43.6)	13	(6.0)	149	(32.0)
25 – 29	104	(31.9)	154	(27.9)	53	(24.3)	143	(30.7)
30 – 34	83	(25.5)	69	(12.5)	45	(20.6)	58	(12.4)
35 – 39	53	(16.3)	43	(7.8)	47	(21.6)	41	(8.9)
40 – 44	24	(7.4)	16	(2.9)	27	(12.4)	27	(5.8)
45 – 49	17	(5.2)	18	(3.3)	13	(6.0)	19	(4.2)
50 and above	10	(3.1)	11	(2.0)	20	(9.2)	28	(6.0)
Length of service								
0 – 4 yrs	109	(34.1)	308	(56.0)	50	(24.6)	179	(38.6)
5 – 9	63	(19.7)	145	(26.4)	70	(34.5)	159	(34.3)
10–14	81	(25.3)	48	(8.7)	23	(11.3)	61	(13.2)
15–19	45	(14.0)	27	(4.9)	37	(18.2)	27	(5.8)
> 20	22	(6.9)	22	(4.0)	23	(11.3)	38	(8.1)
Education								
High school	122	(37.3)	291	(52.7)	70	(32.1)	218	(46.4)
Junior college	14	(4.3)	153	(27.7)	13	(6.0)	154	(32.8)
University	184	(56.3)	104	(18.8)	129	(59.2)	95	(20.2)
Others	7	(2.1)	4	(0.7)	6	(2.7)	3	(0.6)
Marital status								
Single	130	(39.9)	465	(84.2)	79	(36.2)	352	(75.4)
Married	195	(59.8)	73	(13.2)	137	(62.8)	93	(19.9)
Separated	1	(0.3)	14	(2.5)	2	(0.9)	22	(4.7)
Entry								
Fresh graduate	202	(61.8)	402	(73.0)	146	(67.3)	332	(71.2)
Mid-career	125	(38.2)	149	(27.0)	71	(32.7)	135	(28.8)
Total (N)	327	(100.0)	552	(100.0)	218	(100.0)	470	(100.0)
(Population)	(1,526)		(1,879)		(1,323)		(1,431)	

Note: As missing observations (no responses) are excluded from the computation, the total number of male and female sample in each category may not be precisely the same as the total sample (N) indicated at the bottom of the table.

1 *Age structure:* The share of those aged under 24 had declined. This is especially the case of the female sample which reflects the reduction of employment of new recruits as full-time regular employees since the early 1980s. The relative share of men aged 35–39 and above had shown a remarkable increase. In the case of women, there is no increase in the share of those aged 30–34 and only a mere one percentage point increase of those aged 35–39. This implies that there had been little change in the retention rate of women in their child-rearing years. The relative share of women aged 40 and above, similar to that of men, had almost doubled between 1984 and 1988.

2 *Length of service:* The average length of service of both the male and female samples had gone up. For men, it was 9.0 years in 1984 and 10.7 years in 1988 and for women it extended from 5.9 years to 7.8 years.

3 *Education:* The overall educational level of the sample in 1988 was higher than that of 1984; the proportion of high school leavers had declined while that of university graduates had crept up.

4 *Marital status:* In both the 1984 and 1988 samples, the majority of women were single while about two-thirds of men were married. But the proportion of single women had declined over time and those who were married or separated had increased.

5 *Entry to the company:* The majority of the male and female employees joined the company directly after their school or university education. At both points in time, the share of male mid-career entrants was higher than that of women. However, the relative share of male mid-career entrants had declined over time while that of women had remained more or less unchanged.

Appendix B

ANOVA and multiple classification analysis

Multiple classification analysis (MCA) results can be requested from the ANOVA procedure in the SPSSx processes. The MCA output consists of the grand mean of the dependent variable and a table of category means for each factor expressed as deviations from the grand mean. The category means expressed as deviation convey the magnitude of the effect of each category (e.g., age groups) within a factor (e.g., age).

In an MCA table, deviation values are presented in three forms: unadjusted; adjusted for main effects of other factors; and adjusted for main effects of other factors and co-variates, if applicable. The adjusted values show the effect of a certain category within a given factor after variation due to other factors, and sometimes other co-variates, has been taken into account.

The MCA table contains several measures of association. First, a correlation ratio, the *eta* statistic, is associated with the set of unadjusted category effects for each factor in the MCA table; the square of *eta* indicates the proportion of variance explained by a given factor (all categories considered). *Beta* is a statistic associated with the adjusted category effects for each factor. More specifically, *beta* is a standardised regression coefficient in the sense used in multiple regression. Finally, multiple R appears at the bottom of the MCA table. Just as in multiple regression, the multiple R squared appearing at the bottom of the MCA table indicates the variance in the dependent variable 'accounted for' by all factors, co-variates and factor-by-factor interaction terms (see *SPSSx User's Guide*, chapter 26, McGraw-Hill, 1983).

The MCA results from the analysis of variance on the employees' job status in chapter 9 are presented in Tables B.1 and B.2.

Table B.1 Multiple classification analysis (1984 data)

Dependent variable: Job status (grade group)
Grand mean = 1.77

Variable + category	N	Unadjusted Dev'n	Eta	Adjusted for independents Dev'n	Beta
Age					
1 Under 24	273	−0.77		−0.35	
2 25–29	256	−0.29		−0.26	
3 30–34	151	0.56		0.33	
4 35–39	92	1.01		0.60	
5 40–44	35	1.20		0.63	
6 45–49	32	1.29		0.68	
7 50–54	14	1.51		0.92	
8 Above 55	3	0.89		0.43	
			0.84		0.47
Length of service					
1 0–1 year	108	−0.74		−0.43	
2 2–3	215	−0.67		−0.37	
3 4–5	168	−0.17		−0.05	
4 6–7	72	−0.07		0.01	
5 8–9	59	0.29		0.25	
6 10–15	142	0.83		0.39	
7 16–20	58	1.21		0.60	
8 Above 21	34	1.52		0.85	
			0.81		0.43
Education					
1 High school	406	0.10		−0.05	
2 Junior college	166	−0.24		−0.03	
3 University	284	−0.00		0.10	
			0.14		0.08
Sex					
1 Male	314	0.52		0.21	
2 Female	542	−0.03		−0.12	
			0.45		0.18
Multiple R squared					0.81
Multiple R					0.91

Table B.2 Multiple classification analysis (1988 data)

Dependent variable: Job status (grade group)
Grand mean = 2.11

Variable + category	N	Unadjusted Dev'n	Eta	Adjusted for independents Dev'n	Beta
Age					
1 Under 24	162	−1.06		−0.68	
2 25–29	194	−0.24		−0.16	
3 30–34	102	0.28		0.15	
4 35–39	88	0.76		0.50	
5 40–44	52	1.01		0.66	
6 45–49	29	1.16		0.86	
7 50–54	33	0.88		0.55	
8 Above 55	12	0.59		0.26	
			0.83		0.54
Length of service					
1 0–1 year	92	−0.93		−0.39	
2 2–3	92	−0.63		−0.20	
3 4–5	95	−0.44		−0.15	
4 6–7	90	−0.03		−0.01	
5 8–9	84	0.16		0.06	
6 10–15	99	0.51		0.18	
7 16–20	68	1.88		0.27	
8 Above 21	53	1.17		0.56	
			0.73		0.29
Education					
1 High school	285	0.09		−0.07	
2 Junior college	166	−0.31		−0.01	
3 University	221	0.11		0.01	
			0.20		0.08
Sex					
1 Male	209	0.62		0.29	
2 Female	464	−0.28		−0.13	
			0.46		0.22
Multiple R squared					0.75
Multiple R					0.87

Notes

1 Introduction and background

1   The concept of an internal labour market refers to the existence of a set of rules and procedures governing labour allocation and relative wages within the firm. It is distinguished from an external labour market whereby labour allocation and wages are governed by market forces. An internal labour market stresses the primacy of career progression within the firm and the importance of employment continuity. Firms with well-established internal labour markets often have rigid rules and requirements governing entry, confining external recruitment to certain recognised 'ports of entry'. A more detailed explanation of the concept is provided in chapter 2.

2   The poor working conditions of wage workers in the Meiji period are well documented in the following two publications: *Shokko Jijo* (Conditions of Workers), published in 1903 by the *Noshomusho* (The Ministry of Agriculture and Commerce); and *Nihon no Kaso-shakai* (Lower-Class People of Japan), written by Gennosuke Yokoyama in 1899.

3   From the Tokugawa period until the end of World War II, the Japanese family system was governed by the concept of *ie* (home or family), which followed the samurai ideal and was legally recognised in the Meiji Civil Code. The major function of the *ie* was to preserve the family from generation to generation. The household head, invariably a male, was the link between the generations and it was usually the eldest son who succeeded to the headship. The family head was the ultimate authority in all family decisions. The position of women was extremely low in the traditional *ie* system. They could neither conduct ancestral rites nor were they permitted to play a public role in society (Lebra *et al.* 1976: 13–14; Hendry 1987: 21–9).

4   The labour force participation rate of Japanese women is higher than that of several western European countries such as France (45.8 per cent in 1987), West Germany (42.0 per cent in 1986), and Italy (35.0 per cent in 1987) (ILO, *Year Book of Labour Statistics*).

5   A high proportion of women still go to two-year junior colleges (*Tanki-daigaku*). In 1990, 22.2 per cent of female high school leavers went

to junior colleges and 15.2 per cent attended four-year university degree courses. In comparison, 33.4 per cent of male high school leavers attended four-year university degree courses and only a negligible 1.7 per cent went to two-year junior colleges.

3 Sexual inequality in the Japanese employment system: discriminatory company practices

1   The Japanese legislation on equal pay differs from that in western countries. Article 4 of the Labour Standards Law merely states that 'The employer shall not discriminate women against men concerning wages by reason of the worker being a woman'. There is no specification in the law concerning the precise meaning of 'equal work'. Unlike legislation in many western countries where the meaning of 'equal work' and the criteria for comparing work are usually clearly spelled out, the term 'equal work' is not even mentioned in the Japanese legislative text.

2   The Basic Survey of Wage Structure (*Chingin Kozo Kihon Tokei Chosa*) provides data on ninety-nine male occupations and forty female occupations. Comparison between male and female wages in these occupations is difficult because only eighteen of the occupations covered in the survey present male and female wage data. This reflects the extent to which male and female jobs are segregated.

3   Kawashima found that the male and female workforce were not evenly distributed in different sectors of the labour market. In her study, she makes a distinction between the labour market in the concentrated sector (or the non-competitive sector) and the labour market in the competitive sector. The two economic sectors are defined according to the degree of concentration of market power. The two sectors differ in terms of labour characteristics, employment patterns and wage structures. Her study found a significant difference in the distribution of men and women between the sectors. Men were equally distributed between the two sectors (50.1 per cent in the competitive sector and 49.9 per cent in the concentrated sector); in contrast, a high proportion of women were found in the competitive sector (64 per cent compared with 36 per cent in the concentrated sector). A more striking phenomenon is that women with university education were almost excluded from the concentrated sector; only 18.7 per cent of them worked in the concentrated sector, in contrast to 81.3 per cent in the competitive sector. Their male counterparts were distributed 60.5 per cent in the competitive sector and 39.5 per cent in the concentrated sector. According to Kawashima, the concentrated sector, particularly large firms which have well-developed internal job hierarchy, avoid hiring women with higher education for jobs connected to higher positions on the promotion ladder. They hire a small number of women with junior college education for clerical or specialised jobs with little chance for promotion. The competitive sector composed of smaller firms offers more job opportunities to women with higher education. Women with higher education face job discrimination against them. Higher education does not increase job opportunities for

them, but on the contrary, places them in a labour surplus market even when labour is generally in short supply (Kawashima 1983).

4 In Britain, for example, the seniority practice was identified as unlawful in the case of Steel v. Union of Post Office Workers (O'Donovan and Szyszczak 1988: 101–2). In the Leeds Permanent Building Society formal investigation case, the Equal Opportunities Commission states that 'the Society might in the future act unlawfully if it believed that seniority was a justifiable criterion for promotion when this would have had a disproportionate impact on women . . . ' (Equal Opportunities Commission 1985: 47).

5 Legislating for change? The Equal Employment Opportunity Law

1 In 1975, the Childcare Leave Act was enacted as a result of persistent demand from working women. The Act enabled women teaching at national and public schools of compulsory education, nurses and day nurses at medicare and social welfare facilities, to take one-year childcare leave for taking care of children aged under one.

2 According to the Labour Ministry Ordinance, 'supervisors or managers' are defined as 'the chief of a minimum unit of organisation which does work, or a person whose position is superior to the chief and who gives directions and orders on work'. As with regard to the scope of professionals and specialists, the ordinance has designated the following fourteen occupations as requiring 'expertise, specialised or technical knowledge': (a) certified accountants, (b) doctors, (c) dentists, (d) veterinarians, (e) lawyers, (f) first-class registered architects, (g) pharmacists, (h) real estate appraisers, (i) those engaged in research which requires sophisticated scientific knowledge at research facilities, (j) those engaged in the analysis or design of information processing systems, (k) those engaged in covering articles of editing at newspaper or publishing companies, (l) those engaged in covering and editing for the production of broadcasting programmes, (m) those engaged in designing apparel and industrial products, interior decorating and advertising; and (n) those engaged in producing or directing in the production of broadcasting programmes and movies (JIL 1986a).

3 Originally the law was entitled 'Danjo Koyo Kikai Byodo Ho'. The word Byodo means equality. At some stage during the debate, the word Byodo was replaced by Kinto which can be translated as 'equalising' or 'progress toward equality'. Some Japanese critics suggest that the change of the title from Byodo to Kinto signifies a compromise of the government to the opponents of the legislation. The present title suggests an effort toward equalising opportunity rather than a commitment to achieve such equality (Edwards 1988: 243).

4 During the drafting stage of the bill, three possible options regarding the form and position of the EEO Law in the Japanese legal system were suggested. It could be: (1) included as part of the Labour Standards Law by introducing 'discrimination on grounds of sex' to section 3, as

suggested by the labour side; (2) an independent new law or (3) joined to the Working Women's Welfare Law. Both the first and the second options were rejected. The EEO Law turned out to be largely a revision of the Working Women's Welfare Law with a number of new measures introduced to eliminate discrimination.

5   According to the guidelines (MOL 1986: 49–52), the following three types of jobs can be treated as exceptions to the equal opportunity requirement. First, where the essential nature of the job calls for a man for reasons of physiology, or where physical strength or stamina is required or other jobs which by nature of religion or customs would require a man. Second, where the normal operation of the job would require working overtime or late at night for which it would be illegal to treat women equally as men because of the requirements of the Labour Standards Law. The Ministry of Labour's interpretation of the 'normal operation of the job' is rather broad. It includes not only the present, but also future jobs. That is, if there are expectations in the future that the job or rotation to other jobs is going to involve overtime or late-night working, employers can limit the recruitment to men only. This gives employers strong discretionary power in restricting a broad categories of jobs to men only because they can argue that these jobs are, in the future, going to involve overtime or late-night working. Third, where the working environment or social situations such as custom and practices of a country would make it difficult for women to realise their abilities. Here, the major reference is to working in foreign countries. This exception can severely limit the recruitment of women to jobs which would require periods of working overseas. Similar to the second category, it includes not only present jobs but also jobs which, in the future, as a result of job rotation, will require overseas assignment.

6   According to Upham, the rule-centred model emphasises the role of rules. It hypothesises a legal system where legal professionals use specialised techniques to find and apply unambiguous rules to clear fact situations independent of external influences. Under the rule-centred model there is a clear differentiation of law from other sources of normative learning, and law eventually supersedes all other state-sponsored forms of conflict resolution. The judge-centred model emphasises the role of judges as political actors and litigation as the forum for broad-based social controversies. Although the assumptions of the judge-centred model lead to greater power for the process of litigation and for the judiciary as an institution, they weaken the independence and insulation enjoyed by the parties in the rule-centred model and render impossible the uniform penetration in society of formal legal norms. Despite the fundamental differences between these two heuristic models, they have one common characteristic: the limited role of the state in litigation. Under the rule-centred model, the legislature provides the legal rules but then loses all the control over the degree and speed of their penetration into social life. Under the judge-centred model, the state is an active party to the decision-making process, but is only one party (Upham 1987: 7–11).

7   This point was made to the author in an interview with Ryoko Akamatsu

who was Director of the Women's Bureau at the Ministry of Labour at the time of the passage of the EEO Law. She pointed out that there was an implicit agreement at the time the law was enacted, that the government was to review the situation in five years' time following the implementation of the law. She also emphasised that future revision of the legislation was to be expected as the EEO Law was a 'developing' piece of legislation.

6 The management response

1   The survey was based on a questionnaire conducted on a random sample of 7,200 firms (with thirty or more employees). In the survey, firms were asked to indicate the extent to which they had introduced changes in personnel procedures and practices in response to the implementation of the EEO Law.

2   In this survey, firms were asked to indicate their utilisation policies on women during the three years before 1985 and for the three years following 1985. The survey covered 6,750 firms with 100 or more employees but only 2,018 firms responded.

3   Companies operating a network of branches over the country such as department stores or supermarket chains tend to use the extent of commitment to the mobility requirement as a main criterion for classifying their employees into different career tracks. For example, Ito Yokado, a major supermarket chain store corporation, has introduced a more sophisticated system of classifying their employees into three different career tracks, namely, 'national employees' (mobile all over the country), 'area employees' (semi-mobile within a certain area or district) and 'store employees' (non-mobile). Each career track has its own grading and career structure among which only the 'national employees' are eligible for promotion to top management.

4   In April 1986, the Ministry of Labour set up a 're-entry subsidy fund' to provide financial incentives for firms to introduce the re-employment system for their female employees. Also in 1988, a 'childcare leave incentive fund' was set up to encourage employers to introduce childcare leave schemes for their female employees.

7 The Seibu case: an introduction

1   Seibu is widely quoted as a pioneering Japanese company in promoting equal opportunities for women. For example *The Economist* (1988) and J. Woronoff (1982: 141). *The Financial Times* (11 July 1988) also described Seibu as a 'pioneer' among Japanese department stores in promoting equal opportunity for women.

2   The Seibu Department Stores Group is part of the larger Seibu Group of Retail Enterprises which changed its name to Saison Group in 1985, symbolising a major restructuring and expansion of the group. Until 1983, the retail group was composed of four divisions: department stores, superstores, real estate/leisure and manufacturing. The group underwent

major restructuring and reorganisation after the mid-1980s, expanding from four to ten sub-groups, aiming at further diversifications in response to changing consumer demands and market environment. All the sub-groups are engaged in related or complementary enterprises. The major activities of the group include: department stores, superstores, real estate/leisure, manufacturing, credit/finance, restaurants/food services, transportation/aero-survey and insurance. In 1986, the group started to implement a 'cross-over system of employment' which allows employees to move between the different sub-groups which make up the Saison Group. The objective is to increase flexibility in manpower redeployment in the face of rapid changes in the retail environment. The group as a whole employed 76,500 people in 1987.

3   The six biggest department stores groups in Japan, besides Seibu, are Mitsukoshi, Daimaru, Takashimaya, Matsuzakaya and Isetan.

4   This phenomenon is not unique to Japan. Studies in the United States also suggest that department stores should adapt their retailing strategies to the changing perceptions, values and needs of women (Hunt et al. 1981; Joyce and Guiltman 1978).

5   In the early 1980s, department stores in the major cities reported difficulties in recruiting 'good saleswomen' due to the growing competition from the mushrooming specialised shops and boutiques in such fashionable districts as Harajuku and Aoyama (*The Japan Times*, 20 October 1983). Such growing competition for good quality saleswomen was one of the major factors prompting big department stores to add some attractive characteristics to the sales jobs by opening up opportunities to move into specialist roles such as fashion advisers and co-ordinators, etc.

8 The Seibu case: changing company practice

1   Tsuda (1981) points out that the nature of Japanese personnel management is not conducive to the formation of 'specialist' or 'professional' functions in the western sense. A strong emphasis on the collective performance of the work group and task flexibility based on frequent job rotation means that individuals are not encouraged to identify with a specific task or specialist work role for a long period of time.

10 Equal employment for women in the Japanese employment system: limitations and obstacles

1   In October 1984, *Keizai Doyukai* (Japan's Council of Economic Organisations) published an article calling for the formation of an 'intermediate labour market', pointing out that 'a new adjustment mechanism is urgently needed to cope with the growing influence on employment brought about by technological progress in office computerisation'. The council proposed to the government the formulation of policy measures to assist the rapid formation of an

'intermediate labour market'. Eight months after the appearance of this article, the Employee Dispatching Business Law was enacted (for details of the law, see JIL 1986b). The law recognises the legitimacy of temporary workers' dispatching agencies which were previously prohibited under the provisions of the Employment Security Law. One result of this law has been the mushrooming of new employment agencies which dispatch workers to companies as 'temporaries'. According to the Ministry of Labour, companies authorised by the government as temporary employment agencies and those whose application for accreditation was received by 1 June 1987, totalled 7,286. There were only 2,518 agencies at the time when the law went into effect. The law has resulted in an almost threefold increase in the number of temporary employment agencies in one year (JFWA 1987: 74–7).

According to the Ministry of Labour, the objective for formally recognising these agencies which have been burgeoning in recent years is to impose strict requirements upon their operation and to stipulate detailed control provisions for effectively conducting administrative supervision. In practice, the law merely specifies the scope of operations of these temporary agencies in a very loose manner. It initially recognised twelve types of occupation as legitimate for operation, in accordance with general legal standards prescribed by the law; occupations that (a) require professional knowledge, skills and experience and (b) by special nature require a special kind of personnel management. Many agencies and companies were able to exploit the loose meaning of these prescriptions to expand the types of jobs to be operated by 'temporary' workers. Three years after the enactment of the law, the type of occupations recognised as legitimate for operation under manpower dispatching agencies increased from twelve to sixteen. The greatest increase in the number of temporary workers has been in the category of 'clerical and general administrative workers', over 90 per cent of whom are women. Recently, many large firms in the banking and financial sectors started to set up their own 'temporary workers' agencies' within the enterprise group which re-employed their own retired aged workers and women employees (*Gendai Frii Uwaku Kenkyukai* 1986: 24). In practice, the law has little effect in protecting the working conditions of these workers. Evidence shows that working conditions of these workers have deteriorated. A recent survey shows that the average hourly wage has declined by thirteen percentage points between 1986 and 1989 (*Nihon Keizai Shimbun*, 24 July 1989). This is partly because the scope of occupations carried out by the dispatched temporary workers has expanded to increase many low pay clerical jobs. Many companies have been externalising jobs which were previously conducted by full-time regular employees to external dispatching agencies or agencies within their own enterprise group.

2   In October 1987, the Ministry of Labour issued a report outlining an expert study group's proposals for part-time workers. It represented the most detailed and influential statement on government policies on part-time workers since the first report on the utilisation of women as part-time workers was published in 1964. The report specifically proposes the introduction of comprehensive and systematic measures for

recognising part-time labour as an employment form vital to the Japanese economy. Policy revisions in six areas were proposed: first, the assurance of minimum working conditions through administrative guidance; second, the provision of welfare measures, including re-examining the employment insurance system which has mainly been designed for full-time regular workers and the introduction of a special mutual aid system corresponding to the retirement allowance system; third, measures for ability development and employment assurance; fourth, the consolidation of the labour market and the provision of labour information; fifth, the promotion of mutual transition from part-time to full-time work and sixth, the revision of the taxation system.

This report was the major official document to call for the more effective utilisation of part-time workers through consolidating their position in the labour market. The purpose is to confer better 'welfare' to the part-time workers, according to the Ministry of Labour. There is, however, no mention of the harmonisation of the working conditions between part-time and full-time workers. The report also proposed the introduction of a part-time worker welfare law. One of the most controversial points raised by the report is the definition of part-time workers. It excludes the 'pseudo part-time workers'. At present, at least over one-third of the so-called part-time workers are in fact 'pseudo part-time workers'. They actually work full-time like the regular employees but are classified as part-time in terms of status. The word 'part-time' in Japan is less a description of working hours and more a 'label' for employment status and a terminology for labelling many low status job traditionally performed by women. The report proposed to exclude these 'pseudo part-time workers' outside the scope of the new policies.

3   In 1985, the government reduced the national treasury's contribution to the childcare unit cost from 80 per to 70 per cent. It was further lowered to 50 per cent in 1986.

4   Under the government's tax reform in 1987, a married man with a non-working full-time housewife or with a wife working part-time earning an annual income of less than ¥57,000 is entitled to a special married man's allowance (¥35,000), on top of the existing married men's allowance (¥35,000). If the wife's annual income is beyond the threshold of ¥57,000, the special allowance is reduced in proportion eventually reaching zero when the wife's annual income reaches ¥92,000. This new tax policy is widely criticised as discouraging women from working full-time by offering extra privileges to full-time housewives and those working part-time (Ishibashi 1989: 55; *Nikkei Shimbun*, Evening, 6 February 1989)

5   In the 1984 national survey by the Prime Minister's Office, 36 per cent of Japanese women agreed with the statement 'men should work and women should stay at home', 41 per cent disagreed and another 23 per cent replied 'don't know'. In the 1987 survey, 37 per cent agreed with the statement, 32 per cent disagreed and the proportion of those who replied 'don't know' increased by eight percentage points up to 31 per cent. These results were often dramatically taken up by the mass media as

evidence that Japanese women have become 'more conservative' in recent years. An article in the *Independent* (12 March 1988) described the results as showing that 'Japanese women go for hearth and home'. The Japanese government predicted that, unlike in some other industrialised countries, in Japan women would continue to put marriage and children ahead of their careers, even beyond the year 2000 (PMO, 1987). However, what deserves greater attention from the survey results, similar to our finding at Seibu, is that more Japanese women now exhibit an ambivalent attitude to the traditional sex role distinction.

Bibliography

Abegglen, J.C. (1958) *The Japanese Factory: Aspects of Its Social Organisation*, Glencoe, Ill.: The Free Press.

Abramovitz, M. (1972) 'Manpower, capital and technology', in I. Berg, (ed.) *Human Resources and Economic Welfare, Essays in Honor of Eli Ginzberg*, New York: Columbia University Press.

Aigner, D.J. and Glen, C.C. (1977) 'Statistical theories of discrimination in labor markets', *Industrial and Labor Relations Review*, 30 (2) pp. 175–87.

Akamatsu, R. (ed.) (1977) *Nihon Fujin Mondai Shiryo Shusei* (A Collection of References on Women's Issues in Japan), Tokyo: Domesu Shuppan.

Amsden, A.H. (ed.) (1980) *The Economics of Women and Work*, Harmondsworth: Penguin Books.

Arrow, K.J. (1973) 'The theory of discrimination', in O. Ashenfelter and A. Rees (eds) *Discrimination in Labor Markets*, Princeton: Princeton University Press.

Barker, D.C. and Allen, S. (eds) (1976) *Dependence and Exploitation in Work and Marriage*, London: Longman.

Barron, R.D. and Norris, G.M. (1976) 'Sexual divisions and the dual labour market', in D.C. Barker and S. Allen, (eds) *Dependence and Exploitation in Work and Marriage*, London: Longman.

Becker, G.S. (1957) *The Economics of Discrimination*, Chicago: University of Chicago (2nd edition, 1971).

Becker, G.S. (1964) *Human Capital*, New York: Columbia University Press.

Beechey, V. and Whitelegg, E. (1986) *Women in Britain Today*, Milton Keynes and Philadelphia: Open University Press.

Blau, F.D. and Jusenius C.L. (1976) 'Economists' approaches to sex segregation in the labour market: an appraisal', in M. Blaxall and B. Keagan (eds) *Women and the Workplace: The Implications of Occupational Segregation*, Chicago: University of Chicago Press.

——(1984) 'Discrimination against women: theory and evidence', in A.D. William Jr. (ed.) *Labor Economics: Modern Views*, Boston: Martinus Nijhoff.

Blaxall, M. and Reagan, B. (eds) (1976) *Women and the Workplace: The Implications of Occupational Segregation*, Chicago: University of Chicago Press.

Block, W.E. and Walker, M.A. (eds) (1982) *Discrimination, Affirmative Action and Equal Opportunity*, Vancouver, British Columbia: The Fraser Institute.

Blumrosen, A.W. (1972) 'Strangers in paradise: Griggs and Duke Power Co. and the concept of employment discrimination', *Michigan Law Review* 71 pp. 59–110.

Boulding, K.E. (1976) 'Toward a theory of discrimination' in P.A. Wallace (ed.), *Equal Employment Opportunity and the A.T. and T. Case*, Cambridge, Mass.: MIT Press.

Brown, C. and Pechman, J.A. (eds) (1987) *Gender in the Workplace*, Washington, D.C.: The Brookings Institution.

Burgess, J. (1985) 'Sexism works, and new law won't undermine that', *The Japan Times*, 20 July.

Burstein, P. (1985) *Discrimination, Jobs and Politics: The Struggle for Equal Employment Opportunity in the United States since the New Deal*, Chicago: University of Chicago Press.

Clark, R. (1979) *The Japanese Company*, New Haven and London: Yale University Press.

Cole, R.E. (1971) *Japanese Blue-Collar*, Berkeley and Los Angeles: University of California Press.

——(1979) *Work, Mobility and Participation: A Comparative Study of American and Japanese Industry*, Berkeley and Los Angeles: University of California Press.

Cole, R.E. and Tominaga, K. (1976) 'Japan's changing occupational structure and its significance', in H. Patrick (ed.) *Japanese Industrialization and its Social Consequences*, Berkeley and Los Angeles: University of California Press.

Cook, A.H. and Hayashi, H. (1980) *Working Women in Japan: Discrimination, Resistance and Reform*, Ithaca, New York: Cornell University.

Craig, C., Garnsey, E. and Rubery, J. (1985) 'Labour market segmentation and women's employment: a case study from the United Kingdom', *International Labour Review* 124 (3) pp. 267–80.

Crosby, F. (1976), 'A model of egoistical relative deprivation', *Psychological Review* 83 pp. 85–113.

——(1982) *Relative Deprivation and Working Women*, Oxford: Oxford University Press.

Denkiroren (1985), 'Denki rodosha jukka-koku ishiki chosa' (A ten country survey on electrical workers' attitudes), *Chosa Jiho* 204, December.

Dex, S. and Shaw, L.B. (1986) *British and American Women at Work: Do Equal Opportunities Policies Matter?*, London: Macmillan.

Doeringer, P.B. and Piore, M.J. (1971) *Internal Labor Markets and Manpower Analysis*, Lexington, Mass.: D.C. Heath.

Dore, R. (1973) *British Factory – Japanese Factory*, London: George Allen & Unwin.

Dore, R., Bounine-Cabale, J. and Tapiola, K. (1989) *Japan at Work: Markets, Management and Flexibility*, Paris: OECD.

The Economist (1988) 'Japanese women: a world apart', 14 May pp. 21–4.

Edwards, L.N. (1988) 'Equal employment opportunity in Japan: a view from the West', *Industrial and Labor Relations Review* 41 (2) pp. 240–50.

Edwards, R.C., Reich, M. and Gordon, D.M. (1975) *Labour Market*

Segmentation, Lexington, Mass.: Lexington Books.

Eguchi, K. (1984) 'Seibu Ryutsu Gurupu jinji senryaku' (Personnel management strategy of Seibu Retail Group), *Jitsugyo no Nihon* May pp. 40–4.

EPA (1971) *New Economic and Social Development Plan: 1970–1975*, Tokyo: Economic Planning Agency.

Equal Opportunities Commission (1985) *Formal Investigation Report: Leeds Permanent Building Society*, February.

Fuchs, V.R. (1968) *The Service Economy*, New York: National Bureau of Economic Research.

Gable, M., Gillespie, K.R. and Topol, M. (1984) 'The current status of women in department store retailing: an update', *Journal of Retailing* 60 (2) pp. 86–103.

Galenson, W. and Odaka, K. (1976) 'The Japanese labour market' in H. Patrick and H. Rosvsky (eds) *Asia's Giant: How the Japanese Economy Works*, Washington, D.C.: The Brookings Institution.

Gendai Frii Uwaku Kenkyukai (1986) *Jinzai Haken* (Manpower Dispatching), Tokyo: Yuhikaku Bijinesu.

Gordon, D.M. (ed.) (1971) *Problems in Political Economy: An Urban Perspective*, Lexington, Mass.: D.C. Heath.

——(1972) *Theories of Poverty and Underemployment*, Lexington, Mass.: D.C. Heath.

GR (1979) 'Beteran joshi hanbai-in no ikashi kata' (Utillilisation of experienced female shop assistants), *Gekkan Rikuruto* May pp. 47–9.

——(1980) 'Tayoka suru joshi no senryokka' (Growing diversity in the utilisation of women), *Gekkan Rikuruto* October pp. 19–35.

Halliday, J. (1975) *A Political History of Japanese Capitalism*, New York: Monthly Review Press.

Hanami, T. (1986) *Gendai no Koyo Byodo* (Equality in Employment), Tokyo: Sanshodo.

Hartman, H. (1976) 'Capitalism, patriarchy and job segregation by sex', in M. Blaxall and B. Reagan (eds) *Women and the Workplace: The Implications of Occupational Segregation*, Chicago: University of Chicago Press.

——(1987) 'Internal labor markets and gender: a case study of promotion', in C. Brown and J.A. Pechman (eds) *Gender in the Workplace*, Washington, D.C.: The Brookings Institution.

Hasegawa, M. (1984) 'Danjo koyo byodo ho wa bunka no seitaikei o hakai suru' (The law for sexual equality in employment will destroy our cultural ecosystem), *Chuo Koron* May pp. 78–87.

Hayashi, Y. (1986) 'Myth and reality: institutional reform for women', *AMPO: Japan–Asia Quarterly Review* (The challenge facing Japanese women) 18 (3) pp. 18–23.

Hazama, H. (1971) *Nihon-teki Keiei* (Japanese Management), Tokyo: Nikkei Shinsho.

——(1976) 'Historical changes in the lifestyle of industrial workers', in H. Patrick (ed.) *Japanese Industrialization and its Social Consequences*, Berkeley and Los Angeles: University of California Press.

——(1982) 'Historical overview of cultural supposition in Japanese business management', *The East* 18 (11–12) pp. 53–63.

——(1989) *Keiei Shakai-gaku* (Sociology of Management), Tokyo: Yuhikaku.

Hendry, J. (1987) *Understanding Japanese Society*, London: Croom Helm.

Hideo, T. (1976) *The Japanese Legal System*, Tokyo: University of Tokyo Press.

Hiroki, M. (1988) 'Childcare and working mothers', *Resource Materials on Women's Labour in Japan*, No.3, June, Tokyo: Centre For Asian Women's Workers' Fellowship.

Honda, J. (1984) *Danjo Koyo Kinto Ho towa nanika* (What Equal Employment Opportunity Law is all about?), Tokyo: Daiyamonda-sha.

Hunt, S.D., Burnett, J. and Amason R. (1981) 'Feminism: implications for department store strategy and sales behaviour', *Journal of Retailing* 57 (4) pp. 71–85.

Ichikawa, K. (1984) 'Japan's women just want a square deal', *The Japan Times*, 24 June.

Ido, K. (1980a) 'Daisotsu joshi no saiyo to katsuyo' (Employment and utilisation of women graduates), *Gekkan Rikuruto* September pp. 44–8.

——(1980b) 'Seibu hyakkaten no joshi shain kunren' (Training of women employees at Seibu Department Stores), *Kantokusha Kunren* April pp. 10–12.

——(1985) 'Joshi rodo mondai' (Women's employment issues), *Keieisha* April pp. 54–7.

ILO (1972) *Legislative Series, 1972, Japan – 1*, Geneva: International Labour Office.

——(1975) *Equality of Opportunity and Treatment for Women Workers*, International Labour Conference, 60th session, Geneva: International Labour Office.

——(1986) *Legislative Series, 1985, Japan – 1*, Geneva: International Labour Office.

——(1990–91) *Year Book of Labour Statistics*, Geneva: International Labour Office.

Inagami, T. (1989) *Tenkanki no Rodo Sekai* (The Labour World in Transition), Tokyo: Yushindo.

Inagei, N. (1983) *Josei to Riidashippu* (Woman and Leadership), Tokyo: Yuhikaku Sensho.

Ishibashi, C. (1989) *Danjo Koyo Byodo no Shinjidai* (A New Era of Equal Employment between Men and Women), Kyoto: Horitsu Bunkasha.

Ishida, H. (1985) 'Skokuba no josei: sono shoraizo' (Women in the workplace: a future perspective), *Asahi Shimbun*, 14 January.

——(ed.) (1986) *Josei no Jidai: Nihon Kigyo to Koyo Byodo* (Woman's Era: Japanese Companies and Equal Employment Opportunity), Tokyo: Koubundo.

Ishikawa, H. (1980) 'Koyo kozo no henka' (Changes in the employment structure) in H. Ishikawa and K. Ando (eds) *Nihon-teki Keiei no Tenki* (Japanese Management in Transition), Tokyo: Yuhikaku Sensho.

Izumi, K. (1989) 'Employment practices with respect to women workers in Japan and Japanese-owned firms in the UK', unpublished MA thesis, University of Warwick.

Jain, H.C. and Ledvinka, J. (1975) 'Economic inequality and the concept of employment discrimination', *Labor Law Journal* 26 (9) (September) pp. 579–84.

Jain, H.C. and Sloane, P.J. (1981) *Equal Employment Issues: Race and Sex*

Discrimination in the United States, Canada and Britain, New York: Praeger.

JERC (1987) *Koyo Kinto Ho no Eikyo to Kigyo no Taiou* (The Impact of the Equal Employment Opportunity Law and Company Responses), Nihon Keizai Kenkyu Sentaa (Japan Economic Research Centre), No.58, May.

Jewson, N. and Mason, D. (1986) 'The theory and practice of equal opportunity policies: liberal and radical approaches', *The Sociolgical Review*, 34 (2) (May) pp. 307–34.

JFWA (1987, 1988) *Fujin Hakusho* (White Paper on Women), Nihon Fujin Dantai Rengokai (Japanese Federation of Women's Associations), Tokyo: Horupu Shuppan.

JIL (1986a) 'Ordinance and guidelines for implementing the Equal Employment Opportunity Law', *Japan Labour Bulletin* (Japan Insitute of Labour) 25 (4) pp. 5–8.

——(1986b) 'Outline of government and ministerial ordinance for implementing the Employee Dispatching Business Law', *Japan Labour Bulletin*, 25 (7) pp. 6–8.

——(1987) 'The impact of the Equal Employment Opportunity Law at its first stage of enforcement', *Japan Labour Bulletin* (Japan Institute of Labour) 26 (10) pp. 5–8.

——(1989) *Shukan Rodo Nyusu* (Japan Institute of Labour), 16 October.

——(1991) *Shukan Rodo Nyusu* (Japan Institute of Labour), 11 February.

Joyce, M. and Guiltman, J. (1978) 'The professional women: a potential market segment for retailers', *Journal of Retailing* 54 (2) (Summer) pp. 59–70.

JPC (1985) *Joshi Rodo Shinjidai to Koyo Kanri no Shishin* (Women's Employment in a New Era and Guidelines for Employment and Management), Tokyo: Nihon Seisansei Honbu (Japan Productivity Centre).

——(1987) *Rodo-shijo no Henyo to Sogo Jinzai Kanri* (Changing Labour Market and Total Human Resource Management), Tokyo: Nihon Seisansei Honbu (Japan Productivity Centre).

JT (1984a) 'Proposed law stirs debate on equality', *The Japan Times* 25 March.

——(1984b) 'Equal work rights negotiation fail', *The Japan Times*, 27 March.

——(1984c) 'Working women neutral to equality law', *The Japan Times*, 6 June.

——(1986) 'Ministry explains new employment law', *The Japan Times*, 6 April.

Kanto Management Association (1986) *Danjo Koyo Kikai Kinto Ho to korekara no Koyokanri no Hoko* (The Equal Employment Opportunity Law and the future direction of personnel management), Tokyo.

Kawahashi, Y. (1983) 'Chingin no josho to danjo chingin kakusa' (Rises in wages and the male–female wage differentials) in H. Takahashi N (ed.) *Kawari Yuku Fugin Rodo* (Changing Pattern of Women's Employment), Tokyo: Yuhikaku Sensho.

Kawashima, T (1967a) *Nihonjin no Ho Ishiki* (The Legal Consciousness of the Japanese), Tokyo: Iwanami Shoten.

——(1967b) 'The status of the individual in the notion of law, right and social order in Japan', in C.A. Moore, (ed.) *The Japanese Mind: Essentials of Japanese Philosophy and Culture*, Tokyo: Charles E. Tuttle Company.

Kawashima, Y. (1983) 'Wage differentials between men and women in Japan', unpublished Ph.D. thesis, Stanford University.

——(1987) 'The place and role of female workers in the Japanese labour market', *Women's Studies International Forum* 10 (6) pp. 599–611.

Keizai Shingikai (1969) *Rodoryoku Jukyu no Tenbo to Seisaku no Hoko* (Labour Force Demand and Supply: Prospect and Policy), Tsusansho (MITI).

Kendrick, J. (1981) 'Politics and the construction of women as second-class workers', in F. Wilkinson (ed.) *The Dynamics of Labour Market Segmentation*, London: Academic Press.

Knowles. L. and Prewitt, K. (1969) *Institutional Racism in America*, Englewood Cliffs, New Jersey: Prentice-Hall.

Kobayashi, T. (1976) *Fujin Rodosha no Kenkyu* (A Historical Study of Women Workers), Tokyo: Jichosha.

Koga, H. (1984) *Seibu Zuno Shudan* (The Brain of Seibu), Tokyo: Paru Shuppan-sha.

Koike, K. (1983) 'Internal labor markets: workers in large firms' in T. Shirai (ed.) *Contemporary Industrial Relations in Japan*, Wisconsin: University of Wisconsin Press.

——(1988) *Understanding Industrial Relations in Japan*, London: Macmillan.

Komatsu, H. (1980) 'Tokyu Toyoko-ten ni okeru purozekkuto katsudo ni tsuite' (Project team activities in Tokyu Toyoko Stores), *Shokugyo Kunren*, October pp. 12–19.

Kondo, D.K. (1990) *Crafting Selves: Power, Gender and Discourses of Identity in a Japanese Workplace*, Chicago: University of Chicago Press.

Koyo Shinko Kyokai (1986) *Koyo Kikai Kinto no Genjo to Kadai* (Equal Employment Opportunity: The Present Situation and Issues), Tokyo: Sangyo Rodo Chosa-sho.

Kurihara, T. (1980) 'Joshi saikoyo to senmonshoku seido: hyakkaten gyokai ni miru joshi rodoryoku no kanri' (Women's re-entry and the specialist system: Management of the female workforce in the department store industry), *Gekkan Rodo Mondai* 273 (April) pp. 60–4.

Lam, A.C.L. (1985) 'Nihon-teki koyo kanko to kigyo-nai ni okeru danjo sabetsu kozo: aru hyakkaten de no jirei chosa yori' (Japanese employment practices and the structure of sex discrimination: a case study at a department store), *Sekai no Rodo* (World Labour) 35 (3) pp. 2–14.

Lebra, J., Paulson, J. and Powers, E. (1976) *Women in Changing Japan*, Stanford: Stanford University Press.

Lebra, S.T. (1984) *Japanese Women: Constraint and Fulfillment*, Honolulu: University of Hawaii Press.

McCrudden, C. (1982) 'Institutional discrimination', *Oxford Journal of Legal Studies* 303 pp. 303–67.

——(1986) 'Rethinking positive action', *The Industrial Law Journal* 15 (4) (December) pp. 219–43.

Madden, J.F. (1973) *The Economics of Sex Discrimination*, Lexington, Mass.: Lexington Books.

Marsden, D.W. (1986) *The End of Economic Man?*, Brighton: Wheatsheaf.

Marshall, R. *et al.* (1978) *Employment Discrimination: The Impact of Legal and Administrative Remedies*, New York: Praeger.

Martin, J., Price, R.L., Bies, R.J. and Powers, M.E. (1987) 'Now that I can have it, I'm not so sure I want it: the effects of opportunity on aspirations and discontent', in B.A. Gutek and L. Larwood (eds) *Women's Career Development*, Beverly Hills, California: Sage Publications.

Matthaei, J.A. (1983) *An Economic History of Women in America: Women's Work, the Sexual Division of Labour and the Development of Capitalism*, Brighton: The Harvester Press.

Mayhew, L.H. (1968) *Law and Equal Opportunity: A Study of the Massachusetts Commission Against Discrimination*, Cambridge, Mass.: Harvard University Press.

Meehan, E. (1985) *Women's Rights at Work: Campaigns and Policy in Britain and the United States*, London: Macmillan.

Meguro, Y (1980) *Onna-yakuwari Sei-shihai no Bunseki* (A Feminist Analysis of the Relations between Men and Women), Tokyo: Kakiuchi Shuppan.

Michida, S. (1984) *Danjo Koyo no Byodo* (Equal Employment Opportunities between Men and Women), Tokyo: Shinchosha.

Mincer, J. and Polacheck, S. (1974) 'Family investment in human capital: earnings of women', *Journal of Political Economy*, 82 (2) s76–s108.

Mizuno, A. (1984) *Keizai Sofutoka Jidai no Josei Rodo: Nichi Bei Ou no Keiken* (The Service Economy and Women's Employment: Japanese, American and European Experience), Tokyo: Yuhikaku Sensho.

Mokushi, T. (1980) 'Hitachi kaden joshi-shain no noryoku-kaihatsu' (Ability development for women employees at Hitachi consumer electronics), *Shokugyo Kunren* 22 (10) pp. 6–11.

MOL (1964) *Fujin Rodo no Yuko Katsuyo ni tsuite no Hokoku* (A Report on the Effective Utilisation of the Female Labour Force), Rodosho, Fujin Shonen Modai Shingikai (Ministry of Labour, Council on Women's and Young Workers' Problems).

——(1977) *Joshi Rodosha no Koyo Kanri ni kansuru Chosa* (Survey on Employment and Management of Women Workers), Rodosho Fujin-kyoku (Women's Bureau, Ministry of Labour).

——(1981a) *Joshi Rodosha no Koyo Kanri ni kansuru Chosa* (Survey on Employment and Management of Women Workers), Rodosho Fujin-kyoku (Women's Bureau, Ministry of Labour).

——(1981b) *Rodo Hakusho* (1981 Labour White Paper on Labour), Rodosho (Ministry of Labour).

——(1981c) *Yonensei Daisotsu Joshi no Koyo Kanri Jireishu* (Cases on the Management of Female University Graduates), Rodosho Fujin-kyoku (Women's Bureau, Ministry of Labour).

——(1982) *Koyo ni okeru Danjo Byodo no Handan Kijun no Kangae-kata ni tsuite* (Guidelines on Promoting Equality Between Men and Women in Employment), Rodosho (Ministry of Labour).

——(1984) *Fujin Shonen Mondai Shingikai Fujin Rodo Bukai no Shingi no Tame no Tatakidai* (Tentative plan for discussion at the Tripartite Advisory Council on Women's and Young Workers' Problems), Rodosho (Ministry of Labour).

——(1986) *Danjo Koyo Kikai Kinto Ho Kaisei Rodo Kijun Ho no Jitsumu Kaisetsu* (A Practical Guide and Explanation of the Equal Employment

Opportunity Law and the Amended Labour Standards Law), Rodosho
Fujin-kyoku (Women's Bureau, Ministry of Labour), Tokyo: Romu
Gyosei Kenkyu-sho.
——(1987a) *Nihon-teki Koyo-Kanko no Henka to Tembo* (Change and Outlook
for the Japanese Style Employment System), Rodosho, Daijin Kambo,
Seisaku Chosa-bu (Ministry of Labour, Minister's Secretariat, Policy
Planning and Research Department).
——(1987b) *Joshi Rodosha no Koyo Kanri ni kansuru Chosa* (Survey on
Employment and Management of Women Workers), Rodosho
Fujin-kyoku (Women's Bureau, Ministry of Labour).
——(1987c) *Kongo no Pato Taimu Rodo Taisaku no Arikata ni tsuite*
(Future Policy Measures on Part-time Workers), Rodosho (Ministry of
Labour).
——(1988) *Koreika nado Shita de no Jinji Seido ni kansuru Senmon Iinkai
Hokokusho* (An Expert Committee Report on Personnel Management in
the Ageing Society), Rodosho (Ministry of Labour).
——(1989) *Rodo Hakusho* (1989 Labour White Paper on Labour), Rodosho
(Ministry of Labour).
——(1990) *Joshi Koyo Kanri Kihon Chosa* (Basic Survey on Women's
Employment and Management), Rodosho Fujin-kyoku (Women's
Bureau, Ministry of Labour).
Nakajima, M. (1989) 'Pato rodo taisaku no aratana tenkai' (New
developments in policies on part-time employment), *Kikan Rodo Ho* 150
(January) pp. 87–100.
Nakanishi, T. (1983) 'Equality or protection? Protective legislation for
women in Japan', *International Labour Review* 122 (5) (September–October)
pp. 609–21.
Nakayama, I. (1975) *Industrialisation and Labour–Management Relations in
Japan*, Tokyo: Japan Institute of Labour.
Narushima, T. (1978) *Seibu Gurupu no Subete* (All About Seibu), Tokyo:
Nihon Jitsugyo Shuppan-sha.
NIVER (1987) *Joshi Rodo no Shinjidai* (A New Era for Women Workers),
Koyo Shokugyo Sogo Kenkyu-sho (National Institute of Vocational and
Employment Research), Tokyo: University of Tokyo Press.
NNKC (1981) *Joshi Shain no Katsuyo to Noryoku Kaihatsu: Seibu Hyakkaten no
Jirei* (Utilisation and Ability Development for Women Employees: the
Seibu Case), Noryoku Kaihatsu Shirizu, No. 81, Tokyo: Nigen Noryoku
Kaikatsu Sentaa, Zen Nihon Noritsu Renmei.
Noda, Y. (1976) *Introduction to Japanese Law*, Tokyo: University of Tokyo
Press.
Odaka, K. (1984) *Nihon-teki Keiei: Sono Shinwa to Genjitsu* (Japanese
Management: Myth and Reality), Tokyo: Chuko Shinsho.
O'Donovan, K. and Szyszczak, E. (1988) *Equality and Sex Discrimination Law*,
Oxford: Basil Blackwell.
OECD (1973), *Manpower Policy in Japan*, Paris: Organisation for Economic
Co-operation and Development.
——(1977) *The Development of Industrial Relations System: Some Implications of
the Japanese Experience*, Paris: Organisation for Economic Co-operation and
Development.

——(1979) *Equal Opportunities for Women*, Paris: Organisation for Economic Co-operation and Development.

Okada, Y. (1982) *Hyakkaten Gyokai* (The Department Store Industry), Kyoikusha Shinsho, Tokyo.

Okouchi, K. (1958) *Labour in Modern Japan*, Tokyo: Science Council of Japan.

——(1959) 'Reimeiki no nihon rodo-undo' (Japanese labour movement in its early period), *Nihon Rodo Kyokai Zasshi*, April.

O'Neill, J. (1984) 'Earnings differentials: empirical evidence and causes', in G. Schmid and R. Weitzel (eds) *Sex Discrimination and Equal Opportunity: The Labour Market and Employment Policy*, Gower: WZB-Publications.

Osako, M. (1982) 'Dilemmas of Japanese professional women: problems and perspectives', in R. Kahn-Hut *et al.* (eds) *Women and Work: Problems and Perspectives*, Oxford: Oxford University Press.

Ota, Y. (1988) 'Joshi rodosha o meguru saikin no doko' (Recent trends and tendencies of women's employment), in K. Koike and Y. Tomita (eds) *Shokuba no Kyaria Uman* (Career Woman in the Workplace), Tokyo: Toyo Keizai Shimpo-sha.

Ouwaki, M. (1987) *Kinto Ho Jidai ni Ikiru* (Living in the Age of Equal Opportunity Law), Tokyo: Yuhikaku Sensho.

——(1989) 'Parto taimu rodosha o meguru rippo-ron no kadai' (Issues about legislation on part-time workers), *Kikan Rodo Ho* 151 (April) pp. 6–18.

Patrick, H. (ed.) (1976) *Japanese Industrialization and its Social Consequences*, Berkeley and Los Angeles: University of California Press.

Patrick, H. and Rosvsky, H. (eds) (1976) *Asia's Giant: How the Japanese Economy Works*, Washington, D.C.: The Brookings Institution.

Pharr, S.J. (1977) 'Historical changes in the status of women in Japan', in J.Z. Giele and A.C. Smork (eds) *Women: Roles and Status in Eight Countries*, New York: John Wiley & Sons.

——(1981) *Political Women in Japan*, Berkeley and Los Angeles: University of California Press.

Phelps, E. S. (1972) 'The statistical theory of racism and sexism', *American Economic Review* 62 (4) pp. 659–61.

Phillips, A. and Taylor, B. (1980) 'Sex and skill: notes towards a feminist economics', *Feminist Review* 6 pp. 79–88.

Pinchbeck, I. (1930) *Women Workers and the Industrial Revolution*, London: Frank Cass (1969 edition, London: Routledge & Kegan Paul).

Piore, M.J. (1971), 'The dual labor market: theory and implications', in D.M. Gordon (ed.) *Problems in Political Economy: An Urban Perspective*, Lexington, Mass.: D.C. Heath.

——(1975) 'Notes for a theory of labour market stratification' in R.C. Edwards, M. Reich and D.M. Gordon *Labor Market Segmentation*, Lexington, Mass.: Lexington Books.

PMO (1979) *Fujin ni kansuru Ishiki Chosa* (Attitude Survey on Women), Sorifu (Japanese Prime Minister's Office).

——(1981) *Priority Targets for the Second Half of the Period Covered by the National Plan of Action for the Promotion of Measures Relating to Women*, Headquarters for the Planning and Promoting of Policies Relating to Women, Japanese Prime Minister's Office.

——(1983) *Fujin no Genjo to Shisaku* (The Contemporary Situation and Policies for Women), Sorifu (Japanese Prime Minister's Office).

——(1984) *Fujin ni kansuru Seron Chosa* (Public Opinion Survey on Women), Sorifu (Japanese Prime Minister's Office).

——(1987) *Josei ni kansuru Seron Chosa* (Public Opinion Survey on Women), Sorifu (Japanese Prime Minister's Office).

——(1989) *Josei no Shugyo ni kansuru Seron Chosa* (Public Opinion Survey on Women's Employment), Sorifu (Japanese Prime Minister's Office).

Ratner, R.S. (1978) *Equal Employment Policy for Women: Strategies for Implementation in the US, Canada and Western Europe*, Philadelphia: Temple University Press.

Robins-Mowry, D. (1983) *The Hidden Sun: Women of Modern Japan*, Boulder, Colorado: Westview Press.

Romu Gyosei Kenkyu-sho (1986) *Danjo Koyo Byodo Jidai no Romu Kanri* (Personnel Management in an Era of Equal Opportunity Between Men and Women), Tokyo: Romu Gyosei Kenkyu-sho.

Rosei Jiho (1978) 'Hyakkaten ni okeru jinji seido kaitei no choryu o saguru' (Changes in Personnel Management in the Department Store Industry), *Rosei Jiho* 2410 pp. 2–31.

——(1979) 'Seibu hyakkaten no senmonshoku seido to jinzai ikusei-saku' (The Specialist System and Human Resource Development at Seibu Department Stores) *Rosei Jiho* 2456 pp. 41–57.

——(1986) 'Koyo kinto ho e no kigyo no taiou' (Company responses to the Equal Employment Opportunity Law), *Rosei Jiho* 2789 pp. 3–31.

——(1987) 'Kettei shonin-kyu no doko' (Trends in starting wages), *Rosei Jiho* 2834 pp. 2–7.

——(1988) 'Chuken josei shain no katsuyo jirei' (Cases on the utilisation of core women employees), *Rosei Jiho*: 2887 pp. 3–31.

Rubery, J. (1980) 'Structured labour markets, worker organisation and low pay', in A.H. Amsden (ed.) *The Economics of Women and Work*, Harmondsworth: Penguin Books.

Ryan, P. (1981) 'Segmentation, duality and the internal labour markets', in F. Wilkinson (ed.) *The Dynamics of Labour Market Segmentation*, London: Academic Press.

Saison Group (1989) The Office of the Chairman, Saison Group.

Sano, Y. (1986) 'Atarashii jidai no josei rodo' (Women's employment in a new era), in H. Ishida (ed.) *Josei no Jidai: Nihon Kigyo to Koyo Byodo*, (Woman's Era: Japanese Companies and Equal Employment Opportunity), Tokyo: Koubundo.

Sato, G. (1990) *Danjo Koyo Kikai Kinto Ho no Go-nen* (The Equal Employment Opportunity Law in its Fifth Year), Tokyo: Romugyosei Kenkyu-sho.

Saxonhouse, G.P. (1976) 'Country girls and communication among competitors in the Japanese cotton-spinning industry', in H. Patrick (ed.) *Japanese Industrialization and its Social Consequences*, Berkeley and Los Angeles: University of California Press.

Schmid, G. and Weitzel, R. (eds) (1984) *Sex Discrimination and Equal Opportunity: The Labour Market and Employment Policy*, Gower: WZB-Publications.

Seibu (1972) *Katabami*, No. 127 (company newsletter published by Seibu Department Stores Ltd).

Seibu (1973) *Katabami*, No. 13 (company newsletter published by Seibu Department Stores Ltd).

Seibu Nyusha-Annai (1985) (A Guide to Seibu), Seibu Hyakkaten.

Shinotsuka, E. (1982) *Nihon no Joshi Rodo* (Women's Employment in Japan), Tokyo: Toyo Keizai Shinpo-sha.

Shizuka, T. (1983) *Seibu Ryutsu Shudan* (The Seibu Retail Group), Tokyo: Daiyamondo-sha.

Smith, Jr. A.B. (1980) 'The law and equal employment opportunity: what's past should not be prologue', *Industrial and Labor Relations Review* 33 (4) pp. 493–504.

Somucho (1981 and 1990) *Rodoryoku Chosa Tokubetsu Chosa* (Report on the Special Survey of the Labour Force Survey), Somucho Tokei-kyoku (Statistics Bureau, Management and Co-ordination Agency).

——(1982) *Shugyo Kozo Kihon Chosa* (Basic Survey on Employment Structure), Somucho Tokei-kyoku (Statistics Bureau, Management and Co-ordination Agency).

Spence, M.A. (1974) *Market Signaling*, Cambridge, Mass.: Harvard University Press.

Stanback, Jr. T.M. *et al.* (1981) *Services: The New Economy*, Allanheld: Osmun & Co. Publishers, Inc.

Sumiya, M. (1979) *Gendai Nihon no Rodo Mondai* (Labour Problems in Contemporary Japan), Tokyo: Tokyo Daigaku Shuppan (first edition, 1969).

Taira, K. (1970) *Economic Development and the Labour Market in Japan*, New York: Columbia University Press.

Takahashi, N. (ed.) (1983) *Kawari Yuku Fujin Rodo* (Changing Pattern of Women's Employment), Tokyo: Yuhikaku Sensho.

Takanashi, M. (1988) 'Parto taimu rodo o meguru mondaiten to taisaku no hoko' (Issues of part-time employment and the direction of policy measures), *Nihon Rodo Kyokai Zasshi* 343 pp. 34–45.

Takeishi, E. (1987) 'Tayoka suru joshi rodo' (Growing diversity of women's employment pattern), in NIVER *Joshi Rodo no Shinjidai* (A New Era for Women Workers), Koyo Shokugyo Sogo Kenkyu-sho (National Institute of Vocational and Employment Research), Tokyo: University of Tokyo Press.

Takenaka, E. (1983) *Joshi Rodo Ron* (Theory of Female Labour), Tokyo: Yuhikaku Sensho.

Takizawa, T. (1985) *Koyo Kinto Jidai no Jinji Seido* (Personnel Management in an Era of Equal Employment Opportunity), Tokyo: Sangyo Rodo Chosa-sho.

TMLO (1983) *Tokyo no Fujin Rodo Jijo* (Conditions of Women's Employment in Tokyo), Tokyo-to Rodo Keizai-kyoku (Tokyo Metropolitan Labour Office).

Tsuda, M. (1959), *Rodo Mondai to Romu Kanri*, (Labour Problems and Personnel Management), Kyoto: Mineruba Shobo.

——(1977) *Korei Kogakureki-ka no Nihon-teki Keiei* (Japanese Management in an Ageing and Highly-Educated Society), Tokyo: Nihon Keieisha Dantai Renmei.

——(1981) *Jinji Kanri no Gendai-teki Kadai* (Some Contemporary Personnel Management Issues), Tokyo: Zeimu Keiri Kyokai.

United Nations (1985) *The Economic Role of Women in the ECE Region: Developments 1975–85*, New York: United Nations.

Upham, F.K. (1987) *Law and Social Change in Post-war Japan*, Cambridge, Mass. and London: Harvard University Press.

Wada, S. (1981) *Chosen-teki Keiei no Himitsu: Seibu Hyakkaten no Hasso* (The Secret of Strategic Management: Seibu's Innovative Management Concepts), Tokyo: Joho Sentaa Shuppan-kyoku.

Wallace, P.A. and LaMond A.M. (1977) *Women, Minorities and Employment Discrimination*, Lexington, Mass.: Lexington Books.

Watanabe, A. (1984) 'Danjo koyo kinto hoan to joshi no jikangai, kyujistu, shinya rodo' (The Equal Employment Opportunity Bill and women workers' overtime, work on rest days and late night work), *Jurist* 819 pp. 32–9.

Wilkinson, F. (ed.) (1981) *The Dynamics of Labour Market Segmentation*, London: Academic Press.

Williams, K. C. and Faltot, J.C. (1983) 'Research note: a comparison of women in department and specialty store management', *Journal of Retailing* 59 (4) pp. 107–13.

Woronoff, J. (1982) *Japan's Wasted Workers*, Tokyo: Lotus Press.

WVI (1986, 1987) *Shinki Daigaku Sotsugyo-sha Saiyo Keikaku Chosa* (Survey on Recruitment Plans for University Graduates), Josei Shokugyo Zaidan (Women's Vocational Institute).

——(1990) *Kosubetsu Koyo-kanri ni kansuru Kenkyu-kai Hokokusho* (A Survey Report on Career Tracking), Josei Shokugyo Zaidan (Women's Vocational Institute).

Yamate, S. (1972) *Gendai Nihon no Kazoku Mondai* (Family problems in contemporary Japan), Tokyo: Aki-shobo (second edition, 1981).

Yashiro, A. (1986) 'Josei no koyo kanri to kikai kinto ho' (Management of women and the Equal Employment Opportunity Law) in H. Ishida (ed.) *Josei no Jidai: Nihon Kigyo to Koyo Byodo*, (Woman's Era: Japanese Companies and Equal Employment Opportunity), Tokyo: Koubundo.

Yashiro, N. (1980) 'Danjo-kan chingin sabetsu no yoin ni tsuite' (Wage discrimination between men and women), *Nihon Keizai Kenkyu*, 9 pp. 17–31.

——(1983) *Josei Rodo no Keizai Bunseki* (An Economic Analysis of Women's Employment), Tokyo: Nihon Keizai Shimbun.

Yayama, T. (1984) 'Danjo koyo byodo ho wa nihon o tsubusu' (The law for sexual equality in employment will ruin Japan), *Shokun*, May.

Yoshikawa, E. (1980) *Jinzai no Ikusei to Katsuyo* (Development and Utilisation of Human Resources), Tokyo: Waseda University Press.

Young, M.K. (1984) 'Judicial review of administrative guidance: governmentally encouraged consensual dispute resolution in Japan', *Columbia Law Review* 84 (4) pp. 923–83.

Index

Abegglen, J.C. 235, 236
Abramovitz, Moses 69
administrative guidance *see gyoseishido*
administration jobs 15
'adverse impact' 42
advertising, recruitment 125, 127
ages of women workers 13–14, 15; and wage gap 48–9
Akamatsu, Ryoko 9, 99, 106–7, 255–6(n7)
'arbeit' workers 56, 225
Arrow, K.J. 30, 62
Asahi Shimbun 127, 131
attitudes towards women, Seibu 172–3, 204
attitudes of women workers 17, 186, 232; career continuity 210–12, 231; consciousness of equality issues 65, 204, 213, 231, 232–4; job preferences 202–4; perceptions of equality 200–1; promotion aspirations and expectations 204–10; Seibu 200–12; to re-entry 138; and women's role 64

Barron, R.D. 41
Basic Survey of Wage Structure (Chingin Kozo Kihon Tokei Chosa) 50
Becker, G.S. 29, 30
Beechey, V. 37, 39
Belgium, wage gap 16

Blau, F.D. 30, 31, 62
Blumrosen, A.W. 42
Boulding, Kenneth E. 29
bureaucracy 114, 240
Burstein, P. 6

Canada, ages and wage gap 49
career conversion system 81–5, 135
'career development programmes' for women 76–85; career conversion system 81–5; female group leader system 78–80; women's project teams 77–8
'career tracking' 128–33, 234
casual day workers (*hiyatoi*) 57
change: economic pressures for 6, 68–70, 150–3, 155–67, 226–7; and EEO Law 110–15; forces for 19–21; and internal labour markets 5–6; Japanese situation 6; resistance to 235–40; strategy for 239–40
childcare: facilities, Seibu 182; leave 94, 102, 137, 226; public facilities 230
Childcare Leave Act (1991) 137
child-rearing 67; and wage gap 48–50 *see also* re-employment
Chingin Kozo Kihon Tokei Chosa (Basic Survey of Wage Structure), MOL 46, 47, 49, 50, 253(n2)
Civil Code 91
Clark, R. 52, 56

clerical work 7, 12–13, 70–1
cliques 64
Cole, R.E. 27, 28, 56, 65, 236
company practice 45–67; 'career
    development programmes' for
    women 76–85; and culture and
    family ideology 64–7; direct
    discrimination 59–61; indirect
    discrimination 61–4; 'Japanese
    employment system' 56–9; job
    segregation 50–2; market
    pressure for reform 68–76;
    part-time employment 53–6;
    response to EEO Law 117–40;
    small firms 52–4; wage gap
    45–50 see also personnel policies
conditions of employment: direct
    discrimination 60; EEO Law
    102, 105–7; EEO Law
    compliance 120, 122, 124, 126–8
consciousness of equality issues 65,
    204, 213, 231, 232–4
Constitution (1946) 9, 90, 92
consumers, women as 72, 150
'contract employee' system 225;
    Seibu 188–93, 234
Cook, A.H. 91, 92
'core' and 'non-core' employees 3,
    225–6, 238
Craig, C. 37, 39
Crosby, F. 201
culturalist theory 235–6
culture, and role of women 64–5
custom, workplace 35–6, 64

Denkiroren Chosa Jiho 17
Denmark, wage gap 16
department stores 144; buying
    function 164–5 see also Seibu
direct discrimination 43, 59–61
discrimination: before EEO Law
    14–19; company practice (q.v.)
    45–67; Constitution (1946) 9;
    definition of 28–9; direct 43,
    59–61; EEO Law (q.v.)
    compliance 122–4; indirect 43,
    61–4, 108; and internal labour
    markets 33–6, 236–9; litigation
    90–2, 111; racial 40; theory

(q.v.) 27–44, 235–9 see also
    inequality
dismissal, EEO Law 102, 104
disputes, settlement of 103
Doeringer, P.B. 5, 31–7, 43–4, 62,
    215, 217, 237–9
domestic work 231
Dore, R. 28, 56, 57, 222, 223
dual labour market 32–3

economic functionalist theory
    235–6
Economic Planning Agency (EPA)
    229
Economist, The 3, 256(n1)
education 73–6 see also graduates;
    higher education; school leavers
Edwards, L.N. 254(n3)
'elite women' 226–9; attitudes of
    210–12; Seibu 177–80
Employee Dispatching Business
    Law (1985) 230
Employment Status Survey (Shugyo
    Kozo Kihon Chosa) 55–6
enterprise unionism 57
Equal Employment Opportunity
    Law (EEO) (1985) 3–4, 19–20,
    89–116; as agent of change
    110–15; draft Bill, problems
    95–100; 'exhortatory' provisions
    (doryoku-gimu kitei) 4, 20, 101–3,
    105–10; guidelines 20, 102, 103,
    106–7, 109, 115, 118, 255(n5);
    historical background 89–95;
    management response 119–25;
    and non-regular workers 230;
    objectives 20, 101, 146; and
    personnel policies 125–36;
    'prohibitory' provisions (kinshi
    kitei) 4, 20, 101–2, 104–5; Seibu
    response 175–83
exploitation of women workers 8

Faltot, J.C. 165
family: division of labour 19, 38–9;
    domestic work 231; government
    policy 67, 74, 230–1; ideology
    66–7, 230–1; law 9
female group leader system 78–80

feminist theory of discrimination 38–9, 44
Financial Times, The 256(n1)
firms, size of 52–4
flexibility of employment system 3, 18, 58, 223–4
France: attitudes of women workers 17; wage gap 16, 49
fringe benefits: EEO Law 102, 104; EEO Law compliance 122
Fuchs, Victor R. 68–9
Fujin Rodo No Jitsujo (Report on Female Workers), MOL 10, 12
Fujitsu 71–2

Gable, M. 165
Gakko Kihon Chosa (Basic survey on education), Ministry of Education 74–5
Galenson, W. 3, 59
Gekkan Rikuruto (GR) 77
Gendai Frii Uwaku Kenkyukai 258(n1)
Germany, Federal Republic of: administration and management jobs 15; attitudes towards women's role 64; attitudes of women workers 17; wage gap 16
giri 112–13
government policy 6, 229–32, 240; family and education 67, 94, 230–1 *see also* legislation
graduates: discrimination 19, 51–2, 60; and economic pressure 71–2, 74–6; EEO Law response 125–6, 127; occupations 75–6; promotion aspirations and expectations 206–7, 209; Seibu 155–6
grievances 118
Griggs v. *Duke Power Co.* 42
group leader system 78–80
growth, economic 68; and women's employment 10–14 *see also* market pressures
guidance, administrative (*gyoseishido*) 106, 117–18, 139 *see also* guidelines *under* EEO Law
Guiltman, J. 257(n4)

gyoseishido (administrative guidance) 106, 117–18, 139; *see also* guidelines under EEO law

Hanami, T. 106
Hartman, H. 37, 38–9
Hasegawa, M. 100
Hayashi, H. 91, 92
Hayashi, Y. 230
Hazama, H. 223, 224, 235
Hendry, J. 252(n3)
Hideo, T. 112
higher education 13 *see also* graduates
Hiroki, M. 230
history of women's employment 7–14
Hitachi 77
Hong Kong, attitudes of women workers 17
'hope hypothesis' 201
hours of work 98
household (*ie*) system 66–7 *see also* family
'housewife role' 64–7, 230–1, 233
human capital theory 29–30; and wage gap 46–7
Hungary, attitudes of women workers 17
Hunt, S.D. 257(n4)

Ido, K. 150, 156, 161, 175
Inagami, T. 224
Inagei, Noriko 78–80
Independent, The 260(n5)
indirect discrimination 43, 61–4, 108
industry: distribution of labour force 11–12, 70; textiles 7–8, 237–8 *see also* labour market; service sector
inequality 29; job segregation 50–2; part-time employment 53–6, 58; small firms 52–4; 'vicious cirle' of 41; wage gap 45–50 *see also* discrimination
institutional theory 31; discrimination 40–3; internal labour market 31–6; society and

household sexual divisions 36–9
internal labour markets 5–6, 31–6,
    44, 217, 236–9; definition of
    31–3; and discrimination 33–6;
    Japanese *vs.* western 27–8 27
'internal redeployment' 28
International Labour Office (ILO)
    15, 16, 94, 252(n4)
Ishibashi, C. 259(n4)
Ishida, H. 62
Ishikawa, H. 3
Italy, attitudes of women workers
    17
Izumi, K. 64

Jain, H.C. 29, 42
Japan Council of Economic
    Organisations (*Keizai Doyukai*)
    257–8(n1)
Japan Economic Research Centre
    (JERC) 117, 119, 131, 134, 136
Japan Federation of Employers'
    Associations (*Nikkeiren*) 92–3,
    96, 137
Japan Institute of Labour (JIL) 127,
    254(n2)
Japan Productivity Centre (JPC)
    57, 224–5
Japan Times, The (JT) 77, 96–7, 98,
    145, 257(n5)
'Japanese employment system' 5,
    17–18, 56–9; resistance to
    change 222–9, 235–6
Japanese Federation of Women's
    Associations (JFWA) 230, 258(n1)
job, definition of 48, 63
job assignment: direct
    discrimination 60–1; EEO Law
    102, 105–7; EEO Law
    compliance 121–2, 124, 133–5
job rotation 18; direct
    discrimination 61; EEO Law
    compliance 121–2, 124, 134,
    136; indirect discrimination 62,
    63; Seibu 168–71
job segregation 50–2 *see also* job
    assignment
Joyce, M. 257(n4)
Jusenius, C.L. 30, 31, 62

Kanto Management Association
    129–30
Kawahashi, Y. 45
Kawashima, Takeyoshi 112, 115
Kawashima, Y. 3, 47, 52, 58,
    253–4(n3)
Keizai Doyukai (Japan Council of
    Economic Organisations)
    257–8(n1)
Keizai Shingikai (Economic
    Council, *MITI*) 94
Kendrick, J. 41
Kitamura, Hiroshi 96
Knowles, L. 40
Kobayashi, T. 8
Koike, K. 27
Kokusei Chosa (Population Census)
    11, 71
Komatsu, H. 77
Kondo, D.K. 66
Koyo Shinko Kyokai 77
Kurihara, T. 174

Labour Force Research
    Committee, Economic Council
    93–4
Labour Force Survey (*Rodoryoku
    Chosa*) 11, 15, 51, 53, 55–6, 58
Labour Inspectorate 91
labour market: changes in 70–2,
    93–4; inequality 45–56; internal
    (*q.v.*) 5–6, 31–6, 44
Labour Standards Law (1947) 9;
    equal wages provision 48, 90–1;
    limitations 91–2; protective
    provisions 92–3, 95–6, 98
Labour Standards Law study group
    93, 94–5
Lebra, J. 65, 252(n3)
Lebra, S.T. 233
Ledvinka, J. 42
Leeds Permanent Building Society
    254(n4)
legislation: and bureaucracy 114,
    240; Childcare Leave Act (1991)
    137; discrimination litigation
    90–2, 111; Employee
    Dispatching Business Law (1985)
    230; Equal Employment

Opportunity Law (*q.v.*) 89–116; international influence 89–90, 100; Labour Standards Law (*q.v.*) 9, 48, 90–3, 95–8; and traditional thinking 112–13; USA and UK 42–3; Working Women's Welfare Law 93–4, 101, 229 *see also* government
lifetime employment 17–18, 57, 59; and family ideology 66; and legislation 96–7, 99; preservation of 222–5; and women 225
litigation, discrimination 90–2, 111

MacArthur, General Douglas 9
McCrudden, C. 40, 43
Madden, J.F. 30
Maitsuki Kinro Tokei Chosa (Monthly Labour Survey), MOL 16
management: resistance to change 222–9; response to EEO Law 119–25 *see also* company practice; personnel policies
market, pressure for change 6, 68–76; Seibu 150–3, 155–67 *see also* labour market
married women workers 13, 229, 231; compulsory retirement of 58, 61, 91–2; part-time employment (*q.v.*) 55; Seibu 173
Marsden, D.W. 33
Martin, J. 186
maternity leave 98
Matsushita 71, 77
Matthaei, J.A. 8
Mayhew, L.H. 40
Meehan, E. 233, 240
Meguro, Y. 67, 233
Meiji period 7, 252(n2); Civil Code 8, 66, 252(n3)
methodology *see* research methodology
Michida, S. 91, 92
Mincer, J. 30
Ministry of Education, *Gakko Kihon Chosa* (Basic survey on education) 74–5
Ministry of Labour (MOL): and

career tracking 128; *Chingin Kozo Kihon Tokei Chosa* (Basic Survey of Wage Structure) 46, 47, 49, 50, 253(n2); discrimination survey 14, 59; and dispatching agencies 230; and employment training 105; female graduates employment survey 51–2, 127; female labour survey 70; *Fujin Rodo No Jitsujo* (Report on Female Workers) 10, 12; guidelines *see under* EEO Law; length of service survey 76, 222; and lifetime employment 222; *Maitsuki Kinro Tokei Chosa* (Monthly Labour Survey) 16; and part-time employment 54, 229, 258–9(n2); and personnel management policies 226; and recruitment of women 105–7, 127, 133; Rodosho survey 119, 120, 122–3, 124, 133–4, 136; and school leavers' recruitment 60; Tripartite Advisory Council on Women and Young Workers 95, 97–8, 99–100; Women's Bureau 94, 107;and women's starting wages 48; Women's and Young Workers' Offices 103, 118; and working women's welfare 101 *see also* Equal Employment Opportunity Law
Mitsubishi Trading Corporation 135
Mitsukoshi 148
Mizuno, A. 19, 68
mobilisation of women, wartime 8–9
mobility, geographical 18, 63–4, 81, 135, 136 *see also* job rotation
Mokushi, T. 77
Monbusho see Ministry of Education
multiple classification analysis 249–51

Nakajima, M. 230
Nakanishi, T. 94
Nakayama, I. 5
National Federation of Small Business Associations 96

National Institute of Employment and Vocational Research (NIVER) survey 119–20, 121, 134, 138
NEC 71–2
nenko system 3, 17–18, 48, 57; economic pressure on 72–3, 223
neo-classical economic theory 29–31; wage gap 47–8
Ningen Noryoku Kaihatsu Sentaa (NNKC) 144
Nihon Keizai Shimbun 258(n1)
Nikkei Shimbun 77, 132, 259(n4)
Nikkeiren (Japan Federation of Employers' Associations) 92–3, 96, 137
Noda, Y. 112–13
non-regular workers 3, 57–8; utilisation of women as 225–6, 238
Norris, G.M. 41
Norway, ages and wage gap 49

Occupation, post-war 9
occupations of women 12–13, 50–2, 70–1; graduates 75–6
Odaka, K. 3, 59
O'Donovan, K. 43, 254(n4)
office work 7, 12–13, 70–1
Okada, Y. 147
Okouchi, K. 7–8
on-the-job training 33, 62, 105; Seibu 169–72
O'Neill, J. 31
Organisation for Economic Co-operation and Development (OECD) 5, 30, 57
organisations, dynamics and employment policies 72–3
Osako, M. 64
Ouwaki, M. 99, 107, 230

part-time employment 53–6, 58, 94, 225; definition of 55–6
patriarchy 38–9
patronage 64
personnel policies 5, 18, 62; 'career development programmes' for women 76–85; changes in

anticipation of EEO Law 123; prospects for further change 223–5; response to EEO Law 125–36; Seibu 155–67 *see also* 'Japanese employment system'
Pharr, Susan J. 9, 65
Phelps, E.S. 62
Phillips, A. 37–8
Pinchbeck, I. 8
Piore, M.J. 5, 31–7, 43–4, 62, 215, 217, 237–9
Polacheck, S. 30
Poland, attitudes of women workers 17
policy *see* company practice; government; personnel
Population Census (*Kokusei Chosa*) 11, 71
'prejudiced treatment' 42
pressure groups 6, 232–3, 240
Prewitt, K. 40
'primary sector' 32, 37, 41
Prime Minister's Office (PMO): attitude surveys on women 64, 138, 231, 232, 259–60(n5); and UN Decade for Women 90
productivity, sex differences in 29–30
project teams 77–8
promotion: attitudes towards 201, 204–10; career conversion system 81–5; direct discrimination 61; economic pressure on 72–3; EEO Law 102, 105–7; EEO Law compliance 121, 123–5, 133–5; indirect discrimination 63; internal 27; merit system 223; Seibu 159–61, 168, 196–9, 214–16

racial discrimination 40
recruitment: advertising 125, 127; 'career tracking' 128–33; direct discrimination 60; EEO Law 102, 105–7; EEO Law compliance 120, 122, 124, 125–8; of graduates 19, 51–2; school leavers 73
re-employment 102, 136–7, 226;

Seibu 173–4, 182
relative deprivation theory 201
research methodology 21–2, 153–4,
    241–51; ANOVA and multiple
    classification analysis 249–51;
    follow-up study 244–5;
    participant observation 242–3;
    questionnaire survey 243–4;
    samples 245–8
retirement: compulsory 58, 61,
    91–2; direct discrimination 61;
    EEO Law 102, 104; EEO Law
    compliance 120, 122, 124
Robins-Mowry, D. 9
Rodoryoku Chosa (Labour Force
    Survey) 11, 15, 51, 53, 55–6, 58
Rodosho survey, MOL 119, 120,
    122–3, 124, 133–4, 136
Rosei Jiho 123, 126, 127, 135, 143,
    144, 158
Ryan, P. 34, 38

Saison Group 147, 256–7(n2) *see
    also* Seibu
Sano, Y. 28
Sato, G. 126, 137
Saxonhouse, G.P. 8
Schmid, G. 40
school leavers 73–4; recruitment of
    60, 73
'secondary sector' 32, 37, 41
segmentation of labour market
    37–9, 234
segmented labour market theory,
    and wage gap 46
segregation of jobs 50–2 *see also* job
    assignment
Seibu Department Stores Ltd
    147–50; attitudes towards
    women 172–3; attitudes of
    women workers 200–12; buying
    function 151–2, 164–5, 202–3;
    career development 168;
    childcare facilities 182; 'contract
    employee' system 188–93;
    diversification 150; employment
    pattern changes 186–8, 228;
    evaluation of personnel policies
    161–7; family and career 173–4,

182–3; graduate recruitment
    155–6; job classification system
    158; job rotation and mobility
    168–71; job status changes
    193–6; limits of reform 174–5;
    management career route 158,
    164–6; management
    development for women 180–2;
    and market changes 150–3,
    155–67; market orientation
    151–3; married women 173;
    obstacles to equal opportunities
    167–75; personnel policies
    155–67; post-EEO Law 175–83;
    pro-women image 144–7, 182;
    promotion system 159–61, 168,
    196–9, 214–16; re-employment
    173–4, 182; specialisation 151;
    specialist career route 151,
    156–61, 163–7; status changes
    for women workers 186–96;
    training 169–72; two-track
    career system ('elite women')
    177–80
Seibu Nyusha-Annai (A Guide to
    Seibu) 149, 152
Seishonen Mondai Shingikai
    (Tripartite Advisory Council on
    Women and Young Workers)
    95, 97–8, 99–100
selection *see* recruitment
seniority 18, 62–3
service sector 3, 19, 68–9, 70
sex role distinction 19, 64–7, 231,
    233, 237
Shinotsuka, E. 3, 63
Shizuka, T. 148, 149
Shugyo Kozo Kihon Chosa
    (Employment Status Survey) 55–6
skill: definitions of jobs 37–8;
    shortages 71, 134 *see also* training
Sloane, P.J. 29
small firms 52–4
Smith, A.B., Jr 43
software engineers 71–2
Somucho Tokei-kyoku (Statistics
    Bureau, Management and
    Coordination Agency) 225
Sony 77

specialist career route, Seibu 151,
  156–61; evaluation 163–7
Spence, M.A. 30
stability, employment, and internal
  labour markets 31–5, 37
Stanback, T.M., Jr 69
Steel v. *Union of Post Office Workers*
  254(n4)
sub-contracting 58
Sumiya, M. 58
Sweden: administration and
  management jobs 15; ages and
  wage gap 49; attitudes towards
  women's role 64; attitudes of
  women workers 17
Switzerland, wage gap 16
Szyszczak, E. 43, 254(n4)

Taira, K. 235–6
Takahashi, Nobuko 17, 28
Takanashi, M. 56
Takeishi, E. 14
Takenaka, E. 7, 94, 230
Taylor, B. 37–8
technology and internal labour
  markets 31–3
temporary workers (*rinjiko*) 57, 225
  see also non-regular workers;
  part-time employment
textile industry 7–8, 237–8
theory, inequality and
  discrimination 27–44, 235–9;
  culturalist and economic
  functionalist approaches 235–6;
  feminism 38–9, 44; institutional
  31, 40–3; internal labour market
  31–6, 236–9;neo-classical 28–31;
  relative deprivation 201; society
  and household sexual divisions
  36–9; wage gap 46–7
Tokyo Chamber of Commerce and
  Industry (TCCI) 93
Tokyo District Court 92
Tokyo Metropolitan Labour Office
  (TMLO) 75
Toshiba 71, 77
training 94, 224; discrimination 62;
  EEO Law 102, 104–5; EEO Law
  compliance 120–2, 124, 136;

firm-specific 18, 62; on-the-job
  33, 62, 105; Seibu 169–72
Tripartite Advisory Council on
  Women and Young Workers
  (*Seishonen Mondai Shingikai*) 95,
  97–8, 99–100
Tsuda, M. 5, 158, 257(n1)
Tsuzumi, Seiji 153
two-track career system ('elite
  women') 221, 234; Seibu 177–80

'unequal treatment' 42
unionism 57
United Kingdom (UK): ages and
  wage gap 49; anti-discrimination
  legislation 42–3; attitudes
  towards women's role 64;
  attitudes of women workers 17;
  department stores 164–5;
  promotion by seniority 63;
  textile industry 8; wage gap 16;
  women's pressure groups 232–3
United Nations: Decade for
  Women 89–90, 98; Economic
  Role of Women in ECE Region
  49
United States of America (USA):
  administration and management
  jobs 15; anti-discrimination
  legislation 42–3; attitudes
  towards women's role 64;
  department stores 164–5; equal
  pay legislation 9; internal labour
  markets 27; legal concept of
  labour market discrimination 42;
  racial discrimination 40; textile
  industry 8; wage gap 16;
  women's movement 6; women's
  pressure groups 232–3
Upham, Frank K. 114, 255(n6)
'utilisation of women' 68, 77–8,
  83, 85–6, 119–21, 227–8; 'elite
  women' 226–9; as non-regular
  workers 225–6; Seibu 152–3, 161

vocational guidance and training
  (*q.v.*) 94

Wada, S. 144, 149–50, 152

wage earners 70; numbers of women 10–11

wage gap 15, 16, 45–50; and economic theory 29–30

wages: EEO Law compliance 126; Labour Standards Law 48, 90–1

Weitzel, R. 40

welfare 93–4, 101; EEO Law 102

white-collar workers 7, 12–13, 70–1

Whitelegg, E. 37, 39

Williams, K.C. 165

Women's Bureau, MOL 94, 107

women's movements 6, 232–3, 240

women's project teams 77–8

Women's Vocational Institute (WVI) 125, 128, 131, 132

Women's and Young Workers' Offices 103, 118

Working Women's Welfare Law (1972) 93–4, 101, 229

World War II 8–10

Woronoff, J. 256(n1)

Yamamoto, Mitsugu 96–7

Yamate, S. 67

Yashiro, N. 14, 28, 46–7, 54

Yayama, T. 100

Yokoyama, Gennosuke 252(n2)

Yoshikawa, E. 72

Young, M.K. 106, 117

Yugoslavia, attitudes of women workers 17

LIVERPOOL JOHN MOORES UNIVERSITY
Aldham Roberts L.R.C.
TEL. 051 231 3701/3634